SHADES OF
GRAY
Tennis Writings
of David Gray

SHADES OF GRAY

Tennis Writings
of David Gray

**Published in Association with
the International Tennis Federation**

Edited by Lance Tingay

Willow Books
Collins
8 Grafton Street, London
1988

Willow Books
William Collins Sons & Co Ltd
London · Glasgow · Sydney
Auckland · Toronto · Johannesburg

First published in Great Britain 1988
© Margaret Gray 1988

BRITISH LIBRARY CATALOGUING IN PUBLICATION DATA
Gray, David
I. Tennis—History—20th Century
I. Title   II. Tingay, Lance
796'.342'09'04   6V993

ISBN 0 00 218304 8

For permission to use the articles reproduced in this book
Margaret Gray and the publishers would like to thank: *The
Guardian*, *World Tennis*, *World of Tennis Yearbook*, Queen
Anne Press, *Tennis World*, The All England Lawn Tennis and
Croquet Club Wimbledon, Programme Publications Ltd and
The Queen's Club.

Typeset by
Ace Filmsetting Ltd, Frome
Printed in Great Britain by
Robert Hartnoll (1985) Ltd, Bodmin

CONTENTS

PREFACE

I'm David Gray. A brief, almost brusque introduction as the burly stranger settled beside me on the sofa. This was in 1956. We were in the lounge of Bournemouth's Highcliff Hotel, the annual end-April habitat of the tournament-playing community. The British Hard Court Championships were staged just a bus-ride away. Then, as now, the national dailies used specialised writers to report the circuit. They were a merry band, our support-group who trailed us and most weeks lived alongside us, from Scarborough at Easter to Torquay in November.

My first conversation with David revealed that he had been tossed into our midst that very day by his editors; a long step from the theatre critiques and local election coverage that were his previous assignments for *The Guardian*. When we met, David was twenty-six and I already forty-six, but this age difference never intruded in our close rapport which began that rainy Bournemouth afternoon and flourished, I feel privileged to say, for the next twenty-seven years.

He soon came to love the potential grace and beauty of tennis, and his political experiences gave him a ready taste for the personal intrigues and machinations that form the perennial backdrop to our ballet of forehands and backhands out front. In addition, he was a committed tourist and a gourmet, always happy to toss a coin in a fountain or argue passionately the relative merits of Europe's Michelin-starred restaurants. In Rome, our late-night discussions included such subjects as the propriety of lay-sisters conducting a heavy traffic in Coca-Cola on the Vatican roof.

On becoming General Secretary of tennis's world-governing body in 1976, David proved exactly the right person to support president Philippe Chatrier's high ideals with some harsher, real-life underpinnings drawn from his own experiences with us on the road.

David' special insight and reporting expertise made a particular contribution to our game in its most turbulent moments. Lance Tingay's sensitive selections from his writings make *Shades of Gray* a fascinating account of tennis's emergence from amateur sport to professional spectacle.

Ted Tinling

FOREWORD

It is with pride as well as pleasure that I contribute this foreword to a collection of David Gray's most perceptive, persuasive and entertaining essays, for over the years I had many opportunities to respect his qualities as a writer, a tennis administrator and especially, of course, as a friend.

David and I first met during the late 1960s when, in company with others in Britain, I was fighting for the introduction of Open tennis. It was that which provided the first of many common bonds between us during the spectacular development of the game in the years which followed. Our mutual love and appreciation of good food and wines meant that our frequent debates and deliberations together, as our tennis paths constantly crossed around the world, were also made that much more pleasurable.

David loved tennis and he loved life. Those feelings shone through constantly in his daily writings for *The Guardian* and I am sure this book will allow many others, including, by now, a whole new generation, to share the pleasure his articles offered at the time. The outstanding quality of David was that his passion for tennis stretched way beyond the spectacle and the appeal of competition on the court. He was fascinated by, and then increasingly involved in, everything that was happening behind the scenes in the game, which is why, in 1976, he was the obvious candidate to succeed Basil Reay as General Secretary of the International Tennis Federation.

It is particularly appropriate that this anthology should appear not only in the twentieth year of Open tennis but also the seventy-fifth anniversary of the International Tennis Federation and the return of tennis as a fully competitive sport to the Olympic Games. Like me, David was also convinced that the inclusion of tennis in the Olympic Games was essential if we were ever to have the opportunity to develop the game effectively in vast areas of the world. So much has happened since David and I attended our first meeting together of the International Olympic Committee! It is just a pity that he is no longer with us to witness and write about such an historic occasion which his initial efforts have helped to bring about, in that special, enjoyable, as well as informative style reflected in this book.

Philippe Chatrier

INTRODUCTION

This book reflects the development of tennis during the most cataclysmic period of its history, when 90 years of rigid amateurism changed to a professionalism where the leading exponents, men and women, can now command incomes counted in millions of dollars. It tells the story of some of the greatest players of all time, giants like Lew Hoad, artists like Ken Rosewall, magicians like Ilie Nastase, miracle athletes like Margaret Smith Court, overwhelming champions like Billie Jean King, rhythmic perfectionists like Maria Bueno. It comes from the pen of an outstanding writer, David Gray.

David died, on 6 September, 1983, sadly before his time at the age of 55, having been since 1976 the General Secretary of the International Tennis Federation, the key post in the administration of the game round the world. He was an able administrator. For twenty years before that he was the tennis writer on *The Guardian* from the columns of which the majority of the pieces are taken. Margaret Gray, David's widow, and I are grateful to the proprietors for allowing the use of their copyright material.

This is but a small selection from many thousands of words penned by David in his career as a journalist. His writing standards were high, literary rather than journalistic. Indeed he was very much a man of letters who adapted his art to the demands of deadlines with rare skill.

As a journalist he was a rounded craftsman. He filled many roles on *The Guardian*. It was the *Manchester Guardian* when he joined, entrenched in Cross Street, Manchester, and redolent of the radical and intellectual traditions of the old days. David covered general news, the theatre (on which he was expert) and could turn his hand to anything. He was appointed tennis writer in 1956, when I first met him. For two decades we were professional rivals and close friends, for such is the nature of Fleet Street that such ties across the divide of one paper and another are common.

David loved all sport and tennis in particular. Because he appreciated its unique harmony between artistry and athleticism he savoured the delights of the women's game. His sympathy for grace rather than muscle is always evident. The British press has always given strong support to the women's game, probably because Wimbledon bestowed equality, while the rest of the world lagged behind. 'Women's Lib' never had cause to find fault with David.

The plan of this book is evident in the list of contents. If Wimbledon takes up a third of the book it is because the happenings at that wonderful tournament are central and basic to the game. The Wimbledon Championships dominate the story of tennis from the beginnings when the All England Club improvised the rules and form that have remained unchanged since 1877. It was moral pressure from Wimbledon that brought the great reform and Open tennis in 1968.

The section I headed 'Political Issues' is also prominent. More than any tennis writer David loved sport's political aspect. No doubt that is why he was so efficient as General Secretary of the International Federation. There was never a period in the history of tennis when politics loomed larger and David loved the wheeler-dealer aspect of committee meetings almost as much as the sight of a perfect backhand drive. (He was, incidentally, an able writer on election issues for *The Guardian* and he travelled widely in the USA for that purpose.)

His colleagues without exception regretted his switch from journalism to the administration of the game he loved. It seemed as if the poacher had turned game-keeper. He was a great poacher and his game-keeping was no less good. He kept his old friends and made many more.

This book is a tribute to a writing skill that deserves some permanence. I have enjoyed putting his work together. He was a dear friend and we shared many joys (and some tribulations) around the courts of the world.

Lance Tingay

WIMBLEDON

Wimbledon and the English

The following essay, found among David's papers, was written in 1981. Here he considers the advantages of grass over other surfaces.

I once knew a man who believed that the most beautiful words in the world were: 'Play will begin at two o'clock upon the lawns of the All England Club at Wimbledon.' That sentence had a special magic. It wasn't just that he liked to be at the heart of the matter, watching history made and champions crowned. That was only a part of his pleasure. What he liked best was absorbing the particular atmosphere of his days at the Championships. The English summer, the rigours of the game, seeing and being seen, the spirit of the place, the colours of SW19. A huge garden-party, he used to call it. And, of course, that was exactly in keeping with the traditions of the game.

Like life, tennis began in a garden. The whole early history of the game seems to be summed up in a *Punch* cartoon of the 1880s. I have forgotten the caption, but the picture shows two ornately dressed ladies, sitting in deck-chairs, rackets within reach, waiting for a perspiring curate to finish rolling the court. Any middle-class garden might have provided the artist with his models. The first Championships were played at Wimbledon in 1877 and the game burst into popularity. It was all very simple and social. You cut, rolled and marked out and suddenly you had a new diversion. It was much more exciting than croquet. 'Who's for tennis?' asked our great-grandfathers, putting on flannels, blazer and straw hat. The grass beckoned. The ball may not always have bounced perfectly, but that was all a part of the game.

A century later, now that the game has spread from Peru to Pakistan and the latest applicants to join the International Tennis Federation are Mozambique and the People's Republic of the Yemen, how far removed are we from our Victorian ancestors? It is one of the ironies of tennis history that grass, once the cheapest surface to maintain, is now being abandoned in certain countries because of the labour costs involved in the preparation of courts. The US Open is now played on cement. Indoor tennis has expanded and boomed. Occasional mutterings about the possibility of a change to an artificial surface have even been reported from Wimbledon. Whole generations of clay-court players, who for years have made ritual comments about grass being fit only for grazing cattle, must have cheered at the prospect.

But in spite of the critics, grass survives. And not only at Wimbledon. Overseas visitors who come to Queen's look at the large expanse of green and reach for their rackets. Clay may have its tremendous attractions. Paris and Rome, Hamburg and Barcelona, may offer a competitor wonderful tests of strategy, accuracy and stamina. There is drama in the dust at such championships. Flushing Meadow, new, brash and noisy, provides massive crowds and great tests of reflexes and concentration. They are all wonderful tournaments, but why is Wimbledon still the championship that most players still want most of all to win? Why does it attract the largest crowds in tennis and the game's most international audience?

The answer may well be that grass, even though its bounces may not be perfect, is still the surface which offers a player the greatest challenge to his skill and provides the spectator with the best chance of entertainment. There are variations. The courts change with the weather. They grow harder and faster as a tournament progresses. At Wimbledon the Centre Court ought to be at its fastest for those last matches when titles are at stake and players ought to be at a peak of form. Would clay provide as much spectacle? Would cement give the same aesthetic satisfaction? With grass, it seems that the game goes back to its roots. At Wimbledon, at Queen's, at Eastbourne and Beckenham, the quality of the tennis is high and yet we can still keep the festival atmosphere. The look of the thing is right. Times change, but the grass keeps on growing . . . .

* * *

Discovering Wimbledon – the Apprenticeship of a Tennis Writer

Like the previous essay the following was found among David's papers and the original *locale* of its publication unknown. It was almost certainly written just before the Wimbledon Championships in 1977.

I was late in discovering Wimbledon. At my school in the Midlands we didn't play tennis. Summer meant cricket until the term ended and then, in those years at the end of the war, we used to go to camps and pick fruit as part of the patriotic effort of recovery. Mostly, that meant learning how to carry long ladders, smoking illicit cigarettes at the top of plum trees, and drinking cider in the evenings.

The years 1946 and 1947 would have been good ones for learning the game because there were successions of long, sunny days. But for us, in Stourbridge, Worcestershire, they were full of cricket. Tennis, if we thought about it at all, belonged to another world. What we did think about was girls and it dawned on us, with our short hair and 'utility' bicycles with wooden pedals, rather slowly that girls played tennis. If you read their autobiographies the great players always seem to discover tennis with blinding flashes of inspiration. They see someone hit a ball with a racket and suddenly there is a kind of mystical electricity and they know what they want to do for the rest of their lives.

I played for the first time because it seemed to be the only way to get to know a tall, blonde girl with – as I found later – a rather good forehand. I used to look at her from a distance, in the library, in the High Street, on the hockey field. Accidentally, I joined the same tennis club. Acciden-tally, I was always there when she needed a partner in mixed doubles. By the same kind of accident, I went with her on the club trip to Wimbledon. There were six of us and the Chairman had the only Centre Court ticket. The Thursday of the first week isn't the most glamorous day at Wimble-don, but it was exciting enough to get up at 6 a.m. and catch a train to London, to carry a rucksack with a mackintosh, sandwiches, a Thermos and a copy of *Little Dorrit* (which luckily I didn't have to read) on the District Line out to Southfields.

It was the Bromwich–Falkenburg year [1948] ... although no one guessed that Falkenburg would win on that first Thursday. I kept the programme. It is full of magic names: Drobny, Patty, Sedgman, Parker, Hart and Brough. Looking back, I don't think we saw many of them. 'We will take turns in the Centre', said the Chairman clutching the ticket, but we never found him until it was time to go home and I never had a seat on the Centre Court until long afterwards when I became a journalist. I can remember walking through the narrow avenues to the back courts. Where are you now, Pallada, 'Tim' [N. R.] Lewis, Grandet, C. M. Jones and Mrs Dawson-Scott? You were all playing in those distant parts of the ground.

For some time we stood in line outside the Centre Court until it seemed silly to watch people in a queue when we might be watching others play. I never walk past Court Two without recapturing the romantic glow that came from that first trip to Wimbledon. We didn't eat strawberries and cream (after all, our mothers had packed those sandwiches). We consulted our programmes judiciously. I bought a copy of the *Dunlop Lawn Tennis Annual* for 1948 and a postcard with a picture of Wimbledon Church. We recognised Tony Mottram as he walked through the crowd on his way home. And, once or twice, at exciting moments, I held the blonde girl's hand in a very British way. At the end I decided that I would go back to Wimbledon another year.

I wouldn't really have discussed that particular memory at such length if I hadn't thought that I was typical of many of the 300,000 spectators who go to Wimbledon every year. Lawn tennis isn't the most important sport in Britain. Soccer, cricket (which always seems to be dying and reviving) and racing occupy far more space in the newspapers. There has not been a British champion in the men's singles since Fred Perry in 1936 – and in the women's singles the two champions we have produced, Angela Mortimer (1961) and Ann Jones (1969), have been skilfully persistent competitors rather than spectacular stealers of headlines. Tournaments in Britain during the summer aren't particularly well attended and the British Davis Cup team usually receives less support than a Third Division soccer side.

Why, then, is Wimbledon such a roaring success? If you look at the situation in cold terms of performance, the British have about as much right to stage the premier tournament of lawn tennis as they have to act as hosts for the world ice hockey championships. Tradition saves us, of course. We were the pioneers. We invented the game and have watched it grow up. It has a broad base (how many other countries have so many small clubs and courts in schools and public parks?). For the period of the Championships, Wimbledon is on television eight hours a day. We have the best theatre for the play and it is still the best-produced tournament in the calendar. Great events in other countries are busily building their own traditions and improving their reputations. No one knows how Wimbledon will stand if the USTA replaces Forest Hills with a new $6 million stadium, with 20,000 seats in the Centre Court, at Flushing Meadow. But at the moment, after a hundred years, the British still lead in the battle to command public interest.

Perhaps it may be that Wimbledon isn't just a tennis tournament. It is what the British call 'a day out'. If you go to Roland Garros, you make the journey only for the tennis. You can hardly rest on the grass and under the trees on that one free triangle of space near Court Five at Roland Garros. An expatriate Englishwoman from Port Washington, who tried to picnic, Wimbledon-fashion, in a corner of Forest Hills, found herself an object of total curiosity as she opened wine and carved a chicken. After ten minutes people were taking photographs of the phenomenon. Elsewhere, you either watch the matches or you go home. At the All England, set in all that expensive green country in south-west London, there is more room to move and more to see.

This goes back to the deep roots of the tournament. The first Championship, an attempt to improve the finances of the most important croquet club in Britain, was a garden party. The 200 spectators paid a shilling each to watch the final. Competitors were charged a guinea. The first print of the scene shows the crowd sauntering past the courts. No one seems to be paying any great attention to the play. There were lawn tennis enthusiasts – they filled the columns of the sports magazines with arguments about whether the volley and the overarm serve were legal shots – but on the whole the first Wimbledon looks exactly like a social occasion. And it was interrupted for another social occasion. The final was put off for two days because of a clash with the cricket match between Eton and Harrow, the most important schools in the country. So much for the importance of the new sport of lawn tennis in 1877.

It has remained part of the social scene. Racing at Ascot, a Test match at Lord's (the Australians are in England again this year), Wimbledon and the Henley regatta. The London season embraces all the best summer sports. 'Ladies' Day', which always used to be the first Tuesday, is no longer a ritual occasion. Flowered hats and white gloves aren't quite so obvious. But the British like dressing up. If nothing else, we wear our best jeans for Wimbledon. And we indulge in our talent for ceremony. Compare the end of a Wimbledon final – ballboys drawn up in two lines, the slow march of the Duke of Kent (or some other member of the royal family) towards the new champion, the chairman of the club and the referee in the positions hallowed by years of practice, photographers kept within restricted limits – with the confusions on the Centre Courts at some other European tournaments. We British may be monsters of indiscipline at football matches, but at Wimbledon, by gum, we are models of decorum. Even Borg's teenage army stands strictly to attention when we salute the winners.

We don't have sponsors and that means that we don't have to make all those speeches of thanks, which mar the middle and the end of Forest Hills [the venue of the US Open from 1968–77]. We go from drinking Pimm's No. 1 on the tea-lawn at lunchtime to strawberries and cream in the late afternoon, absorbing the spirit of the place. The best of the innovations has been the engagement of a military band to play Sullivan and Sousa before play begins on the great days. Why does no one else have a band on a finals day? Perhaps it only sounds and looks right on grass. Could you have military music on a clay court?

We watch the players arrive, driven to the club door. Again the public are kept at a very slight distance by a rope-barrier. 'It *is* Nastase', says a middle-aged lady triumphantly. The accent is from the far north of England. If you work on the tournament circuit, you see faces familiar from tournaments all over the country. At the end of June, we make our pilgrimages to the All England, carrying our sandwiches, our Thermos flasks, our books of reference and hoping that we glimpse Mark Cox threading his way home through the crowds.

It is a strange two weeks. The British absorb every scrap of information about Wimbledon for two weeks and then, it seems, the tennis season is merely confined to a few club and seaside matches as the grass wears out. Wimbledon itself becomes a shell. The members play on into the twilight; public schoolboys and juniors take part in tournaments on the clay courts; sometimes there is a Davis Cup match. But the atmosphere, which it has taken a century to create, is never the same. Wimbledon only comes alive, only fulfils its destiny, during the Championships. In the other weeks of the year it is empty, almost forlorn. That is the strangest part of its magic.

*   *   *

Reporting Wimbledon

No one knew more about reporting Wimbledon than David. In this essay he illuminates the craft of writing lawn tennis, the hows and wherefores of a specialised world. It may be noted that it was written before 1983, when the Championships were extended to thirteen days, and the final day moved back to the second Sunday.

Reporting Wimbledon is rather like taking part in a twelve-day bicycle race. A long period of preparation, a slow beginning, a hard slog and then, when you are drained of energy and you have supped full of excitement, you have to summon up all your critical faculties for the final sprint at the end. The training period, whether it is in the frozen wastes of Philadelphia in January or in the sun at Monte Carlo in April, matters. No matter how sound you are on technique and strategy, how knowledge-able on statistics or how adept at summoning those smart phrases which sum up a match in a nutshell of wit, if you are the tennis critic, if it is your job to write your paper's main despatch from SW19, it isn't really possible to present these Championships properly to your readers unless you have spent some time on the circuit, watching its actions and passions, assessing the latest vagaries of form.

On the whole – and more, perhaps, than any other British sport except golf – Wimbledon is a place for specialist reporters. There are many other journalists here, armed with cuttings and bright ideas for features ('Could you get hold of Bjorn Borg and ask him whether he thinks the beard is here to stay?'). Columnists arrive, fresh from the wicket, the ringside or the nineteenth hole. Gossip columnists buzz around the frayed edges of conversations, discussing new angles and old twists.

But as far as the main body of the inhabitants of the press-room are concerned, these are fringe figures. Tennis for them is confined to the Wimbledon fortnight. For the hard core of tennis writers, those who can tell the difference between Kathy Kuykendall and JoAnne Russell, the season lasts throughout the year and Wimbledon is its topmost peak. This is the time of maximum public interest in the game. Players know that a good Wimbledon establishes them more than success in any other tournament. It is the same for journalists. You can write gracefully about a match at the Cumberland Club and with precise wit about the French and Italian Championships, but no one in the office will dream of putting out a placard. You come to Wimbledon and even the circulation managers of papers which usually think of tennis in terms of lace on pants take an interest in forehands and backhands, conscious of millions of television viewers who know almost everything that happens on the main courts in what Giles's Grandma once called 'the two weeks of bonk, bonk, for-tay fifteen'. This is a national festival and, like the Olympic Games with their similar time-span, for those of us who cover it it seems to go on for ever, denying any freedom outside the business of reporting sport for a fortnight. It is a wonderful test of concentration, ubiquity, staying-power and good contacts. 'Don't those guys ever choke over their typewriters?', Rod Laver asked Bud Collins, that shrewd and witty American commentator, as he read the prose that had flooded from the press-room about his 1969 victory here.

The answer is that there isn't much choking – someone will always write a first sentence for you if you are stuck and afterwards habit and the pressure of time brings inspiration – but that most of the second week feels like a very long fifth set. Journalistically, particularly when you are working for a paper which requires two elegant columns, the first day is the worst. It is hard to find a rhythm and a routine. There are too many minor matches. If there are upsets, they usually occur at 8 p.m. on Court 14 and happen immediately after you have dictated a piece which was almost good about two players whom a few of your readers will know, but which was totally un-newsworthy and which you wouldn't have written at all if anything fractionally better had caught your fancy before you fell into a panic about all your empty space.

Thereafter, with any luck, the matches improve and your instincts usually carry you towards Wimbledon's drama and sensation. Obviously, you have favourite players, usually those you tipped to win in that foreword which you wrote on the preceding Sunday instead of going to Hurlingham and listening to the band under the trees. Your sports editor, you remember with a flush of shame, made you harden your prophecies to a point which extended far beyond any hope of equivocation.

The first Saturday is always the most crowded and chaotic day in the press-room. Daily-paper journalists relax, like prisoners on weekend leave, and the Sunday men always look as though they are trying to do seven days of work in one. And the middle Sunday is a real holiday, which gives you a chance to write a foreword to the second week in which you can conveniently forget the suggestions you made in your first dip into the future. 'After her problems in the early rounds, it was always certain that Mrs Edgington would have difficulties with Miss Morton.' Always look for liberal doses of hindsight in the morning papers of the second Monday. Most years I drove away to the woods beyond Dorking to produce my exercises in hindsight and predictions about a dwindling field. Once I had to break off because a complete scout camp assembled itself around my car. Another time I wrote a piece from a riverside at Cambridge in which I assured everyone that nothing could stop Roy Emerson from winning the men's singles for the third time. Almost immediately he skidded into the umpire's chair and retired against Owen Davidson.

In the second week interviews become more important. There are fewer matches on the outside courts and more time to question and reflect. Interviews used to be difficult at Wimbledon. They were conducted in a room about 12 ft by 4 ft, which seemed to have been built in imitation of the Black Hole of Calcutta. A hundred journalists used to pack themselves into this concrete cell and try to catch the semi-audible comments of champions and not-quite-champions. It was the only aspect of Wimbledon that ever displeased the *New Yorker's* very polite, very enthusiastic correspondent, Herbert Warren Wind. He never mentioned it in print, of course. He has always been too busy writing wry, funny, sympathetic pieces about what happened on court.

Luckily the All England have now built a new underground interview room, which is much bigger but still crowded throughout the second week. The interviews have improved, too. Open tennis has meant that the players have grown accustomed to answering questions, hard and soft, in formal interviews. Talking to the press is now as much a part of a professional player's job as picking up a racket to serve. This has been good for player/press relations. The critics are given a chance to understand the point of view of the competitor. You learn a lot from watching a match, but post-mortems with a live subject add a great deal of important additional evidence. Particularly about finals. The finalists spend a great deal of the second week in the interview room. You listen to them talk, watch them deal with the cut and thrust of questioning, and you get to know your good players pretty well. Who is the champion at the game of questions and answers? It varies according to mood and occasion, but Christ Evert earns almost as many points at interviews as she does on court.

The tendency of present-day tennis reporting, even at Wimbledon, is for more interviews and perhaps criticism of the play, and that may be the influence of television. If eight million viewers have watched a match at home, it can be argued that the commentators have analysed the play sufficiently for them and that a morning newspaper should merely try to fill the gaps in their knowledge by seeking background information that TV doesn't have the time or the resources to uncover. Doubtless the highly serious newspapers will continue to make Olympian judgements on tennis and these will be read by the kind of people who like to know what the drama critics say before they go to the theatre. They are a sizeable, influential minority. Find a critic whose tastes and opinions are similar to yours and stick to him because he will know what you like. That's the rule ... whether the subject is Shakespeare or Stan Smith.

One of the best features of the circuit is that it is cosmopolitan. The players and the regular members of the tennis press corps are citizens of a common world and Wimbledon is its most important meeting place. Newspapers from every major country except China send representatives here. The reporter from *Sovietski Sport* sits one seat away from the correspondent of *Dunya* of Turkey. *The Hindu* is next to the *Haagsche Courant*.

There are 137 press seats in the Centre Court and the badge-holders have priority in any press seats anywhere in the ground. More than 500 other passes are issued to those who work in the press-centre, but few of those give the right to a seat. The press writing and restaurant rooms have more than doubled in size in the last five years, but still Wimbledon can't accommodate all those who want to report the Championships. The All England sent a polite note to all new applicants for seats in this Centenary year, regretting that they were unable to consider requests from journals which have never previously covered Wimbledon.

* * *

Hoad Takes the Crown

The exploits and outstanding skills of the two Australians, Lew Hoad and Ken Rosewall, dominated the 1950s. The Wimbledon final in which Hoad beat his team-mate in 1956 was a landmark in the game. This was David's first Wimbledon assignment for what was then the *Manchester Guardian*.

After all the final of the men's singles Lawn Tennis Championships here went the way of expectation, for, as in most of their recent meetings, L. A. Hoad beat K. R. Rosewall by three sets to one at 6-2 4-6 7-5 6-4. (To say this is rather like saying that Roland beat Oliver, or that Rosencrantz beat Guildenstern so automatically are their names linked in the public mind.)

For his victory Hoad had to walk warily, conquering waywardness with the strictest discipline for one hour and forty-five minutes, and the title cost him four long and urgent sets. He did not take all the honours. By ingenuity and by skill in trifles Rosewall stole from him today a great many of the trappings of power. Indeed, Hoad won through greater strength and more consistent power in service, but Rosewall provided most of the decorations and luxuries of the match. Hoad took most of his points quickly and swiftly by single blows, Rosewall won the prizes for most of the long rallies.

The contest was exciting – there were those who said that it was the best final since the war – and yet it was oddly lacking in emotion. This was a match that had been played many times before, and it seemed unlikely that the old opponents would be able to surprise each other by conjuring new magic for this latest occasion. The spice of international rivalry was missing, too. Instead of New York versus Sydney, or Paris versus Berlin, this was a matter of Tenshurst versus Glebe and nine miles of Sydney suburbia.

When they walked out on to the court Rosewall, who played in the final two years ago, seemed to be stepping more firmly and in the preliminary knock-up he hit the harder and more surely. Hoad looked pale, and in the first three games he scarcely hit the ball at more than a quarter of his usual power. There was a world watching and even though Hoad is used to collecting national championships – since before today France and Italy made up this year's bag – he seemed bowed down beneath such a heavy weight of curiosity.

The first typical Hoad shot, a fierce smash which Rosewall just managed to reach with his racket but could not return, came in the fourth game. After this encouragement Hoad gained in confidence and levelled the score at 2-all with a powerful drive down the side-line which made the chalk fly like a cloud of white smoke. It was in the next game that he broke Rosewall's service for the first time, and the final point here came on a vicious topspin forehand drive that Rosewall watched like a man who sees an express train go by. This shot was what Hazlitt would have called a singular instance of manual dexterity, and it was notable that in the next few rallies Rosewall, whose face at this time had assumed the kind of expression that Mr Stan Laurel wears when he discovers that he is sitting on his hat, took care to steer play away from Hoad's forehand.

The rallies now began to grow longer. Hoad won his own service in the sixth game and broke Rosewall's again in the seventh. The point of demoralisation here was a fierce point-blank volley which Hoad unleashed in mid-court. There were two more irrecoverable drives in this game, and Rosewall, confronted with so much splendour, could only drop his racket and put an arm round his own neck as though to comfort himself. Hoad, whose face was bleak with concentration, was now completely assured. Once he changed his mind in the middle of a smash, let the ball bounce at the back of the court and won the point with a splendid forehand drive. He had changed horses in mid-stream and had climbed on to the right one.

At the start of the second set there was a quiet spell during which Rosewall served an ace (that is always something worth noting) and then, suddenly, with Hoad ahead and, as usual when he leads, slightly relaxing, the patterns of the match shifted again. The change came after a brilliant spell in the fourth game by Rosewall. Hoad was serving thunderbolts, but Rosewall stole his thunder and in two superbly played rallies, both of which he won with dipping cross-court drives, took the power from Hoad's attack and won the game for 3-1.

After the first of these the applause lasted for two minutes and then, with Hoad as desolate as he always seems when his power fails him at its extreme stretch, Rosewall began to dictate the terms of the set. He led 4-2 and then each player lost two service games. In the seventh game, which Hoad won, the last point came on a net cord which fell tantalisingly on Rosewall's own side. He clenched his fist and reeled in agony – he is much more dramatic in his gestures nowadays. Then he looked up as though for some huge eclipse of the sun or something that might make the anguish of the moment mightier. Eventually he took the set at 6-4.

Rosewall was chasing everything and frequently passing Hoad, but his points usually came after long rallies and were costly in energy. Hoad was content with two- and three-shot winners and came economically through the dark and doubtful region of the third set. When he is on court there is always a sense of drama. The mind cannot sleep, because the unexpected must always be expected. With Rosewall the movement of the ball comes to an anticipated end and the workings of his mind are plain; but when Hoad is in command the result is amazing and one has to work back from the end to see the means by which it has been achieved, for Hoad's play moves in a world of high imagination. Rosewall is the neater strategist, but Hoad's range of ambition is greater. Hoad broke Rosewall's service for 2-1 and then Rosewall levelled the score in the eighth game. Hoad after hitting a ball out looked at his racket as though it were a false friend. The set ended in the twelfth game at 7-5 to Hoad after Rosewall had suddenly fallen into a fit of negligence. Hoad, who always watched for any relaxation, took full advantage of this.

In the fourth set it was Hoad who made lackadaisical strokes and Rosewall broke through early on and led 4-1. At this score when everything was going wrong Hoad's face wore the strange smile of a clown in some dark Elizabethan comedy. It was bitter-sweet and world-weary. The resigned smile of a man who knows that this is a cruel world in which the tricks of fate must be borne and accepted. The bitterness ended soon after this for Rosewall could not sustain his effort. He lost his service in the seventh game; this was the eleventh game that had gone against service and this high mortality rate was due not so much to inaccuracies as to the fact that Rosewall had the best return of service in the world and one of the weakest services. Hoad drew level for 4-all and finished off the set with a triumphant demonstration of his force and power. At the end he tapped the umpire's knee with his racket and smiled unrestrainedly.

*   *   *

Hoad's Second Win

L ew Hoad won Wimbledon for the second time in 1957 in the absence of Ken Rosewall, who had turned professional. Hoad overwhelmed another Australian, Ashley Cooper, 6-2 6-1 6-2 in a devastating display. The match was played on Friday, 5 July, and on the following Monday Hoad signed a professional contract in New York and did not appear on the Centre Court again until ten years later in the special professional tournament that was staged in August 1967.

It could not have been done better. That is the exciting truth about L. A. Hoad's victory over A. J. Cooper at Wimbledon yesterday. It cost him only five games and less than an hour of time, and the story of the match is the story of a murder, a ruthless and violent lawn tennis assassination – the shortest final since Vines smashed Austin in 1938. [Perry beat Von Cramm in an even shorter final in 1936.] This great success brought to Hoad the honour of being the first man to win the title for two years in succession since Budge in 1938. Playing as he did yesterday no player in the world, amateur or professional, could have beaten him. The match was a complete demonstration of power and purpose, grace and speed, and it ended as any great work of lawn tennis art should, in a most majestic climax. The memory of the last three games will last for years to come. Other champions may have won closer Wimbledon finals, they may, indeed, have been better players, but there had not been such a dashing and decisive victory for years. All through this Championship it has been Hoad first and the rest nowhere, and when he reached the winning-post yesterday afternoon one had to look a long way down the course to see where the second runner stood.

For Cooper, left so far behind, the match must have been a matter of continual despair. Normally there is a kind of sacred simplicity about his game. Rhythm comes quickly and he wins his points with handsome, forceful shots. He has no great subtleties. He is not a great strategist, but everything is open and free and done with a studious calm. If he is sometimes slow – he is not like Hoad, a strong man who moves lightly – he is always resolute and steadfast. Determination and steady strength are the keys to Cooper's game. Against any ordinary player these virtues look formidable enough, but they could not stand against the fierce power of Hoad yesterday.

Cooper played his first Wimbledon final with desperate strength – when he served, his face was pale and twisted with effort – but Hoad, like a magician, stole that strength and used it for his own purposes, turning fine shots from Cooper into winners of his own. Even when Cooper did succeed in putting the ball far away from him, the result frequently turned out to be little happier, for Hoad was devastatingly, unspectacularly swift in recovery and with a few quick easy steps and a great deal of positional sense he guarded the whole of his court.

At the end he used this art remarkably well. There were shots that were remembered and spoken of afterwards in hushed, wondering voices. Once Cooper served fiercely down the centre line. It was a ball that few players would have seen, let alone returned. Hoad put a racket to it and the force of it swung him round. The ball went back to Cooper, who played a comfortable drop-shot and the point seemed to be won, but suddenly Hoad, then in full cry for success, dashed in and flashed the ball quickly across the court yards out of Cooper's reach. Cooper, robbed of one of few successes, flung up his arms in despair and walked back with the air of a man counting up money that he had lost.

* * *

Flame and Fire –
Maria Bueno

M aria Bueno captivated the tennis world for a decade. At her international début in 1958 she won the Italian Championship when she was eighteen, and her first of three singles triumphs at Wimbledon came at her second attempt in 1959. In the final she beat the American, Darlene Hard, with whom she formed a notable doubles partnership. In her home town of Sao Paulo, Brazil marked her success by erecting a statue, and a postage stamp featuring her portrait was issued.

For almost the whole fortnight Wimbledon was on the verge of flames. With the sun furnace-hot and the grass fast and dry, everything was ready for a great blaze of spectacle and excitement, and yet the days went by without anyone ever striking a match in exactly the right way. All the time there were interesting smoke-clouds in different corners of the Championship, but there was never enough light and heat for anyone to rise out of the ashes into greatness. Olmedo calmly collected his title and it seemed that although Wimbledon, 1959, was better in general standard than its two immediate predecessors, it was going to be remembered mainly because form was so close and because [in the men's Championship] so many seeds fell in the first week. Every night, travelling back over Putney Bridge one looked down at the water, and every night the river still ran softly. No one had set the Thames on fire, and the number of stanzas in the song was beginning to come to an end.

Then at ten minutes past two on Saturday afternoon Miss Bueno, slim, dark, swift, and super-feminine in her inconsistency, her love for a fine dress and for a quick cry of admiration, began to serve in the third game. Suddenly everything worked. It is always the big moments that call for power and passion, and Miss Bueno was artist enough to know that the time had come for her to fill the Wimbledon stage. The points came easily. Miss Hard, that chunky and cheerful American who was runner-up to Miss Gibson in the final two years ago and who had beaten the Brazilian in six previous meetings, scarcely put a racket to a ball and, although she may not have realised it at the time, that confident flourish of service-power settled everything. Unless something extraordinary happened to put out the fire, this was going to be one of Miss Bueno's bright, fierce days.

The truth is that her hardest battles are always against her own temperament. A player of imagination and instinct, she has often wasted matches by aiming too high or reaching too far and falling into dejection at her own failures. With a little restraint, concentration, and self-control, she might manage matters by degrees, but time and again she has tried to do too much too quickly. Against Miss Hard, Miss Bueno came early to the cross-roads and, once she had shown that she was in the proper mood to win, skill, imagination, and ease of movement all came to guide her to victory. She conquered herself and the rest was easy.

The weapons were service and volley and, apart from a dropped service game at 3-2 in the first set, Miss Bueno was always attacking and always dictating the moves on the chessboard. She made the odd error and Miss Hard, looking at her as a hunter might look who suddenly finds herself shot by the bird, tried hard to fight her off at the net, but always the American's court seemed to be two or three times larger than the Brazilian's. Miss Bueno, moving in with graceful determination to take her low volleys, always seemed to be able to find wide open spaces. It was almost as if Miss Hard was defending Texas. When they came to crucial points, Miss Bueno was the tougher player. Miss Hard, serving to save the first set at 4-5, was so nervous that she could scarcely throw up the ball and finished with the exasperation of a double-fault. All through the second set she was under calm, confidently produced pressure. When there was a rally, she never seemed to be able to read her executioner's mind. She could only watch the blow falling. At the end Miss Bueno, who had played such a great and beautiful match, burst into tears and covered her head with a towel.

There is just one postscript. Three years ago, talking at Beckenham, Miss Hard said: 'Believe me, the best junior in the world is a seventeen-year-old [sixteen-year-old] Brazilian named Maria Esther Bueno. One day she will win Wimbledon.' On Saturday she accepted the fulfilment of her prophecy sportingly and well. Determination was not enough to carry her to the title.

For the rest, Fraser and Emerson won a long, monotonous, and sometimes exciting doubles final from Mark and Laver. Miss Hard and Miss Arth showed themselves to be a real partnership, which Miss Truman and Mrs Fleitz were not, and then Laver and Miss Hard beat Fraser and Miss Bueno in the mixed doubles final. The calculating machines in the press box reckoned that by the time he gained his title Laver had played 299 games lasting for eleven hours 33 minutes on the Centre Court in four days. In the whole fortnight he played 553 games. The junior boys' event went to Lejus, a sixteen-year-old Russian, who beat Barnes, an eighteen-year-old Brazilian Davis Cup player, 6-2 6-4. That looks like a sign of things to come.

* * *

A Champion Totters – Neale Fraser

The left-handed Australian, Neale Fraser, was competing at Wimbledon for the seventh time when he won in 1960 at the age of 26. His quarter-final survival against the American 'Butch' Buchholz was perilous, and he became the eighth of the men's singles champions to survive match-points.

'Dramatic' suddenly became an overworked word at Wimbledon yesterday. So did 'unlucky'. For it was only a sudden turn of ill fortune that prevented Buchholz (United States), the eighth and youngest of the seeds, from putting out Fraser (Australia), the favourite. At 15-14 in the fourth set, after holding five match-points and leading by two sets to one, the nineteen-year-old American chased a ball along the baseline, collapsed with cramp, fell, and twisted an ankle. He played on for one more painful point in the next game. Then Legge, the referee, standing by the court-side, looked at the umpire and threw in the towel for him. The score was 4-6 6-3 4-6 15-15 to Fraser. It was a sad end to a fine match.

Then in the late evening Mackay, the second favourite and the other great hope of the United States, went out to Pietrangeli (Italy), the fifth seed and the man in form, 16-14 6-2 3-6 6-4, after the Italian had fought back from 2-5 in the first set and 2-4 in the fourth. Art triumphed over strength there, and now Pietrangeli meets the winner of the all-Australian contest between Laver and Emerson in one semi-final. Fraser will play the survivor of today's duel between Krishnan (India) and Ayala (Chile) in the other.

When Buchholz's crash came, Fraser had lived close to defeat for an hour. He had been under pressure all the time; he had always been forced to regain lost ground. Buchholz, tall, loose-limbed, and crew-cut, went into the match with the confidence of having beaten him in the United States Indoor Championships earlier this year, and he played his way through the short, sharp, service-and-volley exchanges, which went on for nearly three hours, with a great deal of ease and poise. Buchholz gave little away in his service (in a sequence of five games in the fourth set he served so well that Fraser could take from him only an average of a point a game), whereas the Australian, who served a great many faults in crisis, was always struggling to hold on. In a match full of attacking strokes Buchholz was much the more efficient player. Fraser's play was full of desperately brave shots and hair-breadth escapes, but he never had the American's assured self-command. Buchholz approached the match rather like a bright young nephew determined to teach a nervous uncle how to suck eggs.

The American took the first set with a break to love in the eighth, and he might have taken the second as well – he had three game-points on Fraser's service in the fifth game and another after Fraser had presented him with two double-faults in the seventh. Fraser surprised him, in return, in the eighth, and that was enough to make it set-all. In the third set the tenth game mattered. At 30-30 Fraser was passed by a cross-court shot. He thought the ball went out, and the linesman thought it fell in. When there was no call he looked back in anxiety and then walked round in a wide circle like a thwarted lion. The self-control was admirable. One remembers Seixas in a similar situation in his semi-final against Rosewall four years ago. When he felt calm enough to serve, all that he could produce was a double-fault. The third set thus went to Buchholz 6-4. All through the afternoon Fraser's judgement of a ball to the line was not particularly good, and that point might have been another Australian error.

And so to the fourth set and the end. With 3.52 on the clock and 5-4 to Buchholz on the scoreboard, Fraser put a backhand volley into the net (Buchholz had worked away at that powder-puff backhand of the

Australian's) and it was match-point to Buchholz for the first time. Fraser came in hard and punched home a high forehand at the net. That was salvation for a time. At 6-5 and 15-15 he opened a door to Buchholz again by serving two double-faults. One stop volley took him to 30-40, and then he played another. That time there was rather more volley than stop. Buchholz, who had been over on the far side of the court, ran over to put it away on the bounce, but with the wide open spaces in front of him, he put the ball into the net.

After that, for a time, the walls of Fraser's tight corners were not quite so close. At 9-10 he was down 0-30 on his own service, but Buchholz put a forehand volley, which would have given him three more match-points, out over the sideline, and Fraser got away again. Buchholz did not seem to like that decision, and when they towelled down at the next changeover he gesticulated like a disappointed fisherman. At 4.41 and 13-14 Fraser saved himself twice more – on both occasions by power of service. Then two games later came the accident and the court was suddenly full of officials and first aid men. Buchholz pushed them away once, but in the end they and luck and the injury were too much for him.

* * *

Fraser's Triumph, Laver's Loss

After the all-Australian contests in 1956, 1957 and 1958, an Australian-dominated pattern was taken up again in 1960 with the final between Neale Fraser and Rod Laver. The Peruvian-born Alex Olmedo had broken the pattern in 1959 when he beat the unseeded Laver in the last match, and a year later Laver, now 21 and five years junior to Fraser, was again a finalist. The outcome proved to be a landmark: it was the last time for many years that Laver was beaten at Wimbledon.

Fraser, who had been trying for seven years to win the men's singles title at Wimbledon, succeeded at last yesterday. He reserved for himself a place in lawn tennis history as the last of the all-amateur champions by beating Laver, another Australian and another left-hander, 6-4 3-6 9-7 7-5 in a match that lasted for two hours and five minutes and which provided more entertainment and more excitement than most spectators can possibly have dared to expect.

From previous examples it might have been a dreadful afternoon. Fraser's last final, which he lost to Cooper in 1958, was a dreary service-and-volley affair which lulled the Centre Court into bored slumber, and the match which Laver lost to Olmedo last year was, on the whole, a pallid, shapeless affair, full of nervousness and errors. But yesterday, on one of the most royal occasions Wimbledon has known for years, the two Australians played a match that was full of big services and strong, risky volleys. It was blunt and direct, plain and straightforward. There were few subtleties and few intricacies of strategy. Frequently it amazed and excited, but it never wandered into the highest reaches of the art of lawn tennis. It was fine for those who like that sort of thing, but for those who were still under the spell cast by Miss Bueno on Thursday it was something of an anticlimax.

More than anything else the day was a sentimental occasion. Like Drobny, Fraser is a part of the Wimbledon scene. When he finally won the title, the crowd knew that he had come through difficulties to the crown because for so many years they had seen him in so many of his sufferings. In 1954, when he came over for the first time, he lost in the first round to Rose, whom he might just as well have played in Australia, and the next year he was a first-round victim again, going down to Stewart (United States). Cooper, who almost always defeated him when they met as amateurs, beat him in the semi-finals in 1957 and held him off in the final the next year. Last time, although he won some fine and important matches in other parts of the world, once again success at Wimbledon eluded him. Mackay put him out in the quarter-finals.

This year it was obviously going to be now or never. For all his strength and dogged virtues, no one would really expect Fraser to have a great deal of chance against the pick of Kramer's men and, after he has been one of the most consistent and the most sporting runners-up Wimbledon has known in recent years, there is a kind of justice in the fact that at long last the greatest honour has come to him. At times during the fortnight it seemed that fate loaded the dice for him. Of all the seeds he had the easiest draw to the quarter-finals; Buchholz held six match-points against him and then retired with cramp and an ankle injury; and in the semi-finals Krishnan, who had played skilful and subtle lawn tennis all through the tournament, suddenly lost all his strength and speed. Like the Red Sea in front of Moses, this Wimbledon suddenly opened up in front of Fraser and he was given a clear path to the final. When there were rumours before the match that Laver was suffering from an injured thigh muscle, it seemed that things were going to be very easy indeed for him.

Fortunately Laver soon showed that the strain was not going to cut down his speed. The service-and-volley pattern became plain at once, and service was so dominant that 24 minutes and eight games went by before either man had a game-point for a break. Then Fraser angled a dipping backhand return past the sad-faced, red-haired man at the net and reached 30-40, and a lob finished the job. That made it 5-4 to Fraser, and he served out for the set. Laver accepted the blow and counter-attacked. Soon he was 4-1 up and, although Fraser came back to 4-3, he made it set-all.

The third set decided everything. Laver, leaping for his smashes and running furiously to turn forlorn hopes into profitable ventures, broke for 3-2. Then, when he served again, came the longest game of the match. He began by carelessly throwing points away with shots that he would never be allowed to play if he were in the professional circus. Then at 30-40 the battle was joined. Laver saved the game-point, and then Fraser had three more points for a break. After that Laver lost after what seemed to be a service winner had been judged a fault. Fraser attacked, Laver hit out twice, and the score moved on to level pegging at 3-3.

Fraser broke, in his turn, for 5-3, but when he was serving for the set at 5-4 and deuce the rain, a rare visitor on men's finals days, came down. They went off court for 55 minutes, and when they came back Fraser's service had lost its sting. Laver won two easy points, and it was 5-5. For a time it seemed that Laver was setting the pace, but in the sixteenth game Fraser jumped to 40-0 on his service, and he was defending again. He saved two set-points with service winners, and then came a long rally which he won because Fraser suddenly lost courage. Instead of going for the ball he returned it tamely, and Laver hit his way out of trouble.

But, once out, he was soon struggling. A volley into the net gave Fraser another set-point. Then came the moment of drama, and once more the luck was on Fraser's side. Laver served, and Fraser's return was high and poor, but as he ran to get into position on the base-line he slipped, and Laver, watching him instead of the ball, put an easy smash into the net. That set was a real gift from fortune. The tension slackened after that. Laver seemed to sense that doomsday was near, and he took only six points from Fraser's service in the fourth set. At the end it was by a series of lobs that Fraser forced a way through his defence.

* * *

All-British Women's Final

A rare happening, an all-British final at Wimbledon, took place on Saturday, 6 July, 1961. Both the heroines of that occasion later changed their identities, Christine Truman becoming Mrs Gerald Janes and Angela Mortimer becoming Mrs John Barrett.

'At last' and 'British' were the words most used at Wimbledon this year. At last, for the first time since 1938, a British player reached the semi-finals of the men's singles. At last, after 47 years, there was an all-British women's singles final, and at last, at the tenth attempt, Miss Mortimer won the women's title, and became the first home singles champion since Miss Round in 1937.

Compared with a golden year like 1949, the standard of play was not particularly high. Otherwise, how could a raw youngster like Sangster have reached the semi-finals? Or how could a player who moves as sluggishly as the Venezuelan Pimental have survived until the second Monday? Wimbledon is still closed to Mr J. Kramer's company of champions-cum-lawn tennis business men – thanks to Australia, it looks as though the door will be shut again on Wednesday in Stockholm – and this time there was no Bueno to issue royal commands to the ball in the women's singles. But the home comforts and excitements have been almost enough to compensate for those absences. For the first time for years, the British played a major part at Wimbledon. They kept the interest blazing to the end.

And what a brave, dramatic, and moving end it was. On Friday Laver took the men's title with an aggressive, impressive singles performance. That was a victory to admire. The women's final, in which Miss Mortimer beat Miss Truman 4-6 6-4 7-5 was something different – a match to feel. For those who had been even slightly involved in the world of British lawn tennis, it became difficult to watch as it moved to its tense finish. There were so many memories. There were the two best British players of their generation, meeting on the greatest of all lawn tennis occasions. It was no wonder that there were mixed feelings on the Centre Court. It would have been much simpler if Miss Smith or Miss Reynolds or Miss Schuurman had come through to the final, to meet one or the other of the British pair.

The players came to the match as old rivals. They had met ten times on less important days in the last three or four seasons, and in seven of those encounters Miss Mortimer's quiet groundstroke skill had prevented Miss Truman from using her power, and had bewildered her into defeat. Miss Truman won on the occasions she managed to combine strength with accuracy for the whole of a match – at Connaught just after Miss Mortimer returned from Australia, in a hard-court championship semi-final and in a Hurlingham final. Then Miss Truman broke out of her chains and scored points swiftly and confidently. On those days Miss Mortimer could make no answer to her attacks.

It seemed beforehand that the result of the match would depend entirely upon Miss Truman. If she was nervous and negative, if she allowed Miss Mortimer time to find a length and a rhythm, and to work away profitably at her backhand, and if she continually followed indifferent approach shots to the net, she would lose easily. If she was able to attack at once, if her first service was strong and accurate, and if her forehand found its range, she would win. She once said, 'If my forehand is working, it does not really matter very much about my backhand'. If Miss Truman hit a winning streak at the start, Miss Mortimer would not be able to do very much about it.

And so, on a bare, patchy Centre Court, which was full of bad bounces, the match began. It took a little time for the players to settle down, and then Miss Mortimer moved ahead to 2-0. Then came a crucial game. Four times Miss Truman saved game-points on her own service to hold on for 1-2. Her power was showing itself, but besides power she also seemed to have a greater appreciation of the correct shot to attack upon. This sharper sense of match-strategy had been noticeable in her semi-final against Miss Schuurman. There were none of those wild, nervous charges to the net. It was as though she had suddenly learnt the meanings of the words discretion and patience. This obviously surprised Miss Mortimer.

Miss Truman saved a point for 1-4, and then broke the Devon player's cramped, poked service (which is certainly not a champion's delivery) for 4-4. Resolutely Miss Mortimer tried to chain her to the back of the court, but Miss Truman, who can never have volleyed better, showed a fine ability to hit a good shot in a crisis. Miss Mortimer, on the other hand, failed to take advantage of winning positions.

Miss Truman collected the reward of the first set, and then, after one point had been played in the second, the rain came down. After 40 minutes they came back to court, and Miss Mortimer was forced to defend all the time. Miss Truman struck away to 4-3, and it seemed that she must win. Miss Mortimer was still in the match, but the tide was running against her. Suddenly it turned. Miss Truman failed with one game-point to break service for 5-3 and then a double-fault gave her another. A shot from Miss Mortimer hit the net cord and as Miss Truman moved for it she slipped and her leg twisted beneath her. She stood up and it was plain that she was in distress. She limped her way to another game-point, but again the net cord was against her. Miss Mortimer won the game, and then against an opponent who could only run forward and who found it difficult to turn, she dropped only one more point in taking the set.

Miss Truman has always seemed to be a player who hoped to be lucky, and who often was, but on Saturday cruel luck robbed her of a title that was almost within her grasp. The injury – she said later that it was a slight cramp – enabled Miss Mortimer to escape from a dangerous and difficult position and by the time the cramp wore off Miss Mortimer was more or less in command of the match. At the end Miss Truman was still limping, but she was still attacking all the time.

The final set must have been the most difficult that Miss Mortimer has ever played. The whole Centre Court grieved for Miss Truman, and the Essex player, who came up from 1-3 to 3-3, improved all the time, but her first service was not going in as it had done in the early part of the match. Towards the end she was breaking Miss Mortimer, but she could never hold her own service. Finally, at 6-5, Miss Mortimer served her way to 40-0, lost a point and then won the title with a shot that went low to the middle of the court. She had been lucky, but then she was owed a certain amount of luck.

Her victory on Saturday was the end of a long fight against ill health. Four years ago it seemed that her chance of winning Wimbledon had gone for ever. Only a stubborn, persistent player who loved the game could have gone on for so long and have suffered so much disappointment. As for Miss Truman, she is now talking about the possibility of retiring. That would be a pity. If she can continue to play in the firm bold fashion that she did in this match the future belongs to her – Bueno or no Bueno.

* * *

Latin Magic – Santana v Osuna

This is a graphic description of a match that took place on Wimbledon's Centre Court in the third round in 1963. Manuel Santana, the second seed, whose ultimate success came in 1966, was to lose in the semi-final to the unseeded Fred Stolle. The fast-moving Mexican, Rafael Osuna, was later to win the US title in New York, but in singles at Wimbledon he was thrice a quarter-finalist, never better. Sadly he was killed in an air crash in 1969.

The Santana v Osuna gem of 1963 was noteworthy in that not only did each contestant win the same number of games but also the same number of points. In this year the singles title was won by Chuck McKinley, seeded fourth, who played no other seed. Nor did any of the other seven seeds play each other.

The match of the year was played at Wimbledon yesterday. It may seem early to make this claim, but if 1963 produces such another contest, it will be a year of wonders. Santana, the Spanish No. 1, and the second seed, won it. After taking only two games in the first two sets, he outwitted and outplayed Osuna (Mexico). It was swift, brave and beautiful lawn tennis and at the end of the excitement and emotion, the score was 2-6 0-6 6-1 6-3 6-4.

For the spectator, it was rather like drinking a year's supply of champagne in 100 minutes. There are always those who complain that the standard at Wimbledon is declining, that the days of the great champions have gone. The modern game made part of its reply this afternoon. It was high art, produced at a gallop, a match to remember on cold days of winter, when there is no lawn tennis to see. Apart from the majesty of Laver's play, the last few years at Wimbledon have belonged to the women. Santana and Osuna did something to reassert masculine superiority yesterday.

On one side of the net there was speed, and on the other wit and imagination. Jack Kramer once said that Osuna would make a wonderful lawn tennis professional, and he attacked yesterday in a way that any professional would approve. Santana invariably starts slowly, and his shots take a little time to find their edge and accuracy. Osuna had won four games yesterday before he showed any signs of alertness. The Mexican was commanding the net, volleying, passing, lobbing, and smashing at will. Santana, lips slightly parted, and teeth gleaming in the sunshine, watched him warily. The set ended and Mexico had struck the first blow – and a pretty spectacular blow it had been.

In the press box, Santana's admirers said that the second set would be different. Osuna won his first service game and then came a game that developed into a real struggle for ascendancy. There were nine deuces. Santana, serving, reached game-point eight times and Osuna took the game eventually on his second game-point. After losing that battle, Santana retreated. He did not win a point in the next two games, and he won only five in the last four games – 6-2 6-0 to Osuna. The seeding committee, already bludgeoned and bleeding, must have stirred unhappily in their seats.

Afterwards, it was easy to say in cold blood that this was the moment when Osuna ought to have redoubled the strength of his attack. The axe was in his hands, but he was not quick enough to complete the execution. In the first game of the third set, Santana served and won his service to love. Then he broke Osuna, and suddenly the score was 3-0. Osuna tried to counter-attack, but the speed he needed did not seem to be there. Instead of scoring, he was making mistakes; instead of leading the race, he found that he was merely chasing the ball. Santana began to lob and volley superbly. His groundstrokes began to tell. He looked a complete player. Osuna, for all his brilliance at the net, seemed to be working from a much smaller store of talent.

The third and fourth sets were Santana's, and it seemed for a time that he would win the fifth without Osuna challenging again. But, at 5-3, Santana lost his service and the match was back on the knife-edge. Osuna, who had been looking like a tired panther, became swift again. At 30-all in the tenth game anything might have happened, but everything that did was just as Santana designed. A volley from Osuna fell out and then, with Osuna on the net, Santana conjured a back-hand, cross-court volley, angled for the emptiest of spaces, for victory. Both men moved to the net. For a moment it seemed as though Santana would try to jump it. But he did not. The match itself had been complete. There was no need for an extra flourish.

* * *

Maria beats Margaret

D avid never ceased to be inspired by the artistry of Maria Bueno nor to be moved by the athleticism of Margaret Smith Court. Each won Wimbledon three times. In 1964 their clash in the final brought a momentous match and gave Maria her third singles title. Margaret, who had not yet become Mrs Court, was to avenge her defeat in the same match a year later and to take the title for the third time in 1970. The rivalry between Maria and Margaret was the *leitmotif* of women's tennis for a decade.

The Wimbledon of 1964 was always interesting and intriguing, but it was not dramatic or extraordinary until its wonderful last day. Then, in the women's singles final, admiration and emotion were set free: Miss Bueno, stirring the Centre Court as she did in the first dazzling days of her royalty, won the title for the third time by beating Miss Smith, the Australian champion and the holder, 6-4 7-9 6-3.

Miss Bueno's other victories were in 1959 and 1960. Then a year of illness, during which it was feared that she might never play lawn tennis again, ended her reign. She returned to Wimbledon in 1962, but although she still possessed the style of a great champion, strength and confidence had deserted her. She could play beautiful strokes, but she had lost the power to dominate a court. Her ability to concentrate seemed to have disappeared completely on the day that Mrs Sukova beat her in the semi-finals two years ago, and last year, in a quarter-final against Miss Moffitt, she played as though she was her own ghost. When she lost then, dismally and nervously, it seemed beyond belief that she could ever win a great singles title again.

Oddly that match marked the end of her journey into the wilderness. A few days afterwards she and Miss Hard regained the women's doubles title at Wimbledon, by beating Miss Smith, who had just become the new singles champion, and Miss Ebbern, in the final. Miss Smith may not have realised it then, but the pursuit was beginning. At Forest Hills, two months later, the danger must have been clear when Miss Bueno, wiping out a long Australian lead in the second set, and advancing from 1-4 and 0-30 in the third, took the United States title away from her. When they met again, in the French final, a month ago, Miss Smith won when Miss Bueno faltered after a good start. From the moment when Miss Bueno arrived in England to prepare for Wimbledon, it was clear that, as Miss Hard had turned professional, she was concentrating upon singles.

The grand confrontation of the two best women players in the world took place on Saturday, as the seeding committee had arranged, and the British lawn tennis public had hoped. Miss Bueno, with an easy draw, had advanced quietly until Miss Turner forced her to play superbly in the semi-finals. Miss Smith's journey to the final had been more spectacular. Fierce and accurate bombardment had destroyed the defences of such useful competitors as Mrs Susman, the champion in 1962, Miss Baylon, and Miss Moffitt.

Thus the scene was set, but what no one expected was that Miss Smith would suffer so dreadfully from stage fright. She missed lines that she would have hit with thunderous effect; her service constantly betrayed her, falling short and inviting Brazilian punishment, or sailing yards out of court, and her forehand, always a weakness, looked more vulnerable than ever.

All through the match Miss Smith was struggling to make proper use of her power, and the fact that Miss Bueno, constantly turning the screw of pressure, prevented the Australian from breaking loose and hitting freely, was the key to the Brazilian victory. Even when Miss Smith led 4-0 in the second set she was unable to summon up the resolution to continue to attack.

As the match was so difficult for her, it must have been galling for her to see Miss Bueno scoring points with capricious ease. The Brazilian spent points as wastefully as ever, but in the crises of the match she invariably found it possible to produce luxurious quantities of shots which were rich and imaginative, graceful and deadly. She was the more effective server; she did not miss a smash and, in the recollections of even the oldest members, no woman has hit so many beautiful and piercing forehand volleys. Her volleying from the backhand was not quite so good.

Miss Bueno soon gained the initiative. Both women suffered from the line-judges in the first set. A call that raised almost every eyebrow in the crowd cost Miss Bueno a lead of 4-2, and then Miss Smith endured what seemed a dreadful injustice when Miss Bueno reached set-point. The Australian, attacking an opponent who played two careless games, was at her best in the middle of the second set, but then Miss Bueno, in control of her strokes and herself again, moved from 0-4 to 4-4, and the wonder was that Miss Smith, living through crisis after crisis, was able to deny her the set. When Miss Bueno let it slip, amid almost unendurable tension, in the sixteenth game, the time seemed to have come for Miss Smith to accelerate and snatch victory, but the last surprise was the ease with which Miss Bueno, playing with great firmness and accuracy, regained command. She broke service in the seventh game, and that was the end of the battle.

When it was all over, Miss Bueno leapt high, burst into tears, and then walked from the umpire's chair back into the middle of the court. Wimbledon belonged to her again.

* * *

The Beloved Champion

The victory of the Spaniard, Manuel Santana, at Wimbledon in 1966 was a surprise in that he was one of the many continental players who were prone to bring out the old cliché: 'Grass is only fit for cows'. As a hard-court specialist he won the French title in 1961 and 1964; then, in the autumn before his famous Wimbledon excursion, he won the US title at Forest Hills on turf less good and more demanding than that at Wimbledon. Throughout his career he warmed spectators by his captivating personality, cheerful and sporting to a rare degree.

After twelve years of failure, Europe recaptured the men's singles title at Wimbledon yesterday. Santana, the greatest public favourite for years, beat Ralston, the 23-year-old United States No. 1, by 6-4 11-9 6-4, to become the first Spanish champion of the lawn tennis world. In some ways, it could not have been better done: this was as pleasant a final to watch as there has been for years, full of high grace and elegance, wit and spirit. 'A sympathetic match', said someone at the end, and that seemed to sum it up. It lacked the drama of some of this week's long journeys to the edges of cliffs and the high peaks of excitement, and it was a little short of that crushing pace and rugged efficiency which has played such an important part in so many of Australia's Wimbledon successes – but, as a contrast in style and personality, it could not have been bettered.

Everyone always suffers with Santana. Centre Court crowds all over the world make a habit of clasping him to their warm-hearted bosoms, whereas Ralston, crop-headed, awkward, unrelenting, always, it seems, angry with himself, and with life, is one of the difficult children of the family of lawn tennis. There have been times in the past when he has allowed his temper to run away with him, when the USLTA, not the most liberal or the most understanding of official bodies, have found it necessary to suspend him. His semi-final against Drysdale on Wednesday did not exactly endear him to Wimbledon, and at the start yesterday, as he strode about the court, erect and grim-faced, he seemed perfectly cast as the villain of the piece. When Rosewall lost to Drobny in the 1954 final (Europe's last victory), he said afterwards that he felt as though he was playing against 14,000 opponents. Ralston must have understood what he meant, yesterday.

Santana had both the game – variety, delicacy, sudden bursts of boldness and imagination – and the manner to please. He only had to hit a good shot and Madrid must have heard the noise that London made; if he smiled, tension was broken; and, by the third set, when it was clear that he was going to win, and that the crowd (his 14,000 supporters) could look forward with bright anticipation to a happy ending, he was able to relax and float gently to victory on a great wave of popular emotion.

The first time that I ever heard anyone talk about him was ten years ago, when he was eighteen. 'He's small and frail, but with the most lovely shots. They all worship him in Spain', said a leading British player who had been beaten by him. As he padded about the court, scuttling to the net, hair unruly, and shoulders broader now but slightly hunched, there still seemed to be a good deal of that wonderful small boy about his performance. Some older, colder players treat their lawn tennis like poker, but if you looked at Santana's face yesterday you could tell exactly what kind of stroke he had played, and whether it had pleased him. Impish delight, definite anxiety, and relief at the successful completion of a risk followed each other quickly.

To play so much and still have such enthusiasm for the game must be a great thing. 'Nothing will speak to your heart with the sweetness of the man of strings', said the old musician in the Hardy novel. There were times yesterday when Santana made such a direct appeal of joy and beauty that any violinist alive would have envied him his skill. It is to Ralston's credit that he tackled his battle against the odds with sturdy courage. He went closer to winning than the score suggests. In the first set he had two points to break service in the eighth game, but Santana beat him first with a service and then with a high backhand volley. An ace at deuce left the American looking doubtful, and then came a superb forehand, taken early on the rise, which dropped and died in Ralston's backhand corner. Immediately afterwards Santana broke service for 5-4, and that gave him the set.

The second set was long and arduous, and for a long time there seemed the possibility that Ralston's plain aggression and greater strength would enable him to outlast Santana. Might the Spaniard become dispirited, as he had done against Fletcher and Davidson in sets in which the magic failed to work? Ralston led 3-1, and everyone waited. Santana replied by counter-attacking and breaking back in the seventh game. Thereafter there was no flickering of concentration. All was strict, all was disciplined, as he advanced towards the great prize. He seemed to jar his back as he moved for a lob in the eighth game, but it only pained him for a moment or two. He saved a set-point at 5-6 with another flashing service, and then broke through for 10-9. In the previous game three pigeons had swooped across the court in front of Ralston. The message seemed to be that Santana was going to win.

In that crucial nineteenth game, which Ralston lost, he served two double-faults, and in the whole match he served nine. He served more accurately than usual, but his service, always flat and always ambitiously fast, is still not reliable enough. He must improve it if he is going to win the title next year. It betrayed him again in the third set, but by that time

Santana was in complete command. The last shot was a forehand volley which Ralston could only watch. Santana threw away his racket and danced a kind of mambo. The applause was loud and long. At his press conference he talked happily for a long time. Among other things he said that he would not turn professional, and that he would return to defend his title next year.

* * *

The First Open Scorches

The first Open Wimbledon, in 1968, was a challenge to every tennis writer who took pride in his craft. In this article David records happenings at the halfway stage.

Rosewall, Newcombe, Emerson, Stolle . . . the temperature at Wimbledon rose to 100 degrees on the Centre Court and in the sudden fierce heat half the great names of professional lawn tennis and of the Australian game were burnt away. There has never been a day like it in the history of the tournament. More than 500 spectators fainted and for long torrid hours every court seemed to be in a state of crisis.

'Enjoy Wimbledon' said the posters outside. There was no time to do that. Too much happened. Even the tournament's record doubles set – the 32-30, which Alex Olmedo and the 47-year-old Pancho Segura took from Abe Segal and Gordon Forbes (South Africa) – passed without proper attention. The courts, sodden for so long, were suddenly scorched and so were one or two reputations. At the end of it all only two Australians, Rod Laver and Tony Roche, who are at opposite ends of the draw, were left in the men's singles and the Americans, with Dennis Ralston, Arthur Ashe, Clark Graebner and Earl Buchholz surviving, are having their best Wimbledon for years.

The afternoon became a matter of deciding which funeral pyre one attended. Fred Stolle, who had always been marked for burning, was the first to go, beaten 6-1 7-5 7-5, by Graebner, the conqueror of Santana, in that intimate little oven which is known as Court Two and which is always the hottest place on the ground since there is no shade at all. On the Centre Court on Saturday the American had generated an astonishing amount of service speed. Santana, on the receiving end, had tried to deal with this for a time and then settled for making a few late gestures at the ball.

From the Court Two press box, which is five yards from the players, it was possible to understand why. Stolle, who has hammered down a few in his time, was reduced to a respectful silence. He saluted the first few of the American's thirteen aces but then found himself behaving like a guardsman on duty at Buckingham Palace, marching slowly from side to side and springing to attention at regular intervals, and he gave up the habit. The exchanges were violent. At the end one felt rather as though one had been on a day trip to Stonehenge 3000 years ago. The umpire, who wore a yellow carnation, waited a long time for a rally. When one came – in the ninth game of the third set – he flung up his hands and beamed with delight. Stolle, who lost that point, merely looked sad. Soon afterwards he met his inevitable end.

The decline of Stolle, which was a comedy for those who think, was followed quickly by the defeat of Rosewall, which was a tragedy for those who feel. Tony Roche had beaten him in four sets in the professional tournament in Boston a fortnight ago in the first battle between the two pro groups and there was never a chance for the smaller, lighter, older man yesterday. Roche, serving his first ball at threequarter pace in order to get it into court ('His return is so good that I knew I would be in trouble with my second') and chipping down both lines and across court in order to make Rosewall move as much as possible, set a fierce pace from the start.

He was relieved to find Rosewall missing the kind of shot he usually finds possible and he reckoned that he himself made fewer errors than he used to in his amateur days because the strict VASS points for cash system which the 'Handsome Eight' use has tightened his game. He went in boldly and effectively. When it came to the post-mortem, Rosewall discussed it all a little sadly. Perhaps the change in the weather had destroyed his normal precision of shot. 'I missed a lot of volleys', he said, shaking his head. 'If I hit them high they went out. If I hit them lower they went into the net.' He paid a rueful groundstroke player's tribute to a server and volleyer. 'Tony plays his game to perfection. The speed of the ball off his racket kept beating me. I kept feeling that he was not hitting firmly and yet I could not get near it. He has a vicious swing service, and if you are a little bit off like I was today you poke at it and he has plenty of time for a good volley.'

That was how it looked. Roche dominated the net and Rosewall tried vainly to keep him away from it. He was in trouble all the way through the first set and eventually lost it: he had no luck with the net cord and, as always happens when the tide is running against one, even less in his dealings with the line-judges.

There was some controversy about a let which was not called at 7-8 in the first set, the game which cost Rosewall the set, and a fiercer argument in the eighth game of the second, which Rosewall lost to be 3-5 down. He was serving and it was Roche's advantage. Rosewall volleyed into the corner and the ball skidded across the line. The linesman gave it out and the umpire awarded the game to Roche. Both players thought the ball was in and wanted the point played again, but nothing could be done about it. This break of service on a blazing day ended Rosewall's resistance. If he had been going to win, he would have to have done it in four sets. Certainly, he did not look as though he possessed the stamina for a fifth. He put on the kind of cap that Buster Keaton might have worn to protect him from the sun, but the real weakness was in his arm which had lost so much of its usual cunning. In this way the winner of the first two major Open tournaments failed to win the biggest prize of all.

Someone asked him whether he thought Wimbledon was a specially unlucky tournament for him. No, he said, playing here was just like playing anywhere else, but when you looked at him you felt that he did not really believe that. There are some Australians who are sentimentalists, just as there are a great many people who go to Wimbledon who wanted this particular master of the game, who is so skilful and so sporting, to win the title. He will be 34 next year – even older, but not much, than Drobny was when he beat Rosewall in the 1954 tournament.

There was a kind of interlude in the main action after this – a whole hour without a sensation. Ray Moore, the psychedelic player, beat Tom Edlefsen, the unknown American, in five sets; Ralston struck a blow or two for capitalism by disposing of Alex Metreveli; and Rod Laver beat the gallant Mark Cox 9-7 5-7 6-2 6-0. The second set, which Cox won, must have been the best played by a British player for a couple of seasons. There was never much hope of another great surprise there, but Cox kept going and Laver showed once again that he is not really happy against another left-hander.

It was possible to see Ashe win on Court No. 1 and then race along the corridors of the Centre Court to watch the streamlined Dutchman [Okker] sweep to the fourth great amateur success of the day. It is astonishing that the amateurs are still level with the pros as we come to the quarter-finals. It is also interesting that there is not a player over 30 in the last eight. The Wimbledon of the old hands has turned into the Wimbledon of the young men.

That neglected event, the women's singles, again failed to produce any real surprises. The professional women proved more reliable than the men – Billie Jean King, who rebuked her umpire in her best Red Queen manner, Ann Jones, Françoise Durr and Rosemary Casals all won. Besides Mrs Jones, there are two other British survivors. Joyce Williams beat Janine Lieffrig (France) and Shirley Brasher, now the mother of three and ten years from her great performances on the hard courts of Europe, beat Vickie Rogers, the eighteen-year-old US No. 10. I was talking about this match with her on Saturday evening. 'I know how to beat her', said Mrs Brasher, 'but I don't think I shall have the stamina'. She did, and she had. Some of the lobs and drop shots were gorgeously reminiscent of her best days.

Two Great Women's Semi-finals

There was little prospect of any British man doing much at the first Open Wimbledon in 1968, but among the women Ann Jones was outstanding. The previous year she had given her best singles performance when she reached the final, where she went down to her old rival, Billie Jean King, and in 1968 she climbed to the last four for the seventh time.

While she had an outstanding match against Mrs King, the ebullient Australian Judy Tegart, who had beaten Margaret Court in the quarter-finals, equally thrilled with her semi-final against the Texan, Nancy Richey. In the final two days later Mrs King was to win the title for the third time.

The Fourth of July at Wimbledon: but the Americans only succeeded in half-celebrating the occasion. Judy Tegart will meet Billie Jean King, their champion and the winner of the title for the last two years, in the women's singles final. It will be Australia v United States; amateur v professional; and tomorrow's match may well turn out to be the most robustly aggressive women's final for years. If you like to see women volley and smash, 1968 could be your year. Miss Tegart, attacking with more ferocity and control than one had ever seen from her before, beat Nancy Richey, the leading amateur, 6-3 6-1, and Mrs King defeated Ann Jones 4-6 7-5 6-2, after the British player had served for the match at 5-4 in the second set.

Only the British will be disappointed by the way the affair has ended. Mrs Jones, who lost to her great American rival in the final last year, seemed to have learnt how to beat her in the course of her three months of professional touring. Before yesterday they had each won three matches, and for more than an hour on the Centre Court, it looked as though Mrs Jones, seven times a semi-finalist, and one of the finest hard-court players in the world, might have the best of all her chances of winning the greatest of the grass-court titles.

For those who have watched their other duels – at Wimbledon, in the Wightman Cup, and in the final at Forest Hills last year – yesterday's contest seemed curiously unrelated to anything that had gone before. A stranger might have thought that Mrs Jones had a long record of confident aggression behind her, and that Mrs King was habitually uneasy, and liable to miss her chances at the net. Mrs Jones spoiled as cleverly as ever, and volleyed more purposefully than she did in her amateur days. She had always been a shrewd strategist, using her head as well as her racket. Travelling with Mrs King seemed to have given her a new and deeper knowledge of where the American would place her shots.

She was tidy and efficient. Mrs King seemed depressed, and – this is a word which one never expected to use about her – lethargic. Before the tournament she had withdrawn from Beckenham and Queen's, and flown home to California because she was feeling tired and ill. In her previous four matches she had not lost a set, but she had hardly seemed to be her normal self. No bounce; no zest; she wasn't even talking to herself when she lost points; there was no sign of the old bespectacled eagerness, or of that hungry bird look which used to come over her face whenever there was a volley to be snapped up.

Mrs Jones won the first set, and moved easily, almost lightly, to 5-3 in the second. There were no agonized glances towards the players' stand; her chin, which had drooped all the way through the final last year, jutted belligerently ... and yet, as what seemed to be the finish drew nearer, memories of their past meetings, of long British leads which melted suddenly, began to rear ugly heads. 'We are not safe yet', said a tall man in a mustard hat and coloured suit. Suddenly it was noticeable that there was a briskness and determination in the way that Mrs King picked up the balls to serve in the next game. She won that ninth game of the set to love, for 4-5. ('Ann played a bad game. She slugged every return.' *'But you were getting your first serve in and serving harder, weren't you?'* 'It had to go in some time. It was getting late.')

Then came the crisis. Mrs Jones served. At 15-all she hit a ball wide to Mrs King's forehand. The shot might have beaten the American, but she scrambled it up for a lob. Mrs Jones might have killed the ball, and nearly did, but Mrs King, topping it slightly, drove across court from her backhand. It found a gap of about a foot between Mrs Jones's forehand and the sideline, kept low, and skidded off the line – spectacular winner, and a warning of the challenge that was to come. The British player won one more point in that game and then lost the next thirteen. The sleeping tigress was awake. Mrs Jones began to look as though the ghosts of matches past were appearing before her one by one.

Regular readers can skip this paragraph. The final set followed a familiar pattern. Mrs Jones kept on volleying, but shots that had been going in fell out, and her first service lost its accuracy. ('A semi-final at Wimbledon isn't the place to start practising your first service', she said tersely.) She thought that she had still had a chance at this time, but the Centre Court's crowd quickly lost its optimism, and at 2-4 it was clear that the end was near. ('When you are playing someone as good as that, if you don't take the opportunity when it arrives, you don't often get another chance.')

At the end Mrs King looked so confident that you would not have thought that she had ever been in the slightest danger of defeat. Just one more near miss for Mrs Jones. In the end it was not even as close as their final at Forest Hills last September.

That was a revival. Miss Tegart put on a completely new show. She has always been one of the most attractive players on the circuit, hitting freely and happily in all circumstances. Give her a racket and a ball and she likes the sight and sound of them colliding. She is broad-shouldered, optimistic, and enthusiastic. If she played cricket, Somerset would want her to qualify for them. In Melbourne she used to be an audit clerk, and her tennis is exactly what you would not expect from an accountant. It is generous, roughly accurate, and hearty. Certainly, there is often more red ink than black in some of her margins. She hits, and she does not always count the cost.

There was even something haphazard about the way she arrived at the ground yesterday. The official car which was carrrying her to the All England Club broke down a mile from the ground, and she thumbed a lift. That kind of thing would never have happened to the sober and diligent Miss Richey, who works for her points, patient enough to win the French title (which Miss Tegart isn't), and is only happy when she is hitting hard, often and accurately. On form, Miss Richey ought to have won yesterday, but she gained only four games. Miss Tegart kept her under pressure from start to finish. There was no rest, and no chance for Texas. In this match, as in the other semi-final, the bold stroke-maker took command of events.

Those who have to play Miss Tegart know that, if you can only hold out long enough, her control is liable to slip – as it did against Mary Ann Eisel in the third round. She was a little wild at the start yesterday, and Miss Richey's lobs baffled her, but she decided to go on attacking, and her courage was rewarded. By the end, she had given one of the most brilliant displays of free hitting that has been seen from a woman on the Centre Court for years. She clouted the ball meatily; she took risks; and the points flowed to her, and she did not make her usual quota of mistakes. 'Like Marble' said someone, as she put away a series of brilliant volleys. Miss Richey, as much a spectator as the rest of us, must have felt that her feet were encased in clay. She led in four of the games that she lost in the second set, but each time her lead was hammered away from her. It was the best piece of Australian opportunism since the jumbuck was put into that tucker-bag, and at the end one expected all the fountains of Wimbledon to flow with Foster's Lager.

* * *

Muddled Aftermath

If the pre-Open scene was rife with dissension and political manoeuvre, that following the reform was little better. Here David reflects on the first Open Wimbledon in 1968 and his comments echo the uncertainty that was to remain for many years.

For anyone with a taste for irony, and the way that the whirligig of time brings in his revenges, there could have been nothing better than the last day of the first Open Wimbledon. Night fell on the Centre Court with two Russians, Alex Metreveli and Olga Morozova, whose national federation has violently opposed Open tennis, gallantly failing to wrest the last title from two highly paid Australian amateurs, Margaret Court and Ken Fletcher.

Three weeks earlier, Mrs Court had – or so she thought – defied the Lawn Tennis Association of Australia by accepting prize-money at Beckenham, although since then the LTAA, who have spent most of the past six months turning political somersaults, have been able to avoid the unpopular step of disciplining her by saying that they had not refused to let her play for prize-money, but had only issued a warning – later withdrawn – that she might be jeopardizing her amateur status. As for Fletcher, he has been in dispute with the LTAA for so long that no one can remember the original cause of the quarrel. It was all symbolic of the confused state of the game's administration.

Throughout the week Bill Edwards, the President of the LTAA, once the outspoken leader of the anti-Open party, but now pro-Open on the theory that 'if you can't beat them, you have to join them', had occupied two seats in what seemed to be a rather isolated position at the corner of the Royal Box. One wondered whether he had been received with absolute cordiality by those British officials whom he had threatened and attacked for six months before he changed his mind, and how he could still continue to hold the Australian Presidency after his council had rejected the views which he put forward so tenaciously for so long. Australia's new policy will help Britain's attempts to reform the game, but if the LTAA had looked further and spoken more clearly earlier in the day, the International Lawn Tennis Federation would not be in its present state of confusion. Edwards must take some responsibility for that, as he also must for the threatening message brought by Ben Barnett, the Australian delegate, to the annual meeting of the Lawn Tennis Association here in December. That did nothing to help the situation.

In the international box was Giorgio de Stefani, the President of the ILTF, who threatened Britain with expulsion in January because he thought he owed a duty to lawn tennis's particular but outworn concept of amateurism, and believed that the rest of the world would agree with his view that the game was not ready for Open tournaments, and that, in any case, Open competition would only benefit the professionals.

De Stefani's appearance at Wimbledon was a sign that the British – and the bulk of the lawn tennis public in every country – had won. Two months ago de Stefani was saying in Rome that there was no general demand for Open tournaments. If – thanks to the weather, and the rail strike, attendances at Wimbledon were down by 24,000 this year – the publicity throughout the world, and the tremendous success of the first Open in Paris in May must be regarded as proof that the ordinary spectator wants Open tennis.

De Stefani has shown himself to be out of touch with the general development of the game so far. He has a chance to remedy the situation at the annual meeting of the ILTF, which begins at Monte Carlo on Wednesday. This is unlikely to be as momentous as the special meeting in Paris in March, when the British gained about 70 per cent of what they wanted, but there are a good many anomalies to be examined. The British, who have abolished the distinction between amateurs and professionals, and the Americans, who hope to keep it strictly, are both at variance with the ILTF's acceptance of the new category of 'registered players', who can earn money from the game and yet are not regarded as professionals.

The Federation will have to re-examine their relationship with the professional promoters. Since the first Open tournaments have been so successful, the demand for more than the restricted number laid down in Paris is bound to increase. The ILTF may not make a formal statement of policy on this, but the management committee may well feel themselves able to grant more. One reason why Open tournaments were rationed was a fear that the professionals would win everything – and become too powerful. Wimbledon has shown that most of the contract professionals are not powerful enough.

Amateur national associations will now work hard to prevent leading players like Okker, Ashe and Graebner from joining the pros. To do that, they will have to have the kind of money at their disposal which comes from success in the Davis Cup, or from staging attractive tournaments – which means a good gate, high sponsorship, and probably the professionals. In this paradoxical fashion, the amateurs can probably keep their best players under their control by staging Open tournaments, for no one is going to join a professional group if it is possible to make more money and live more easily by staying as a freelance.

In the end, too, a general acceptance of this situation would mean that the promoters no longer had to stage tournaments of their own, and could act as agents for players who were back again under the control of amateur federations. Some such arrangement has already been put forward as a solution to the problems of the 'Handsome Eight', the Texan group, whose operations so far have not proved profitable, and the matter will have to be pursued much further if, as Australia have proposed, all professionals are allowed to play in the Davis Cup.

All the titles except the mixed, which Fletcher and Mrs Court won for the fourth time, went to professionals on Saturday. Billie Jean King took the women's singles for the third successive year – which only Louise Brough and Maureen Connolly have done since the war – by beating Judy Tegart, the Australian No. 1, 9-7 7-5. Miss Tegart's fierce blaze of riot, which had destroyed Nancy Richey in the semi-finals, did not last. The pressure of playing in the final took a good deal of the zest from her hitting, and for a time she looked quite subdued. She never led, and she served eleven double-faults.

Occasionally it looked as though she might batter her way into the ascendancy, but in times of danger Mrs King always managed to produce the right kind of shot. This is one of her great strengths and probably something produced by living in Southern California. There you have to be aggressive to survive, otherwise all those bustling competing people, driving high-speed cars along eight-lane highways, would grind you into the ground. Technically, she may not be the greatest of Wimbledon's recent women champions, but even when she is playing badly she still looks mighty formidable in a crisis.

Sadly, this was just what Ann Jones was not in the women's doubles final. She and Françoise Durr have been beating Rosemary Casals and Mrs King regularly on the pro tour, and they won the first set on Saturday, but then they lost the initiative, and in the final set Mrs Jones missed all the best chances of regaining it. In the end the Americans won 3-6 6-4 7-5.

The men's doubles final was dour and all-Australian. Tony Roche and John Newcombe regained the title they won in 1965 by beating Fred Stolle and Ken Rosewall 3-6 8-6 5-7 14-12 6-3. So the 'Handsome Eight' salvaged something, but it was a long business.

* * *

The Longest Match

The setting for Wimbledon's longest match, in terms of games, was the Centre Court in the first round of the men's singles in 1969, on Monday, 23 and Tuesday, 24 June. The tie-break, which has largely ended such extended struggles, was then unknown, as was the provision of chairs on which players can now rest when changing ends. Gonzales, seeded twelfth, went on to win two more rounds before losing to fellow-American Arthur Ashe in the fourth round. Twenty years earlier, in 1949, as an amateur, he had failed to justify his second seeding against the Australian, Geoff Brown, at the same stage.

After the longest singles contest ever played at Wimbledon, the old man had triumphed in one of the finest and most emotional matches on the Centre Court since the war. Pancho Gonzales, aged 41, and former champion of the world but never at Wimbledon, beat time, weariness, and expectation in defeating Charlie Pasarell, the best first-day player in the tournament, as both Santana and Rosewall remember, 22-24 1-6 16-14 6-3 11-9. Overnight he had been two sets down, and altogether he played for five hours and twenty minutes, and for a total of 112 games – nineteen more than Jaroslav Drobny played against Budge Patty in Wimbledon's previous longest match sixteen years ago.

It was a match that cannot be discussed in ordinary lawn tennis terms. Here was Gonzales, gaunt and greying, the great player, fighting desperately. On Tuesday night, complaining bitterly about being forced to play on in semi-darkness, he had been booed by sections of the crowd. Yesterday, there was only cheering. Pasarell, younger and stronger, challenged him all the way, and reached match-point seven times. Gonzales was so tired that he could scarcely hold his racket, but he saved himself – twice from 0-40 – and went on to win the match. It was the kind of match that took your breath away, and moved you to tears at the same time.

For a long time it seemed that Pasarell must win. When Gonzales, taking the last eleven points, finally beat him, it was absolutely the right result. The crowd had watched Gonzales hold on and crawl uphill until, finally, stricken with cramp in the final set, and moving only when necessary, he reached the winning post. In the end he had to win. Any other result would have been emotionally wrong.

The tremors of Tuesday night's argument about whether or not Captain Mike Gibson, the referee, was right to allow the second set to be played in the fading light had scarcely died away when they went on to the court, and the crowd was clearly divided into pro- and anti-Gonzales sections. In the first half of the third set he drifted close to danger. Around the eighth game there were signs that his service was shortening, and all the pressure was coming from Pasarell. The change began four games later when, at 6-5, he held the first of his nine points for the set. There Pasarell produced a service of the utmost ferocity into his stomach, which made him double up defensively. Oddly, Pasarell was using fewer and fewer of the lobs which had served him so well in the first set. When chances came his way he tended to hit his forehand nervously, and missed two crucial chances of breaking service at 8-8 and 10-10. At 13-14, Pasarell served three aces, one of them saving Gonzales's seventh set-point, but at 14-15 he served two disastrous double-faults.

Once Pasarell's service had gone, his confidence followed. As he said afterwards, he found Gonzales difficult to play because Gonzales had coached him and knew his weaknesses and had earned his respect. Gonzales, who had always moved as economically as possible, attacked with swifter purpose as he saw Pasarell wilting mentally. The fourth set hung on its seventh game, which was a disaster for Pasarell. Gonzales left him looking forlorn with an angled lob and by producing as many angles as Euclid in one rally. Pasarell finally lost it with a double-fault.

By now the match was rather like the end of a marathon. Bruce Tulloh, having run across America, can hardly have looked more exhausted than Gonzales at the start of the last set. Time and again he leant on his racket. He regarded every good shot that Pasarell hit with a kind of dismal death's-head face. The fascinating thing at this point was to see that both men were still capable of using every possible variation of service – spin, slow, short, deep, fast, cut, angle, or straight – to suit the situation, and in the rallies they were stroking the ball rather than hitting it. If bodies were tiring, brains were still alert. At 4-5, after three tired points, Gonzales was 0-40 on his service and Pasarell was beginning to lob again. But two lobs went inches out, and Gonzales saved his third match-point with a centre-line service. This agonizing game went to deuce seven times.

At 5-6 he was down at 0-40 again and the crowd became wilder as, with a smash, a sweetly angled volley, and a service, he destroyed every one of Pasarell's chances. Could he last any longer? All the time Pasarell seemed to be getting closer. He missed his seventh match-point at 8-7 when he lobbed out. By this time it looked as though Gonzales could only serve. When Pasarell served, the older man seemed to have lost control of his racket. Yet suddenly he used his last reserves of energy. Pasarell cracked, and lost eleven successive points for the match. To Wimbledon, Gonzales has always been a world champion by repute. His great matches have been played elsewhere. Yesterday he showed the Centre Court what it had missed in the years when he had been unable to play there.

* * *

Laver and Ashe Renew their Rivalry

From the earliest times there was acute rivalry between American and Australian players. The onset of Open tennis fanned the flames anew and they were never hotter than when the precision of Arthur Ashe was brought against the perfection of Rod Laver in 1969.

Wimbledon came to its great confrontation yesterday. Arthur Ashe, the United States Open champion and the leader of the new generation, came up against Rod Laver, the holder, the world champion and the most professional of the professionals. For one set Ashe ravaged the court, breaking Laver's service three times with the fastest and fiercest returns of the week. Then, gradually, Laver broke the force of the storm. Doggedly he asserted his strength. Forcefully he showed that his brilliancies were the more devastating. In the end, after the most spectacular hour and a half of the week, he won 2-6 6-2 9-7 6-0. He took the last nine games and the fourth set lasted only fourteen minutes. Ashe, the poised begetter of lawn tennis lightning, was destroyed, but his destruction was a work of art. The speed of the exchanges was breathtaking; the risks were fantastic, and the margins for error were infinitesimal. If Laver and Ashe have dictionaries at home, it is unlikely that either of them contains the word 'safety'.

The first set struck everyone dumb. A month or so ago, those who saw Ashe win at Forest Hills last September were finding it difficult to convince people who had only seen him struggle on European clay or wave a damaged racket arm on the indoor courts at Queen's Club of the firm, serene way in which he had dealt with all his opposition in the US Open. Even at this tournament, his progress had been concealed behind a camouflage of lost sets and erratic extravagance. Marty Riessen ran him close; he lost the first two sets against Terry Ryan, a minor South African; Graham Stilwell served for victory against him and only when he played Pancho Gonzales did Wimbledon suddenly realise what a sharp, tough player Ashe is.

He might look slender, but underneath the apparent frailty there is a core of steel and those spectacles conceal a sniper's eye for small targets. The storm that Laver ran into yesterday was a kind of ambush. Ashe approached his semi-final stealthily and struck so hard that he nearly pushed the champion out of the tournament.

When they played last year, Laver beat him 7-5 6-2 6-4. This time a set had been wrenched away before the champion realised what was happening. Has Laver's service ever been captured three times running in a set? Admittedly, Laver recovered one break but it was only by desperate, instinctive hitting. Afterwards Ashe said that he had never played as well in his life as he did in those eight games and Laver said, with a wry smile, that he had been embarrassed when he went back to serve, knowing the kind of shots, mainly topspin backhands, scarcely visible to the eye and hardly touchable by the racket, that Ashe was going to hit against him.

Certainly, all the Centre Court's old inhabitants tried to remember a similar performance. In the end white-haired gentlemen began to mutter about Vines achieving a similar pace and accuracy. Ashe treated any shot that Laver played, any service, with utter contempt, producing streaks of lightning which were usually aimed at the place from which Laver had played his previous shot. He looked bleak and world weary, but with a champion's logic, and a champion's knowledge of his rivals, reckoned that Ashe could not continue to play with such flair and fury. He began to find his range; his cold arm – the one he has to put ice on before a match to kill its pain – began to grow warm; and his service began to work up to full power. The force of Ashe's challenge stirred him to an equal ferocity. Three aces in the fifth game signalled his counter-attack and in the next he broke for 4-2, and moved on for the set. From then on Laver was more in command than the American. Intermittently, there were gleams of dark, swift skill from Ashe, but for the most part Laver held the initiative. He missed too many forehand volleys for the perfectionists, and his service was still below its old peak, but at the end his domination of the court – both mental and physical – was complete.

John Newcombe, who will be his opponent in the final tomorrow, defeated him at Queen's Club a fortnight ago, but that result in the dress rehearsal for the major tournament does not seem to count for much now. Newcombe also won a four-set match – 3-6 6-1 14-12 6-4 – but his semi-final against his old rival, Tony Roche, lasted nearly twice as long and seemed even longer. Here were familiar Australian acquaintances, and members of the same professional group, who knew each other's strokes and strategies too well for there to be many surprises or much emotion. The Centre Court crowd admired their battle, but it did not stir them. Perhaps Sydney or Tarcutta, New South Wales, the country town where Roche comes from, would have been excited, but the match lacked the spice of international rivalry.

Victory yesterday gave Newcombe, the 1967 champion, a lead of two matches to one in his private battle against Roche in major tournaments this year. The left-hander beat him in five sets in the Australian champ-ionships in January and then Newcombe avenged that defeat in the Italian final in April. He won because his service was more secure, because his lobbing was more accurate and because the frailty of Roche's backhand was gradually revealed. Two double-faults cost Newcombe his service in the sixth game of the first set, which Roche duly captured. Then Roche seemed to lose concentration and Newcombe drew level.

Service was broken several times in the third set. Both men were taking the ball early; both were attempting more and more daring angles. At 6-5, Roche held a set-point, played a backhand as he sprinted across the base-line and slipped. Newcombe watched him fall and then turned, with hair and eyebrows raised, to see the ball drop inches out of court. Roche frustrated him when he served for the set at 12-11, but then wasted a series of volleys. Thereafter Newcombe was in command and so the men's singles final will be between Wimbledon's first Open champion and the winner of the title in the last of the old amateur tournaments.

* * *

Triumph of Rosewall

There were dramatic overtones to the men's quarter-finals at Wimbledon in 1971. While the one-time master, Rod Laver, lost to Tom Gorman, another senior Australian, Ken Rosewall, who was destined never to achieve the ultimate, showed renewed life by reaching the semi-finals. At 36 he was four years older than Laver.

This is a story of one of the greatest matches played at Wimbledon since the war. After playing for almost exactly four hours last night, Ken Rosewall, who will be 37 in November, reached the semi-finals of the men's singles for the fifth time by beating Cliff Richey, the 24-year-old United States No. 1, 6-8 5-7 6-4 9-7 7-5 – a score which speaks for itself. The old favourite, the small, dark, graceful man from Sydney, who lost in a final for the third time last year, lost the first two sets and then slowly moved into the lead.

Nothing was ever easy. The sky was dark and a cold wind blew all through the afternoon. The match, with all its shifts of ascendancy and continuing crises, must have been as agonising to play as it was compelling to watch. As a test of stamina it was tremendous. As a clash of character it was fascinating – Rosewall the neat stylist, the maker of beautiful shots, against Richey, sturdy, dogged, and with his great and obvious appetite for points. As sheer entertainment it was a long haul. But the more one watched the more compelling it became. Drobny versus Patty, Gonzales versus Pasarell, Santana versus Osuna – this was another contest for every tennis enthusiast's collection of great Wimbledon memories.

Richey ought to have won it. Rosewall began by lobbing so cleverly, that he made him look like a small boy who had strayed on to the Centre Court. But it was soon plain that he had been a little too clever. Richey started to volley with a great deal of power and penetration and to hammer away when he served at Rosewall's backhand corner. He lost one early break of service in the first set but then broke the Australian again in the thirteenth game. The last point then was a topspin lob to the base-line, which Rosewall saluted by holding up his racket. Then he served his way to the set. In the second set the pattern was similar. An early break for Richey; Rosewall coming back in the eighth game to the first long loud relieved applause of the contest, and then another bleak Australian service game which Richey won.

All through there had been a strange lack of urgency about Rosewall's play. Richey had looked tougher and more determined. He had been faster; Rosewall had looked like a 36-year-old player. Time's winged chariot seemed to have made him nervous and ineffectual. At the end of the match he said: 'I knew that if I could only win a set I would get better. Certainly I could not have become any worse.' All this time the crowd had behaved as though they were at the sick-bed of a dying friend. They stirred optimistically at every moment of possible improvement, but on the whole Rosewall gave them very little reason for optimism.

In the third set Richey led 4-2 and 30-0. The time then was 5.30. The match ended two hours later. Rosewall broke back for four-all, and went on to take the set. Richey looked up at his wife and his sister in the seat below the competitors' box – which are reserved for the friends of those who play on the Centre Court – and the glance was one in which pain, frustration, and appeal were all mingled. It seemed to be the one spot where he was certain of support. The rest of the crowd belonged to Rosewall and the sharper and more efficient Rosewall became the louder they supported him. 'Rosewall could look around for 360 degrees and find support', said the American. 'I could only look at one place.'

After that Australian advance everyone was conscious of the change. They changed service games at the start of the fourth set, but then there was a great deal of perilous living by both players before eventually Rosewall won it. Richey's mistake was that in the crisis he played for safety – instead of attacking. He would produce tame returns to the middle of the court, which set no problems for Rosewall. But he broke for 7-6 only to falter when he served for the match. In the post mortem he regarded his failure to attack then as his biggest mistake. 'I didn't come forward enough. I thought I had learnt my lesson about that last year.'

When Rosewall survived, broke him, and took the set, an Australian victory seemed inevitable but again, with the night growing darker and rain in the air, Richey held on. Again he missed his chances. Seven times he held game-points to break service and always he was frustrated. The glances to his corner of support became more and more anguished. He had trouble with his service – he was foot-faulted twelve times, which inhibited him, to say the least – and at breaking-point (literally for four-three) a side-line judge ruled against him in a very difficult case.

The Centre Court was crowded. It seemed that no one moved except to applaud and as the scores went up on the electric score board outside, there were loud echoes of the applause from those who could not get any nearer to the match. Even though they could not see what was happening, they too, were for Rosewall. The Australian served his way from 15-40 to 5-4 and then came a wonderful game. Four times Rosewall held match-points. Twice he had time to place his backhand perfectly and yet always Richey beat him. The tension was almost unbearable. One just wanted to watch; one didn't want to write about the match.

In the next game Rosewall found himself at 15-40 again, and once more Richey could do nothing when it mattered. It was 6-5 to Rosewall, 30-all and Richey serving. It must end sometime, we said. A forehand volley gave Rosewall his fifth point for the match and suddenly, amid silence, a backhand passing shot finished it all. By the clock, it was three hours, 59 minutes since they had begun. The applause – everyone standing – carried them over the fourth hour and to four hours and five minutes. Richey hoisted himself over the net and Rosewall put an arm round him. 'It was a great match', said Richey. 'I always felt it would be.' All Rosewall's allies in the court saluted him. 'They didn't worry me', said Richey. 'After all, in South America you feel that the spectators have guns. They were very polite to me.'

* * *

Evonne and Chris Make History

The women's semi-final between Evonne Goolagong and Chris Evert on 5 July 1972 enriched the Wimbledon scene. Evonne was the defending holder and Chris was there for the first time. Their ages were twenty and seventeen respectively. On this occasion Evonne thrust back the challenge of the young American only to lose her title to Billie Jean King in the final, and it was another two years before Chris won the title for the first time.

Goolagong v Evert at last and a victory for the champion by 4-6 6-3 6-4 . . . after a year of waiting there was a sense that history was being made at Wimbledon yesterday. The best players of the new generation were meeting for the first time, and the whole world was intrigued by the contest. There hadn't been so much publicity and anticipation about any women's match since Helen Wills was finally allowed to come up against Suzanne Lenglen at Cannes in 1926 or the sixteen-year-old Maureen Connolly played Shirley Fry in the 1951 final at Forest Hills. And the beautiful part of it was that expectation was totally fulfilled.

There could hardly have been a semi-final full of higher excitement or deeper emotion. The tennis had been brave, skilful, dramatic, and full of style, fluctuation and contrast. It was chivalrously won and graciously lost. There could not have been a better advertisement for the new order in the game. Miss Goolagong, the instinctive player, sometimes lethargic and sometimes brilliantly swift and decisive, gradually overcame the slight, neat American, the possessor of the most precise armoury of groundstrokes in the women's game.

If you stretched it, it was a case of athleticism beating discipline and determination, the natural player beating the superbly coached one . . . but at the end no one really wanted to make easy judgments like that. The players had stretched their store of talent and energy to the utmost.

Everything had been given. Devastating returns had been countered by seemingly impossible winners, and the rallies had become anthologies of great shots. The earlier semi-final, in which Billie Jean King had defeated Rosemary Casals 6-2 6-4, had been full of shrewd thinking and spectacular exchanges.

That was a volleyers' match, tennis to appeal to the head. The sight of Miss Goolagong gradually summoning her strength to break up Miss Evert's accuracy, and the American's brave response was stuff for the heart. There is a special magic about matches full of positive ground-strokes, and this was a contest to remember and cherish. 'Like Connolly v Hart', said a French friend at the end, and it was impossible to think of higher praise.

Miss Goolagong won because once again she responded to danger by hitting with increasing pace and discipline. Danger stimulated her as it had done on Saturday when Olga Morozova was within three points of beating her or when Françoise Durr was close to winning either of their two sets in the quarter-final. There were times when her first service betrayed her, when she lost concentration and seemed to be taking part in the dream sequence, when under pressure she started to over-hit her forehand, but she always was able to play herself back into the match.

Miss Evert was never able to rest easily, never able to take the lead without facing a sudden challenge at the end. Against lesser opponents she had turned the screw, waited a little, and then accepted a series of surrenders. This was the victim who didn't give in. Miss Goolagong may have begun untidily, presenting her points with a profligacy which is not usually expected from Wimbledon champions. But she won the match from a set and 0-3 down, and in the crises in the second and third sets she scarcely wasted a point.

'Her attitude was good. She never got mad; she was always smiling', said Miss Evert, looking at her with cool detachment afterwards. 'She moves quickly, probably the best in the women's game. She changed direction with her shots a lot, and she was a lot steadier than I thought she would be. At 6-4 3-0, I did not really feel that I had the match won because I had heard that she was used to losing the first set.' 'It's a challenge, I guess', replied Miss Goolagong when someone asked her about her capacity for recovery.

It was one of the brightest afternoons of this year's Wimbledon. The sun paid them the compliment of shining, and they came on to the court to a battery of cameras. They both curtseyed awkwardly to the Royal Box (that was almost the only less than graceful movement that Miss Evert made in the whole afternoon) and then the test of accuracy, courage, and concentration began. 'I'm going to attack her forehand', Miss Evert had said on Monday and, looking across with shrewd concentration, she proceeded to follow that strategy in the best determined American fashion.

For a time that policy was profitable. Miss Goolagong won the fourth game from 0-40; but she was broken for 2-4, with Miss Evert knocking off the points firmly and confidently. There were some groans from the crowd. At the moment, Miss Evert is a bit too cool to be a popular favourite, whereas Miss Goolagong is obviously human and erratic, and, anyway, she became a part of the Wimbledon mythology when she killed Goliath [Margaret Court] in last year's final. She came back to 4-4, only to lose the first set with a dreadful service game. And at the start of the second there were no great signs of a counter-attack. At 0-3 Miss Evert seemed to be comfortably in control. Afterwards she thought she rushed too much there. 'I should have taken my time, but I wanted to win so badly that I rushed. Perhaps I was a little too confident.' That was the end of her time of supremacy. Miss Goolagong served her first ace at 30-0 in the next game. She began to come in more, and she began to give the American more and more short balls on the backhand. Suddenly she looked like a champion again. The dream sequence was over. She had suddenly woken.

For the first time it seemed that she was playing to a plan. Usually her coach, Vic Edwards, uses indirect methods – 'the odd remark here and there' – to advise her on strategies, but yesterday he gave her direct orders: go to the net and hit short to her backhand to make her lift the ball. 'That is the first time he has ever told me what tactics to use', she said yesterday. These are fairly obvious tactics to use against Miss Evert with her double-handed backhand, and Miss Goolagong might well have worked it out for herself . . . but obviously Vic was intending to make sure. The cloud of concerned smoke over his seat was thicker than ever. During the darker part of the match the furrows in his forehead were deep.

Gradually, they disappeared. From 0-3 she won seven successive games. Then she lost a service game to be down 1-2 in the third set; but she broke back at once. The exchange of services was repeated again immediately. Miss Evert may have lost the initiative, but she was hanging on desperately. All the time, however, Miss Goolagong was playing with greater audacity and authority.

Miss Evert held on in a long game for 4-4, with Miss Goolagong mounting a full-scale attack. Every time she put her first service into court, which was a fine achievement for a seventeen-year-old player in the crisis of a Wimbledon semi-final. But the next time she served, the pressure proved too much. Miss Goolagong was in full cry. The bombardment became fiercer, and the champion became more ambitious and more successful. A drop shot, a forehand which dipped over the net, an American error, and one last wonderful volley settled the matter. It could not really have been a better match.

* * *

Classic Contrast in the First Sunday Final

The imperturbable solidity of the American, Stan Smith, and the flamboyant genius of the Rumanian, Ilie Nastase, had one of their most notable confrontations in the men's singles final of 1972. Because of rain it was postponed until Sunday, 9 July, breaking new ground for Wimbledon. To avoid any possible illegality, spectators were admitted free and were treated to one of the best finals of all time. This was Smith's only singles title at Wimbledon; Nastase never did take it.

Wimbledon's extra day brought a tremendous bonus. For the third successive year the men's singles final went to five sets – and this was the best of the three and the most exciting end to the Championships for years. After two hours and 41 minutes Stan Smith, who had held service from 0-30 at 4-4 in the final set and had missed two match-points in the next game, beat Ilie Nastase, the first Rumanian to reach a singles final at Wimbledon, by 4-6 6-3 6-3 4-6 7-5.

In a breathtaking match, last year's runner-up proved that he was not just a heavy server and volleyer. In the crises he forced himself to play flexible and imaginative shots of a kind which had seemed far beyond his range in the earlier rounds. On the great occasion he became a great player. He produced the determination, strength and skill to defeat the most talented strokemaker in modern lawn tennis. There were moments when Nastase was erratic. But at the end of the third set he began to concentrate properly and mounted a brilliant counter-attack. The last few games were ablaze with great shots; Smith won by the narrowest of margins. 'The end was 80 per cent guts and the rest of it just a little luck. Obviously it could have gone either way', he said at his press conference. His friends had bathed him in champagne and he was still wiping it from his hair.

Wimbledon was in holiday mood. Rain had washed out play on Saturday and for the fourth time in 50 years the tournament had been stretched into a third week. Admission was free and the crowd, having waited, were determined to enjoy themselves. Finals usually begin quietly. Even the opening rallies were applauded loudly yesterday. The Centre Court affections were divided equally. For once, in a final, the crowd were not absurdly partisan. Smith, with his straight bat and quick marching between points (is that all that he has learnt from the US Army?) is a popular figure at Wimbledon. They like his calmness and absence of fuss, the way he obviously enjoys his tennis.

Sometimes, of course, his tennis has been too plain for them and he has been disciplined to the point of dullness. No one has ever been able to say that about Nastase. The Rumanian is the circuit's great entertainer, its spoilt and talented child, who uses his racket as a weapon of wit, and its favourite actor. If steadiness is one of Smith's greatest virtues, the ability to climb to sudden peaks of inspiration is one of Nastase's strengths. But there has to be drama, if his game is to work properly, if the magic lamp is to be rubbed ... just as there has to be someone or something to blame – a line judge, an umpire, a doubles partner, a bad bounce or, as happened yesterday, the stringing of his rackets – when things go wrong. Apparently, his rackets had been newly strung and when he began to play, he found them too tight. He kept looking desperately at his friend, Michele Brunetti, a lawyer from Ancona, who was sitting in the players' box, and talking vigorously in Italian. Once Brunetti and an official of the Rumanian Tennis Federation left their seats in response to urgent glances. It was not until the middle of the third set that he began to settle down and concentrate.

'I thought it was a good sign that he kept changing rackets', commented Smith. 'If you keep changing your racket back and forth, you obviously haven't found one that feels good. When you get into a tight situation like that, it is very easy to look for excuses.' Smith thought that Nastase's concentration had been too brittle: 'When he got a little upset over net cords and line calls, it really hurt his concentration, I think. Overall, he has improved quite a bit as far as temperament is concerned. Today under the extreme pressures of the final it might have bothered him a bit.'

Nastase won the first set while Smith was slowly gathering power and accuracy. By the fifth game battle had been properly joined. He had presented the American with a series of sharp-reflexed challenges and Smith, who had lumbered through many of his earlier matches, surprised the Rumanian's supporters by the speed with which he moved to the ball. His backhand, which had been his major problem against players like Ian Fletcher and Alex Metreveli, suddenly regained a good deal of its old force. The spur of playing in the most important tournament in tennis improved his strokes wonderfully. He began to look sharper and more resilient, getting to low volleys with surprising ease for such a big man and sometimes launching himself across the net to stretch for shots that scarcely anyone else in the game could have reached.

But it took him a little time to set the machinery in motion. In the early stages Nastase was serving with more accuracy and fluency and the American was groping for his returns of service. Nastase broke him in the ninth game to win the first set, but then started to hesitate and to fret about his rackets and Smith was given the chance to take the initiative. He captured the second set and all the time Nastase was looking dismally at the strings of one racket after another. His gestures to Brunetti became more and more dramatic. The Italian sat, looking slightly embarrassed, with a cigarette drooping from his lips. And the more anxious Nastase became, the more confident Smith looked. The Rumanian buzzed about the court. Smith was content to graze on it, profiting from the errors that Nastase made. In this part of the match he was relaxed and unemotionally efficient. Nastase was hurrying too much, missing the kind of shots that he uses to torment his opponent and doing less with the ball than he does on his confident days.

The start of the fourth set was notable for a long baseline rally which Smith won. Equally surprisingly, he was winning the greater share of points from the delicate exchanges at the net. Which of the prophets would have thought that about a final like this? But just when Smith seemed to be advancing comfortably, Nastase's mood changed. He swept in, broke him once and captured the set. Two sets all – suddenly, what had seemed to be an easy American victory became a battle again.

Now it was clear that Nastase thought he could win and confidence came flowing back to him. It was Smith's turn to hang on desperately. The sunlit Californian smile with which he had greeted all the chances and changes of the match began to droop a little. 'In the fifth set it was just a matter for me to get my first serve in. If I could do that, then I could hit a more forceful volley', he said. 'I began to think that he might pull it off and that I would be a bridesmaid again.' His first crisis came in the fifth game, which he called 'exacting and crucial'. That went to deuce seven times. Nastase held two points for it and Smith won it with his seventh point. He breathed again there. But in the ninth game he was in danger again. Nastase passed him on the first point and then beat him with a low lob. Love-30 and very little room for salvation! He served, Nastase hit a return and Smith volleyed off the wood. The ball dropped over the net and Nastase ran into it.

The whole of the fifth set was crucial, but that was the most critical point of all. Smith won the next three points – taking the last for 5-4 by diving for a backhand volley, which was almost the most spectacular shot of the afternoon. He held up his arms after that in a gesture of triumph. Suddenly he looked full of confidence again. Nastase saved a couple of match-points at 5-4. Smith should have got the first, but did not have much chance with the second. 'It flashed across my mind then that my chance might have gone', he said. He served his way safely through the next game and then saw another match-point disappear. He needed only one more. Nastase had a chance for an easy high volley, misjudged it and put the ball into the bottom of the net. It was a sad end to a great battle.

The scene then was tumultuous. Smith received the cup with the broadest of grins and waved it at the crowd. He was the first American winner since Chuck McKinley in 1963. 'When we Americans win we certainly make the most of it', said an American player in the competitors' stand. Nastase sat slumped on a seat behind the umpire's chair. When he received the runners-up medal he showed that to the crowd, too, imitating Smith's gesture of jubilation. There had been so little difference between them – but the difference in the rewards was enormous.

* * *

The Dunkirk Spirit

The run-up to the sixth Open meeting in 1973 was the most traumatic of all time. Because Wimbledon would not defy the International Federation's ban on Nikki Pilic, the Association of Tennis Professionals, then less than a year old, caused its members to withdraw at the last moment (see also page 201). It meant that 79 leading players pulled out. The draw had to be postponed and the seeding done anew.

Despite the reduction of the men's events to second-class status the meeting was successful, with total attendance reaching 300,172, the second-highest since 1967. It began on Monday, 25 June, with everybody wondering how an emasculated tournament would fare. This is the story of that dramatic opening day.

In the crisis, of course, the British became more British than ever. The first day of this depleted Wimbledon was full of the Dunkirk spirit ('who do you think you're kidding Mr Kramer, if you think old England's done?') and the comradeship of the blitz. The sun shone – just like it did in the summer of 1940; the Centre Court was packed, noisy, emotional and bloody well determined to enjoy itself; and the attendance was almost a record for the start of the Championships.

It was pleasure defiantly taken. From standing-room to Royal Box (to which Morecambe and Wise had been invited in case the All England Club needed to be cheered up), there was a tremendous unity. Taylor, Nastase, Borg ... they were the heroes. When Ilie Nastase came on with Hans-Joachim Plotz, an energetic little German, to open the tournament, the applause must have been heard from Wandsworth to Kingston. 'It was as though I had won Wimbledon', said Nastase.

Everyone stood. Everyone cheered. When Bjorn Borg, who had just played a tie-break which ended at 20-18 to finish his 6-3 6-4 9-8 victory over Premjit Lall (India), tried to cross the main concourse to be photographed with Lennart Bergelin, his captain, immediately he was surrounded by 200 schoolgirls, shrieking, thrusting autograph books at him, behaving as though he was Nastase or David Cassidy. The stewards had to rescue him. And the welcome for Taylor was even more rapturous. He had borne the brunt of ATP's pressure and criticism, and with Nastase he was joint saviour of the Championships. The applause was louder than ever. Dark, shoulders broad and brow furrowed, he looked round the court. He might have been in Coventry in the dressing room at Queen's Club last week, but here he was among friends – and grateful friends. 'I suppose it's a nice consolation that someone is glad to see me', he said.

Tennis may be a lonely game for him in the future, but at least he had done what the British expect of their heroes. He had paid a debt to the public, who had encouraged him, applauded him and supported him. Other British players, with less heart and narrower views of the significance of Wimbledon, do not seem to have understood why he felt it necessary to take the step.

All through the afternoon the proceedings on the Centre Court seemed more like a celebration than competition. Nastase's match lasted 68 minutes. He missed a few shots at the start ('the court was faster and softer than the main court at Queen's, and the ball did not bounce'), but he won 6-3 7-5 6-2 amusing himself, teasing Plotz and occasionally falling into a few German traps. Every now and again Plotz would produce a clever drop shot or a good passing shot, but he was never allowed to sharpen his challenge. His comment at the end was: 'The players are not the same, but the atmosphere is.' That was how it seemed for Borg's match. This was the seventeen-year-old Swede's first appearance on the Centre Court and he was meeting an experienced Wimbledon competitor. Now, Lall is one of the best of India's post-war players and in 1969 he came closer than anyone else at Wimbledon to spoiling Laver's Grand Slam. Yesterday he seemed slow at first. He took only two points from Borg's service in the first set and four in the second, but in the third he began to counter-attack.

They played the longest tie-break – 20-18 – in the history of Wimbledon and that also beat WCT's [World Championship Tennis] record, the 19-17 between Mark Cox and Roy Emerson at Dallas two years ago. Throughout these exchanges the crowd roared and applauded. It was just like old and good times. Borg needed eight match-points before he won, and Lall held five set-points. The pace of Borg's serving, the boldness of his volleying and the accuracy of some of his passing shots – all those spectacular weapons helped to turn him into an instant hero. Who is going to miss Cliff Richey or Charlie Pasarell when there are players of this quality to take their places in the centre of the stage?

The British enjoyed some success. If John Paish lost to Marcello Lara (Mexico) after taking the first set, and Stephen Warboys, who had led 3-1 in the final set, fell to John Yuill from Natal by 6-2 4-6 9-7 4-6 6-4, the Lloyd brothers won well. John Lloyd beat François Caujolle, a French contemporary, 8-9 4-6 6-3 6-4 6-3, and David Lloyd beat Corrado Barazzutti 6-2 0-6 6-1 6-1. Barazzutti played here even though Paolo Bertolucci and Adriano Panatta joined the boycott. The Italian Federation is considering disciplining them and Jack Kramer ('Via a casa, Gianni Kramer') is flying to their defence.

The matches on the Centre Court ended quietly. Taylor [was] much too powerful and efficient for Jean Louis Haillet, the son of Robert Haillet, a French Davis Cup player fifteen years ago, and Frank Sedgman, making what must be his last appearance there, went down by 6-0 6-4 7-5 to Jiri Hrebec, an aggressive Czech. Jan Kodes, Czechoslovakia's principal challenger, finished his match with Ken Hirai, Japan's No. 3 – 'What is Hirai? Is he a breakfast food or a brand of chocolates?' said Ion Tiriac, complaining of the anonymity of some of the players on view – with a flourish. He won 4-6 6-4 6-1 6-3, after trailing 2-3 in the fourth set and winning the last sixteen points.

Clay Iles [Great Britain] beat Steve Messmer, a corporal in the US Army, stationed at SHAPE headquarters in Belgium, 7-5 6-2 6-4, and Peter Curtis [Great Britain], who has been working so energetically to return to fitness, beat Graham Thomson (Australia) 6-4 6-4 6-2. Old acquaintances who lost included Istvan Gulyas, the determined little Hungarian, who took a set from Jurgen Fassbender [Germany], the eighth seed; Boro Jovanovic, one of the Yugoslavs who did play in the match against New Zealand which Pilic missed, who went out to Sid Ball (Australia); and John Clifton, the former Scottish champion, who missed his way in the fifth set against Jaime Pinto Bravo [Chile].

Altogether, it was an interesting day. The public did not seem to be particularly worried by the fact that so many strange forehands and backhands had been thrust before them, and they stayed until sunset watching Nicola Pietrangeli [Italy], a late substitute, playing with stately elegance. Wimbledon was like this in the days before Open tennis. This year, as in 1947, 1957, and 1967, there were still a great many worthy amateur talents on view. It just demonstrated how much the standard has improved since the introduction of Open tennis.

* * *

Champions Galore

There was a remarkable clash of outstanding players in the women's singles semi-finals in 1975. Billie Jean King, already five-times champion, played the 1974 winner, Chris Evert, while Evonne Cawley, the 1971 champion, met Margaret Court, three times the winner. Mrs King was the ultimate victor, when two days later she took the Championship for the sixth and last time. Although at the time she announced that in 1975 she was competing in her last Wimbledon singles, she could not resist the allure of her favourite Championships, and was back in action from

1977–80, but never again passed the quarter-finals there in singles. However, she continued to collect doubles titles.

In the train to Eastbourne two weeks ago Billie Jean King, who defeated Chris Evert, the champion, 2-6 6-2 6-3 to reach her ninth Wimbledon singles final yesterday, sat down and wrote herself a letter. One of the things she wrote was: 'Even if you get twenty bad calls, the wind is blowing against you, the sun is shining in your eyes, and everything seems to go wrong, you still have to be willing to give, even if you have nothing more to give.'

She took the lesson to heart. She had never lost to Miss Evert on grass, and she approached the match with her usual assurance and determination. But she lost the first set, enduring all the ill luck on the line decisions (please, Captain Gibson, would you tell your linesmen once again to stop laughing after they have ruled against players in tight moments), won the second, and then trailed 0-3, 15-40 in the final set.

It was a major test of nerve and determination, but she came through it wonderfully to meet Evonne Cawley, who beat Margaret Court 6-4 6-4, in the final. She has said that this will be her last attempt to capture a major singles title. No more Wimbledons, even if she wins tomorrow. No defence of her title at Forest Hills. Elizabeth Ryan won nineteen Wimbledon titles, all in women's doubles or mixed. If Mrs King wins again, she will equal that record. As we watched her, wearing down Miss Evert, destroying the superfine accuracy of the cold girl from Florida, we were conscious again that Mrs King is the most remarkable of all post-war champions. She is the match-player extraordinary. Connolly was greater. Bueno looked more stylish. Mrs Court was stronger. We cared more about Doris Hart. Angela Mortimer and Ann Jones belong to us – but no one has been quite like Mrs King. 'I love Wimbledon. I could hug Wimbledon. I love the atmosphere. The Centre Court. Everything about it', she said yesterday. How could Miss Evert, the fair Miss Frigidaire, prim and accurate, hope to counter a player who cared as much as that?

The match was as astonishing as its winner. In the first set Miss Evert seemed invulnerable. Only twice did she miss with her first service. Mrs King tried to play her from the base-line but abandoned that strategy after a long rally at 1-2 and 15-30. She lost her service for 1-3 and the set disappeared. Mrs King was trying to get to the net and she was being lobbed. But the picture changed at once in the second set. Miss Evert needed three second services and was broken in the first game, and although she came back to 2-2, Mrs King smashed with all her old accuracy. The crowd were cheering her too ('I was very conscious that they were aware that this is my last Wimbledon. They were really nice and I appreciate it. It meant a lot to me'). She won four successive games for the set, snapping them up like an angry sharp-beaked bird. There is something decidedly ornithological about the eager, determined concentration with which she picks up her points.

Then she fell behind again. There were three long games at the start of the third set and Miss Evert won all of them. Mrs King tried checking the pace, kept on attempting drop shots, and was passed frequently again. But Miss Evert was passive, always watching her and waiting for her to make a move. That fitted the pattern of her matches against Lindsey Beaven and Betty Stove ('I was surprised by how little she did', said Miss Beaven). Mrs King held service for 1-3 from 15-40, saving an advantage point, and then broke for 2-3 after two long rallies and a remarkable sprint from the base-line to pick up a drop shot. Who said that she couldn't run any more?

That was the heart of the match. Thereafter Miss Evert was defending and Mrs King was always the attacker. 'When I was down 0-3 and 15-40 in the final set, I thought how embarrassed I shall be if I lost it 6-0. I said to myself I must try and take each point to get back into the match. Then I thought: "This is my last Wimbledon and I just can't lose this match now. I just want to do the whole trip." ' She broke for 4-3 after another of those fierce sprints and the rest was comparatively painless. Miss Evert looked as though she simply had not understood anything that had happened in the last six games. At the end she said that she had thought herself safe in the fourth game of the third set. 'I had a good chance, but then I guess I rushed it a little bit. Billie Jean is really a gutsy player and as the set went on I kept thinking about the 3-0 lead which had gone instead of getting on with the match as I should have done. Billie Jean is best when she is down. She always goes for broke. I just hope she plays Forest Hills. This is Billie Jean's last Wimbledon and it means a lot to her. She is like Ken Rosewall in the men.'

By contrast, Mrs Cawley's victory was another demonstration of natural magic. The honeymoon continued. Life was still a joke that had just begun. Perhaps the glorious shots did not quite flow as freely as they had done when she played Virginia Wade; but there was an old inhibition to overcome. The younger Australians always find it difficult to overtake their senior champions. Apart from the remarkable final here in 1971 when Mrs Court was (a) pregnant, a condition revealed shortly after the match, and (b) such an odds-on favourite that she could not help being nervous, Mrs Court has won the great majority of their matches. She had enjoyed a comfortable Wimbledon. She was seeded fifth, which took away the pressure, and she had a leg injury, which the world knew about. But she looked confident, until yesterday she hadn't lost a set, and she had beaten Martina Navratilova, one of the leaders of the younger generation, in the quarter-finals. If Mrs Cawley faltered, Mrs Court would gather strength and steam-roller her way into the final again.

So there was an old domination to be broken. At first it looked as if the usual story might be repeated. Mrs Court broke immediately and led 4-2. She was ruling the net, committing herself early and guessing shrewdly about the destination of Mrs Cawley's shots. But there had been some signs of danger. She won the second game, but she served two double-faults. Like a statue of herself, she stood on the base-line. Even then she was a symbol of frustration. She was hitting powerfully and volleying efficiently. No other woman has such long, strong arms. No one reaches a wide ball like Margaret. She is the most difficult woman in the world to pass.

But she never improved upon her beginning and Mrs Cawley, as she had done against Miss Wade, grew better and better. The first crisis came in the eighth game. Mrs Court led 40-15 and suddenly Mrs Cawley's backhand, graceful, easy, forceful, began to work. She beat her first with a return of service and then forced an error for deuce. There was a wonderful lunge of a volley from Mrs Court for advantage-point and suddenly she served two double-faults. Mrs Cawley accepted the gifts, passed her again to make it 4-4, and captured the initiative at the same time. She swept through a service game, reached 40-love on Mrs Court's service at 5-4, saw the older Australian save four set-points, and then two forced backhand errors from Mrs Court gave her the set. She lost a game at the start of the second, regained the break immediately, and then exchanged services again in the fifth and sixth games. She was playing beautifully, but she hadn't quite chained down Mrs Court.

It was still a battle until another crop of double-faults (altogether she served nine) betrayed the old champion. 'I had my chances and I let them slip. I had an early break in the second, but I just could not maintain it. If I serve well, I generally play well. Once I serve badly my whole game goes down. I didn't serve well and so I started thinking and worrying about it, and then my timing went', she said at the end. The last game typified her failure.

* * *

Connors Humiliated

Jimmy Connors was 22 when he defended his Wimbledon title in 1975. Arthur Ashe was just short of 32 and his finest glory, when he won the US Open, was seven years in the past. His taking apart of Connors's bravura skills by intelligence and craft became a talking point in the game.

Before Arthur Ashe met Jimmy Connors in the South African final at Johannesburg in 1973, that match which meant so much to him, he wrote in his journal: 'I have a fair right to be confident. My best strokes go to his weaknesses. My backhand is better than his forehand, so I'll play him down the line a lot, or right down the middle and refuse to give him the angles he likes. Also, because he likes to work with speed, I'll try to vary the pace on my shots. I expect to attack his second serve and lob him because his overhead is lacking. I'll hit over the ball, too.'

Connors won that match 6-4 7-6 6-3 after Ashe had held a point for the second set. Never anything but tidy, studious and methodical, he afterwards noted the force and accuracy of Connors's groundstrokes ('I was more impressed than I expected to be'). But he found Connors's serve 'nothing special', and when at last he worked in a few lobs, he felt he could hit with him off the ground.

At Wimbledon, where Ashe at last beat him by 6-1 6-1 5-7 6-4, Connors had left behind a trail of destruction on the way to the final. There had been explosions everywhere. Ashe, who had decided earlier in the year that he would meet him in the final, watched Connors against Raul Ramirez ('Ramirez had the right idea, but he changed his game') and in his devastating semi-final against Roscoe Tanner ('Watching Roscoe told me how not to play him. I knew that I had to be restrained in my game'). For Ashe, with the experience of South Africa and a week of close observation to draw upon, the final was an exercise in the art of taming a champion.

He approached it almost as though he was going to play Connors at chess with a strategy deeply considered and carefully rehearsed. Connors's idea of preparation for the final was to go out to one of Wimbledon's distant courts, watched by a large crowd, and practise hilariously with Nastase, who entertained himself by parodying Ashe's style. Funny, certainly, but would the businesslike Mrs King have allowed Martina Navratilova and Julie Anthony, her sparring partners in the last hour before the women's final, the amusement of imitating Mrs Cawley? 'Connors didn't train for this Wimbledon like he did for his challenge matches at Las Vegas against Laver and Newcombe', said Ashe.

The beginning was important. Connors might have exploded at the start, kicking over the chess board and breaking the pieces before Ashe could lay down the tactical lines. But he seemed to take the match too lightly. It is hard to be an odds-on favourite in an individual sport like boxing or tennis and maybe he had been too dominating in the early rounds. Or perhaps he was over confident because he had beaten Ashe in three previous matches ... Ashe took charge immediately, winning his first service game comfortably.

The first break was dramatic. Connors's lash of a smash was well out, but the linesman did not call and the crowd, who had become so critical of umpiring standards in this country since that disastrous day at Bournemouth, roared and bellowed at him until he told the umpire that he had been unsighted and the point was rightly given to Ashe. There had been a great deal of emotion before the match. The lawsuit and all the other rivalries had added to the tension and that incident enabled the partisans on both sides to show their allegiance. 'Is this Wimbledon? I have been coming here for twenty years and never heard the crowd like that before', said a Turkish journalist.

Connors played the next two points as though he was determined to be revenged on the whole pack of them, but then Ashe took command again, making everything as difficult as possible for him. The South African strategy was plain. Nothing to hit; variations of speed; a great deal of awkward slice, doubly effective on the dry court; lobs in plenty (which must have been a surprise because Ashe is famous for forgetting to use the lob); fine bowled smashes to counter Connors's lobs; accurate serves, particularly those kicks to the left-hander's double-handed backhand, which were such a joke when Nastase counterfeited them ('Playing Roche in the semi-finals gave me the practice I needed for serving to a left-hander', said Ashe); and – most surprising of all – brilliant volleying. He always seemed to be guessing right at the net. He was always in position to put the ball away.

This was Ashe's ninth Wimbledon and up to now the low forehand volley has always been his glaring weakness. Laver in particular profited from it on the Centre Court, but on Saturday against another left-hander he took total command of the net. 'It wasn't difficult to volley well against a guy who just hit the ball at 100 mph. If I put my racket there, it went screaming back', he said. Everything else went according to plan. The lawn tennis thinker was in total intellectual control. Hamlet had spotted Laertes, was thrusting the poisoned cup down the King's throat and winning envenomed points everywhere. Against Roche he had hesitated, but the last act was crammed with dynamic action.

As Connors struggled and Ashe ruled, the crowd became totally involved. Double-faults were applauded passionately and there were so many cries from the galleries that the umpire angrily demanded silence. 'Come on, Connors', shouted one man at 0-3 in the second set. 'I'm trying, for Christ's sake', said the American. One romantic foreign journalist, who clearly had not been reading the gossip columns, thought he said: 'I'm trying for Chrissie's sake.' 'He likes all that stuff with the crowd', said Ashe afterwards.

He meditated between points, shutting his eyes and sitting totally relaxed. Neither his friends nor his opponents were able to do that. Bill Riordan, Connors's manager, kept bounding up and down in the court-side box. Donald Dell, ATP's lawyer and Ashe's agent, was in front of him, almost biting off his own right hand with anxiety, with Marty Riessen. Next to Riordan was an unidentified man, loudly applauding everything that Ashe did. Exasperated, Connors's manager asked him who he was. 'I'm Arthur's personal physician', said the stranger. Mrs Connors made gestures of encouragement to the falling champion, but the second set had gone before he showed signs of coming to terms with Ashe's shrewd attack. All those coaches who criticised the double-handed backhand must have been delighted to see how Ashe exploited the vulnerabilities of the best double-handed backhand in the world on Saturday.

He could have won in straight sets. He broke Connors for 3-2 in the third then lost his service but had half a dozen points to break in other games. Connors had looked at the message of advice that he keeps in his sock, but it had not done much good. Then when Ashe was serving at 5-6 and 30-all, a pigeon flew low over the court. Was it carrying another message for Connors? Certainly, he responded by hitting two fierce forehands to take the set. He led 3-0 in the fourth but Ashe counter-attacked immediately. 'I expected him to break my serve a lot, maybe more than he did. At 0-3 in the fourth, I didn't worry too much. It was only one break against me', said Ashe.

After that the rest was comparatively silent. The odds-on favourite was lobbed, dinked, teased, passed, out-rallied and frustrated. 'Today I just lost. Everyone must realise that every time I go on to court I can lose. You guys in the press have to realise that as much as anyone. He played well and did everything well today. I don't reckon I had an off day. It was just that I was playing a better Arthur Ashe. I can't pinpoint any one thing he did that put me off. His forehand was good. His forehand volley is usually his weaker side, but that was good. He returned well. He served and volleyed well. That sort of thing is pretty hard to play against. I played hard, but it was all in vain. If I could have won that fourth set I felt that I would have been in with a chance. I had a point for 4-1 and I saw the ball well but it came blistering by me. But I walked into this tournament with head high and I go out with my head high.'

The last shot was a smash as Ashe hammered the ball into an empty space with Connors yards away beyond the far sideline, the first cheers coming from William Hill, the official bookmakers. Ashe may have criticised their presence at Wimbledon, but he helped more than anyone to make their experimental appearance at the Championships a huge success.

It was a victory, too, which totally changed the balance of political power in the game. While Connors was the champion, Riordan was able to stage highly profitable challenge matches for television. Another of the so-called 'world title events' has been arranged for February, but now the only credible opponent for Connors is Ashe and he is the President of ATP, one of those whom Connors is suing, and at the centre of the tangled dispute. There is clearly a vast area for negotiation. If Riordan wants the challenge matches to continue, and if CBS are to have the kind of opponent for Connors who will attract a huge television audience in February, there will have to be an agreement of some kind. This may be the opportunity for all parties to end the litigation which has been so damaging to the game. If Ashe's victory – which follows his success in the WCT final at Dallas – brings peace to the game, it will be the most important match won at Wimbledon for years.

*   *   *

Connors Meets his Match

A spectacular upset marked the quarter-finals in 1976, the year Bjorn Borg won for the first time. Arthur Ashe, who fell to Vitas Gerulaitis in the fourth round, was the top seed, and Jimmy Connors the number two. Roscoe Tanner, 24 years old and from Lookout Mountain, Tennessee, blasted his way to the semi-final at the expense of Connors. But there he was stopped by Borg, who was to beat him again three years later in the final.

The trouble with Jimmy Connors is that he is always the victim of his own propaganda machine. His conversations bounce with confidence. He is devastatingly aggressive on the lesser occasions of lawn tennis. He looks and sounds exactly like a champion. But since he won Australia, Wimbledon and Forest Hills in 1974, he has not played in enough of the biggest tournaments and all the best prizes have eluded him. At Wimbledon yesterday the odds against him were 11-10 for the title. He was the overwhelming favourite, just as he had been when he played Arthur Ashe in last year's final, and again he crumbled. Roscoe Tanner, the left-hander from Tennessee, ranked third in the United States, beat him 6-4 6-2 8-6 in one hour and 41 minutes, bombarding him with serves and volleys. He played as well as Connors has talked in the last few weeks and, faced by this relentless bombardment, the former champion was never able to use his talent properly. The expected explosion never occurred.

Tanner's victory was a spectacular piece of revenge. In the semi-finals last year Connors had beaten him 6-4 6-1 6-4 and provided all the forked lightning. The way he played then misled the whole of the tennis world into thinking that he could not fail against Ashe. When he served one quoted Hemingway's description of gunfire: 'You see the flash, then you hear the crack and last the shell comes.' After the first half dozen games yesterday, all the heavy artillery came from the other side of the net. It was a fast-bowlers' wicket. The Centre Court is full of bald, brown patches. If Tanner had been a West Indian cricketer you would have said that this was a holding operation. Connors was bewildered and brushed aside by the sheer pace and variety of Tanner's deliveries. It is a long time since Wimbledon has seen serving of such quality.

The man [born in] Chattanooga in Tennessee gradually worked up to full pace. He had beaten Connors at Beckenham three weeks ago, but there is a great deal of difference between the final of the Kent championships and a Wimbledon quarter-final. As always, he was stern and serious. Connors attempted a little of his usual buffoonery, those Joe Miller jokes and gestures, some of them imitated from Nastase – who can always make old business seem funny – which earn easy laughs and make him feel at home in the cathedral of lawn tennis. He would pretend to be frightened by the naked pace of Tanner's serve, he would grope after shots that had gone by and he would affect considerable delight in his own ability to hit spectacular winners. It all seemed like a flashback to 1975. 'Play it again, Jim', muttered someone in the press box.

By the time he was leading 4-2, Tanner was still failing to control his forehand and had not quite reached full power and accuracy in his serve. His first service was the key to the change in command. He put only four of his first twelve first services into court. By the time he drew level in the eighth game, his ratio of successful first services had reached twelve out of 28. By 2-1 in the third set, it was nineteen out of 37 and at the end it was 45 out of 92 with nineteen aces and six doubles. Considering the pace and fury of his serving and the risks that he took, that was a remarkably consistent performance. But if he bludgeoned and bewildered Connors with his service ('Against Jimmy I tried to vary my serve every time. Whenever you serve two alike to him, he knocks off the second unless, of course, he has knocked off the first one. I tried to mix up my serves, slicing, flat, changing from his forehand to his backhand'), the quality of his returns brought him victory. Connors would lash down a service and Tanner would either return hard to him as he came in or present him with nasty, dipping, floating angled returns which made him stretch on the forehand or caught him off balance on his double-handed backhand.

This was the way Ashe out-manoeuvred him last year. Tanner, a year wiser, no longer the blunt young man who stepped on the accelerator all the time, followed that admirable model. Connors held a point for 5-3 in the first set and Tanner at last beat him with a forehand and, as soon as he drew level at 4-4, he began to attack freely and Connors struggled. A low backhand down the line and a double-fault at set-point gave him the first set.

He broke for 3-1 and again at 6-2 in the second. He led 3-1 and 5-2 in the third and then Connors made a last effort. A few jokes with the crowd, who encouraged him in a way that they would not have done a year ago when he seemed much less vulnerable than he does now, and some brave shots and suddenly he had saved three match-points and the score was

5-5. At 6-7 Tanner beat him with two backhand passes, then Connors took a ball which was going out and missed his volley and another pass from a second serve finished the match.

* * *

Nastase's Magic Fails

Ilie Nastase, an exceptionally gifted touch player, was champion at the US Open in 1972 and at the French Open in 1973, but he never won the Wimbledon singles crown. In 1972 he was beaten in the final by Stan Smith and the following year was top seed at the boycotted Wimbledon, where he failed in the fourth round. Three years later, in 1976, he reached the final for a second time, but Bjorn Borg treated his talent with scant respect.

Strangely the final between Bjorn Borg and Ilie Nastase bore more resemblance to Connors v Rosewall – 1974's slaughter by 6-1 6-1 6-4 – than any other recent finish. It was another case of smash-and-grab by the young, of a brisk, determined newcomer to the final rising to the occasion and exploding with aggression at exactly the right moment, and an older player, for all his experience and the honours that he has won, failing to make full use of his talent. By the end, after Borg had won 6-4 6-2 9-7 in one hour and 51 minutes, Nastase looked as bruised and over-whelmed as Rosewall had done on that sad afternoon two years ago. His supporters – and there seemed far more of them than the Borg people – tried to cheer him on to revival and salvation. But all they were given was a good beginning, in which he held three points for 4-0 and must have won the first set if he had not missed an easy volley, and a counter-attack at 3-5 in the third, when it was much too late.

Those were the rare moments when he held the initiative; otherwise they saw Nastase in retreat, struggling to survive in the face of some of the most devastating attacking tennis that the Centre Court has known. Hoad v Cooper, Laver against Mulligan, Newcombe's victory over Bungert – those were Wimbledon's other recent one-sided finals, star vehicles in which the star drove at a furiously spectacular pace and left his opponent far behind. Nastase wrested a rather better score from Borg than his companions in misfortune had done from their conquerors, but once he had lost his lead in the first set he was not allowed any more hope of winning than the worst of them.

Brilliantly, furiously, and remorselessly as Borg played, it was still bewildering to see the way Nastase let the match slide after he lost the first real battle of wills in the fourth game. Almost immediately something went sadly wrong with his volley. Too often he followed in hopeful approaches and was passed by great clubbing strokes from that double-handed backhand – or he played slack-wristed shots, entirely without sting, which went over the base-line or bounced nicely so that they could be punched away for winners. Borg's violence was cold-blooded and efficient. A boy with long blond hair and a wispy beard lashing a ball and an opponent mercilessly. It is inhuman to play tennis so well.

Nastase, who has so often taunted and ridiculed opponents, took his heavy beating gracefully. Once he gave Borg an ace which a line-judge had denied, and another time he didn't ask for a point to be played again – as he might have done – because the Swede had dropped a spare service-ball on the court in the middle of a rally. The only by-play was, perhaps, pardonable. Borg's damaged stomach muscle has been Wimbledon's most publicised injury this year. For a week he had been having cortisone injections and still managing to play superbly. At first it was thought that he might withdraw, but he still managed to beat Brian Gottfried, Guillermo Vilas, and Roscoe Tanner without making the slightest compromise in his shots. As he thumped down fierce serves, Nastase's eyebrows rose higher and higher. Only a magic doctor could have treated Borg if the injury really had been serious enough to make him think of pulling out on the evening before the fourth round. Occasionally, after some particularly brutal winner, Nastase would appear through a fog of chalk clutching his stomach in mock agony. 'It must have been a miracle', he said at the end. 'Borg could have had a hundred injections and still not served like that if he was injured. What sort of pain was it? I have no pain and still I can't serve like that. I have played him often but he has never served as well as he did today.'

Nastase was, he lamented, never allowed to play his own game. His second serve was vulnerable and he found that he had been mistaken in trying to rally too much from the back of the court. The truth was that Borg hit too hard for him. Nastase was never given time to find his touch (most of his drops were total calamities) and no time for those cut, thrust, parry-and-deceive rallies that he enjoys so much. It was not his kind of tennis.

Just before the end one or two tricks did succeed. The Nastaseophiles on the terraces took heart. He served at match-point at 4-5 in the third set and lived a bright little life until Borg put both hands to the bludgeon of his backhand again and finished him. 'When it was 8-7 I knew that I had to win that game. The first two points were easy and I was more aggressive than I had been at 5-4.' In the next breath he said: 'I think I have learned to be aggressive. That's what you need to win Wimbledon.' Borg felt that he had been too nervous to be 'aggressive'. That was certainly the key word in the Swedish vocabulary on Saturday.

At twenty, Borg has now won Wimbledon, Paris, Rome and Dallas.

Only Forest Hills, Australia, and the Masters, of the great titles, have eluded him. His victory made him the third-youngest Wimbledon champion and he is certainly the richest twenty-year-old in sport. At the end, with his high ambition fulfilled, he threw his racket towards the sky and Nastase jumped the net to congratulate him. This was the great entertainer accepting defeat sportingly and the Centre Court crowd applauded him hugely. As the Duke of Wellington remarked: 'A kindly nation seems to prefer its heroes slightly unsuccessful.'

* * *

Borg's Centenary Win

In this article, written in 1977, David captures the excitement of the suitably memorable final for Wimbledon's centenary year between the reigning champion, Borg, and Connors, who won the title three years previously.

In a hundred years we have learned how to cheer and boo at Wimbledon. The most intriguing picture in the programme on the last day of the Centenary Championships was of the crowd that watched Joshua Pim beat E. W. Lewis in the all-comers' final in 1892. Formal, predominantly male, top hats galore. They might have been dressed for a funeral. Over the years you could hear the polite clapping of gloved hands.

We aren't like that any more. In the age of package tours to Centre Court – did you hear about the group of sixteen from Chicago who arrived suddenly at Charlie Hare's intimate little cocktail party and announced that it was on their itinerary? – there is nothing but partisanship. The institution has changed. If we want to cheer, we cheer. And sing. If we protest, we protest loudly. The band plays 'Land of Hope and Glory' before Virginia Wade's final. Newspapers lead on Wimbledon ('What a Nasty Way to Go!' cried the *Daily Mail* in its largest type). Enough electricity is generated in Centre Court to keep the factories of West Germany at full production for a week. At Wimbledon the cathedral hush has given way to the enthusiasm of popular religion. Top hats off, gentlemen. Nowadays, unrestrained and uninhibited, we tell our geniuses exactly what we think of them.

That was why it seemed quite remarkable that the coolest competitor should win the prize. Disciplined, concentrated, often seeming as remote from the noise and passion as if he were isolated on some Scandinavian island, Bjorn Borg, presenting a bleak face to all the distractions of other people's match play, retained his title by beating Jimmy Connors, the 1974 champion, 3-6 6-2 6-1 5-7 6-4 in a match that lasted $3\frac{1}{4}$ hours.

The heady days of Borgmania – that strange epidemic that swept through English girls' schools in 1973 and lingered for two more years – seem to be over. He still has strong supporters, but he is no longer the commander of the entire gymslip army. He has grown up and he must look to them as serious, as singleminded and forbidding as he does to the players on the other side of the net. Connors could explode and grunt with effort, Vitas Gerulaitis effervesce, and Nastase turn matches into bitter debates about the competence of line-judges. But Borg, the stream-lined player, spent the two weeks of Wimbledon perfecting his strong, quick game. No one could touch him mentally.

'Not a sympathetic player, but one you must admire', wrote an Italian critic after the final. Maybe his executions were a little cold for some tastes. Perhaps he did not dazzle us with imaginative flourishes. But no one could do anything but admire the way he controlled himself, his shots, and his opponents. Borg has become a tremendous tennis machine. His semi-final against Gerulaitis – 6-4 3-6 6-3 3-6 8-6 – which held the crowd in Centre Court until long after supper-time, was as good a match as Wimbledon has seen for years. 'Like Smith–Nastase in the 1972 final', said Dan Maskell, and that didn't seem an unfair comparison. Gerulaitis, who must be a future champion, forced him to the brink and was then beaten by two lobs (one he leapt for and volleyed out and the other left him stranded at the net) in the late evening.

Mark Edmondson also took Borg to five sets; Nikki Pilic, still a pretty good competitor at Wimbledon, tested him shrewdly; and then victories over Wojtek Fibak and Nastase showed everyone that the champion was in the mood to retain his title. Fibak was out-punched and Nastase dominated in a second version of the 1976 final. That was a pleasant, sporting match. The 1977 contest was spoiled by the fact that Nastase couldn't resist the temptation, from the very beginning, to attack the umpire as well as Borg. The Swede did not have to do much more than maintain his concentration. Nastase wasted the match, defeating himself by 6-0 8-6 6-3. When he plays like that, it is rather like watching a talented friend set himself deliberately on the road to ruin. What might have been brilliant entertainment ends in recrimination and boredom. The game needs Nastase, but it wants him to use his skills positively.

His Wimbledon tally this time included a stormy meeting with Andrew Pattison, a contest with Tom Okker in which he played well enough to stir the hopes of his supporters, and a match against Eliot Teltscher, a California qualifier, which caused some anxieties about the safety of Court 14, the new show-court at the far end of the ground. Nastase versus Teltscher didn't exactly sound like the match of the year, but it attracted an enormous fifth-day crowd who jammed the alleyways and over-burdened the barriers around the court. The police tried to cope, but too many people wanted to see Nastase. 'I can't understand it', he said afterwards. 'Why do all these little girls like me? I'm nearly 31, married,

and very ugly.' Under the circumstances he behaved perfectly and won
6-4 6-3 6-1 as quickly as possible. Perhaps he needs the stimulus of total
confusion to make him play well.

Connors also added some extra pressures to the burden of his own
quest for the title. He began with an injured right thumb. Then, instead of
attending the champions' parade at the start of the tournament, he
practised on an outside court with Nastase, leaving almost the whole of
the British Commonwealth of Nations murmuring with resentment. Old
champions travelled from the furthest ends of the tennis world to receive
Centenary medals on Centre Court. The air was moist with nostalgia. The
public had the delight of remembering old allegiances. Here was the
living embodiment of Wimbledon's tradition – and yet Connors didn't
seem to think it important to attend. All kinds of reason were put forward
for his absence – some by his friends ('Jim's here to play tennis') and some
by his critics.

He is accustomed to critics and Mother is usually pretty firm in dealing
with them for him. But what must have surprised him was the strength of
the public reaction. Because of his injury, Wimbledon scheduled his first
match for the second day. When he came onto court with Richard Lewis,
the British left-hander, he was greeted with boos and jeers. No one could
remember any player receiving such a hostile reception. Back in the
1930s, the crowd had thrown cushions onto Court One in protest against
what they regarded as the premature curtailment of a day's play in a
Davis Cup match. But demonstrations against individuals are rare in the
sports played by the British middle class. If the British don't like a
stranger, they tend to look glacially through him. They don't often heave
half a brick at him.

Even on the last day, after Connors had behaved almost perfectly in
what remained of the tournament, some coldness persisted. He always
seemed to be playing underdogs (Lewis, Byron Bertram, and the astonishing John McEnroe) or old favourites (Marty Riessen, Cliff Drysdale, or
good old Stan Smith, who held a point for a 4-2 lead in a match that went
to 7-9 6-2 3-6 6-3 6-3) and that meant that popular support was always
stacked against him. On the day after the ceremony, he said ruefully that
it was impossible to bring back the past, and that sounded something like
a note of regret. Perhaps the real answer was that he hadn't quite understood how important the ceremony was to Wimbledon and those who
enjoy watching great players. Most players have boxes of old medals
stuffed away in cupboards. Is it possible that he regarded Wimbledon's
award as just another meaningless honour? Ah, well, we missed the sight
of him linking arms and singing 'Auld Lang Syne'.

It seemed that he never quite recovered from that false start, from that
failure to understand exactly what kind of a religion Wimbledon holds for
its devotees. He seldom looked relaxed and, in spite of all his hunger and

athleticism, a certain sharpness was missing. He served better and took his risks more confidently in 1974, his championship year. The answer might have been that he hadn't played enough since the great day in Dallas when he won the WCT title. Last year he felt that he came to a peak too early and Roscoe Tanner, a first-round victim of John Lloyd this time, beat him. This year he missed Nottingham and went to Queen's, pulling out because of injury towards the end of the week. Borg, by contrast, had competed regularly. He moved from the Grand Prix to Team Tennis and his attitude to match play had differed from the American's. If he loses in a minor event, it doesn't seem to affect his ability to rise to a great occasion. Connors, on the other hand, seems to feel that his confidence depends on winning all the time. And that must put a huge strain on him, mentally and physically.

He had won seven of his nine previous meetings with the Swede, losing only their first match in Stockholm in 1973 and their last at Boca Raton in January. Notably, he had defeated him 6-4 3-6 7-6 6-4 in the final of the US Open last September – a match in which he had always looked the more enterprising competitor. In Fight Ten at Wimbledon he won the first set after Borg had missed four chances to break service in the third game. The Swede lost his service to love for 5-3. Connors bounced ahead, sportingly conceding that a first serve at set-point might have been a let and the crowd applauded him as though the mishap of the First Day had taken place on another planet. Thereafter, the match depended on Borg's ability to attack. He served better (which was the great difference between the players) and reduced his topspin. He won the second and third sets, lost a little concentration, seemed to tire, and saw Connors edge past him for the fourth. Then he led 4-0 in the fifth. Suddenly, he became tentative again, losing his length. Connors swept back to 4-4, seemed to have the title back in his grasp, and then won only one of the last eight points. Perhaps he had spent too much energy in climbing back up the mountain.

'To beat Jimmy at Wimbledon is something special', said Borg. 'This was the tiredest match I have ever played. I have never been so tired on a tennis court before.' Even so, it seemed that he had more in reserve in those last moments than Connors – psychologically as well as physically. Lennart Bergelin, his coach, thought that he had been tougher mentally than Connors. 'He may appear nice and calm on the surface, but underneath there is fire. He is so tough mentally.' Thus, 1977 was another Borg year at Wimbledon. He joins Hoad, Laver, Emerson, and Newcombe, among post-war champions, in the distinction of defending the title successfully.

* * *

Australian Golden Age

D avid wrote this essay in 1982, when he had ceased to be employed by
The Guardian. It is taken from typescript.

For those of us who are old friends and admirers of the Australians there
has been much too long a break in their habit of successfully pursuing
greatness in the men's singles at Wimbledon. Their Golden Age here
ended a decade ago in 1971 – John Newcombe's last year as champion –
and since then we have been waiting for them to produce once again a
player with that special (and characteristically Australian) mixture of skill,
self-confidence and apparently casual strength which brought them so
many titles.

Australians dominated the Centre Court from the mid-1950s to the
early 1970s. There seemed to be a production line of champions – all
superb athletes, hardened in competition, highly popular with the crowd
and their fellow players, and fascinatingly individual in character. This
was the generation of the good guys. Professional tennis, as we know it
today, was built on the foundations of their talent.

We saw them grow up here, acquiring personality and technique and
finally advancing to heroic and legendary status. A shy, small left-hander
from Queensland would turn into Rod Laver, the winner of all four
Grand Slam titles in 1962 and 1969. A Neale Fraser, pounding away
doggedly with a fast and awkward left-handed serve, would start off in
the qualifying competition and end seven years later [in 1960] by taking
the title.

There was a familiar pattern. Every year a new crop of Australians
would arrive in Europe, struggling on clay in the early tournaments and
then looking bolder and more comfortable as they came to grass and to
Wimbledon. We British felt we had a special relationship with them, that
Wimbledon, next to Melbourne, Sydney or Brisbane, played a particular
part in the education. Here was grass like they had at home. They could
play naturally, serving and volleying and enjoying the freedom to live
dangerously that comes from sharpness of reflex. Many of them achieved
reputations at Wimbledon first and then went out to tackle the problems
of winning on clay.

They waited a long time for their period of control. Until Frank Sedgman won in 1952, there had been only three Australian men's singles
champions at Wimbledon – Norman Brookes (1907 and 1914), Gerald
Patterson (1919) and Jack Crawford (1933). But once they began to take
command, the post-war Australians were irresistible. They handed on
the title from one to another as though it was a baton in a relay race. Lew
Hoad (1956 and 1957) passed the title to Ashley Cooper (1958). Fraser

picked it up again in 1960, defeating Laver, who was playing in his second final. Laver, at the end of his brilliant apprenticeship, held it for two years before turning professional.

When Laver moved on, Chuck McKinley interrupted the Australian supremacy in 1963 and then came Roy Emerson, lean and keen, winning for two years and missing the chance of a hat-trick of victories when he fell and injured a shoulder in a quarter-final in 1966. John Newcombe won in 1967, the last amateur year, and then Laver, returning, resumed the crown for two years, followed by two more years of Newcombe before this astonishing sequence ended. No country had ever taken such command of the Championships before.

In sixteen years six Australian players had taken the men's singles title on a total of thirteen occasions, and only once in that period was there a final without an Australian contender. That was in 1966 – the year of Emerson's injury – when Manuel Santana beat Dennis Ralston. There were ten all-Australian finals (1956–58, 1960, 1962, 1964–65, 1968–70). In 1957–58 and 1969 Australia provided three semi-finalists and all four in the strange year of 1962 when Dr John Fraser [brother of Neale] proved that it was possible for a Melbourne holiday-maker, coming to Wimbledon with no greater ambition than that of merely playing in the tournament, to reach the semi-finals. Martin Mulligan, an Australian who settled in Italy and won Rome twice, beat him in one semi-final and Neale Fraser lost to Laver in the other. It was the first time that brothers had stayed so long in the tournament since the days of the Dohertys.

In this period the Australians did not only produce singles champions. Between 1956 and 1971 they won the doubles eleven times – Newcombe shared in five of those victories, Tony Roche in four and Emerson in three – and that was merely following a post-war tradition which had been set by Sedgman and John Bromwich in 1948 and continued thereafter by Bromwich and Adrian Quist (1950), Sedgman and Ken McGregor (1951–52), Hoad and Ken Rosewall (1953), Rex Hartwig and Mervyn Rose (1954), and Hartwig and Hoad (1955). Men's doubles sometimes seems like one of the neglected arts. Great players of our day have been known to restrict themselves to singles, but the Australians of the Golden Age did not neglect this event. Comradeship in the locker-room was reflected in partnership on court, and it was rarely that the trophy could be prised from their grasp.

It was not only in victory that they set an example to the rest of the world. The Australian Golden Age also gave us two of the most popular and talented runners-up in the history of the tournament – Ken Rosewall and Fred Stolle, both of whom had a deep hold on the affections of the crowd. Rosewall, defeated in four finals between 1954 and 1974, entertained and charmed the Wimbledon crowds from his youth to his middle-age. The older he grew, the more supporters he collected. His astonishingly long period of near-ascendancy was a remarkable testimony to the skills of one of the most elegant competitors Wimbledon has known.

Playing his first final at the age of 19 against Jaroslav Drobny, Rosewall endured almost every possible Wimbledon experience. He appeared here first [in 1952] as the lawn tennis equivalent of a child prodigy, sharing with Hoad the honour of leading the new wave of young giant-killers who came to cut down the established leaders of the post-war game. He and Hoad began by winning the doubles in 1953, a year in which he also took the singles in Australia and France.

At the next Wimbledon he found himself confronted by the 32-year-old Drobny in the final. There could hardly have been a more difficult opponent for the young Rosewall. He was fighting against national sentiment. Exiled from Czechoslovakia and often disappointed at Wimbledon, Drobny, the winner in the previous year of the famous match against Budge Patty which went to 8-6 16-18 3-6 8-6 12-10, was one of the Centre Court's heroes. Everyone recognised that this was probably his last chance of winning the title. The British had adopted him, and the waves of support and emotion were overwhelming. Rosewall, small and alone, was submerged. He found himself playing against 14,000 opponents and one of them, Drobny, beat him in four sets.

Two years later Hoad, his great rival at home, frustrated him in a final that went to 6-2 4-6 7-5 6-4. There was a regular pattern to matches between Hoad and Rosewall at this time. When Hoad was hitting the ball with full power and majesty, Rosewall found great difficulty in containing him. When he was inconsistent and erratically brilliant, Rosewall took command. Hoad's victory gave him three legs of the Grand Slam that year, but in the fourth, the US Championships at Forest Hills two months later, Rosewall stopped him in the final and then turned professional.

It was not until 1970 that Rosewall played his next final. He had to meet Newcombe, who was then at the peak of his career and who won by 5-7 6-3 6-3 3-6 6-1. Rosewall was 35 and Newcombe, formidably aggressive, was his junior by nearly ten years. It looked like a contest between Man and Superman. Rosewall fought back to take the fourth set but Newcombe, always at his best in crises, dominated the final set. Rosewall avenged that failure by beating Newcombe in the quarter-final in 1974 and, against the odds, reached the final again. The Drobny situation was repeated, but this time Rosewall was the national hero, supported vociferously by the crowd. Connors hardly seemed to notice and beat him 6-1 6-1 6-4. There has not been an Australian finalist since then. That crushing defeat signified that the Golden Age had come to a very final end.

Stolle first attracted attention at Wimbledon as a doubles player and then, relying on serve, volley and return of service rather than mobility, turned himself into a most effective singles player. With Bob Hewitt, then in the Australian phase of his career, he won the doubles in 1962 and 1964, but in singles he lost in three successive finals. McKinley defeated him in 1963 and his old friend and doubles partner, Emerson, thwarted him in 1964 and 1965. Stolle won the singles in Paris in 1965 and the German and US titles in 1966, but Wimbledon eluded him. Gottfried von Cramm, who lost in the 1935, 1936 and 1937 finals, shares his record of disappointment.

In recent years Peter McNamara has raised some Australian hopes. Two years ago he and Paul McNamee won the doubles. But no one has broken the barrier and reached a singles final. The Lawn Tennis Association of Australia has spent a great deal of money and energy on seeking promising players but at the moment there are no obvious replacements for the great stars of Australia's post-war Golden Age.

*   *   *

Ghosts of Wimbledon

This essay, taken from the original typescript, was inspired by the centenary of 1977.

'You will be haunted', said the Ghost of Major Walter Clopton Wingfield, the founding father of lawn tennis, for whom time had drifted away on a court shaped like an hour-glass, 'by three Spirits'.

The Spirit of Wimbledon Past added little to the stock of human knowledge. Too many flesh-and-blood historians had trodden the path before him. The 1877 Championships seemed very sedate, English and polite. Here was the familiar Victorian garden-party, an amble through competition: 22 players, the final postponed from Friday to Monday because of the Eton and Harrow match, rain, a further postponement until the following Thursday and then, even though it rained again, Gore and Marshall dodging showers and slithering on damp grass until Gore, the volleyer, beat Marshall, the base-liner, in order not to disappoint the two hundred spectators who had paid one shilling each. Straw hats and umbrellas – and the Club Committee, huddled in a corner, wondering whether they could find a way to restrict the server's advantage. The newspapers found it less exciting than the annual camp of the Rifle Volunteers on Wimbledon Common.

'That was the beginning', said the Spirit, and vanished back into the All England Club's new museum, leaving a pretty perfunctory set of records behind. Cricket has arranged its history better than tennis. Many of the great tennis matches of the hundred years that followed weren't chronicled in any detail. By contrast, the second visitor, the Spirit of Wimbledon Present, was patriotic ('The Queen's returning in her Jubilee year'), nostalgic ('The old champions have been invited') and very much alive to publicity ('No other annual sporting event attracts so many journalists or so much coverage').

His gestures were prosperous and expansive. The Centre Court, which had seemed such a gamble in 1922 when the club moved from Worple Road to the Church Road ground, had been sold out for every day of the 1977 Championships six months before the first ball was struck, and for the whole of the first week of the tournament the crowds around the outside courts were so closely packed that it was almost impossible to move in the alleyways. 'Wimbledon is so successful that complacency is our only danger. If only Forest Hills challenged us a little more sternly! They caught up to two-thirds of our attendance last year by holding day and night sessions, but Wimbledon's lead is still awfully long', said the Spirit, smiling benignly at the customers, who were advancing towards the courts, eating hamburgers, drinking orange squash from waxed cartons and [carrying] large green and white striped bags of sweets.

The last Spirit was dressed entirely in synthetic black leather and moved immediately to the Championships of 2077. The site at Church Road had been almost completely redeveloped. The car-parks had gone because a monorail service linked the ground directly with the West End of London on one side and the huge new southern conurbation, centred on the obsolete airfield at Gatwick, on the other.

Wimbledon had now become the Supreme Championship of the European Confederation and was still the most celebrated tournament in the world (mainly because the Americans couldn't decide which of their cities should stage the All-American World Series Spectacular). There were four main courts and the vivid green of the artificial turf, contrasting with the grey cliffs of the concrete stands and the light blue tunics worn by both the men and women spectators, was almost the only bright colour. One of the privileges of the members of the All England Club, mostly senior civil servants attached to the Ministry of Sport and Cultural Indoctrination, was the right to wear cummerbunds of this particular 'Wimbledon green'. The old sombre purple and green ties had become outmoded around the year 2015. 'We use that green colour because we understand that at one time they played here on an old animal feeding-stuff called "grass"', said the Spirit of Wimbledon Yet to Come. 'Did you know that the game was once called *lawn* tennis?'

During the tournament play began every morning at ten o'clock. There were three sessions – the first (for evening shift workers) ended at 2.30, the second at 7.30 and the third at midnight, which gave every spectator time to return home before curfew. There were 160,000 seats in the main court and 90,000 in each of the other three show-courts. 'Do you have enough spectators to fill so many places?' I asked. 'Of course', said the Spirit. 'There have never been any empty seats at Wimbledon, even in the strange years of 1972 and 1973 when for an obscure reason so many of the best players were absent from the Championships. If there is ever a danger of an empty space, the authorities simply issue another ration of tourist tickets. This year the tournament is particularly popular with enthusiasts from Papua and Paraguay.'

'One of the virtues of the old Wimbledon used to be that you could see the faces of the players so clearly in even the largest of the courts. You must have lost that intimacy in these huge stadiums.'

'By no means', replied Spirit. 'Every seat has its own television set and spectators follow the play and listen to a commentary. Many of them are happier if events are interpreted for them than if they are forced to make judgements for themselves. In any case, many of them are unable to see the court clearly because of defective eyesight. British vision has deteriorated of late, possibly because too many of the citizens spend too much time watching television in their own homes.'

'Why do they then still come to Wimbledon?'

'It is a tradition and the people keep their traditions. The British are the best watchers of sport in the world. That is a particular point of pride.'

The tournament began with a fanfare – 'Trumpets at Wimbledon', said the Spirit. 'Some people won't like that' – and a parade of the champions. There were a great many Americans. Those from California wore sequins and spangles. The players from the East Coast were more conservative in their dress. Russians, Nigerians, powerful and exuberant, Chinese, South Americans, some in national costume, and at the end a group of very, very old men. 'One or two of those are Australians', explained the Spirit. 'They won all the trophies at one period, but tennis is out of fashion there now. They prefer the greater violence of cricket. Some tennis administrators tried to introduce a hard ball at one time, but the sight of players visibly bruising each other in close exchanges did not add greatly to the excitement of our game. Speed and endurance are still more important than blood and anger in tennis.'

'Are there no British competitors?'

The Spirit looked at me pityingly. 'No British player has won the men's title here since Fred Perry 141 years ago. The women were more successful, but of late the Asian countries have dominated women's tennis. As I told you the British are the best spectators in the world. Look at your fellow-countrymen and tell me whether you think them capable of winning titles or even of playing tennis at all.'

I looked closely at the crowd for the first time. Most of the men were bald, hunchbacked and bespectacled. It was hard to tell the young from the old. The women looked only slightly stronger and healthier. 'Does no British player take part in the Championships? Did no one inherit the skills of Mike Sangster, Roger Taylor and Mark Cox?'

'The authorities allow one home player to compete as an act of grace, a reminder of the fact that the British invented tennis and that Wimbledon was the first great tournament', said the Spirit. 'If it were not for that gesture, the people might forget their past and imagine that every title had always gone to the Americans or the Chinese.'

It began to rain a little. They closed the great transparent roof over the Centre Court. The electronic line-machines were turned on. Play began. The first service was an ace. 'One-zero', said the umpire. 'That ball travelled at 306 kilometres per hour and fell 2.8 centimetres inside the service-court.' All around me the little bald men wrote down the statistics in large books. In the first set there were seven returns of service. Each one was applauded wildly. The blunt and boring pattern of play disturbed me more than anything else I saw at the Bicentennial Wimbledon. Here was blacksmiths' tennis, played only to delight statisticians.

'Answer me one question', I asked the Spirit. 'Are these the shadows of things that will be, or are they shadows of things that may be, only?'

'Change is possible', he replied. 'The British must build more and more courts and clubs. They must teach their children how to play and ensure that they understand the joy of competing. They must foster the old skills and encourage those who play the game with wit, imagination, tenacity and enthusiasm.'

'May I then look at Wimbledon in 2177?'

He pointed into the far distance. A mushroom cloud hung over SW 19. 'Heavens, is it all destroyed!' I exclaimed. 'Oh, no', said the Spirit. 'That is simply the atmosphere at the final between James S. Connors XII and Dmitri Nastase, a descendant of the famous Rumanian multi-millionaire!'

THE US CHAMPIONSHIPS

Match of the Year

The last of the old US National Championships at the West Side Club, Forest Hills, New York, was staged in 1967. A year later the event there was the US Open Championship and the old tournament, for amateurs only, was staged for two more years at the Longwood Cricket Club in Boston.

In retrospect the last of the 'National' meetings at Forest Hills was a nostalgic affair and, in British eyes, memorable for Ann Jones being in the singles final. She met Billie Jean King, then with two Wimbledon singles titles behind her. Neither had taken the US crown but each had previously played in a final – Mrs Jones against Darlene Hard in 1961 and Mrs King in 1965 against Margaret Smith. Mrs Jones never did take the American crown.

Without any doubt, the final of the US Championship, in which Billie Jean King, the Wimbledon title holder, beat Ann Jones, Britain's leading player, 11-9 6-4, was the women's match of the year. There could hardly have been more emotion or drama and if, in the end, Mrs Jones failed – as she usually does when she plays the dynamic American – the contest must be reckoned as the finest losing battle of her career.

For most of the one hundred minutes of the match, she limped from a pulled thigh muscle. She saved nine set-points before the first set was wrenched from her. In the middle of the second she collapsed, and when she returned to the battle she edged her way back from 2-5 to 4-5, and saved four match-points before the end. It was a far closer and more interesting encounter than the one she lost by 6-3 6-4 to Mrs King at Wimbledon, and it was a complete atonement for her dismal performance in the Wightman Cup at Cleveland a month ago.

Her injury was a disappointment. Her conquest of it roused the crowd and gave the match its depth. From the start it had seemed that she would have more chance of beating Mrs King here than at Wimbledon. Forest Hills, starved of American successes, was crying out for the first home win in the women's singles for six years. At Wimbledon it had been Mrs Jones who was under heavy national pressure. Then Mrs King could hit freely, and bound confidently about the court. Today it was Mrs Jones who had nothing to lose, and some part of her Cleveland-battered lawn tennis reputation to regain. Yesterday both players had won their semi-finals easily, and by the same score, 6-2 6-4 – Mrs King beat Françoise Durr, the French champion, and Mrs Jones defeated Lesley Turner, the Australian No. 1.

The start looked depressingly familiar. Mrs King took the initiative, and allowed Mrs Jones only two points out of the first twelve. At 2-0 and 30-love, with Mrs King serving, it looked as though we were going to see a match that was as bleak as the day. A cold wind blew, and the court was damp and slippery. But suddenly Mrs King made a sequence of errors from the backhand ('The wind was bad', she said afterwards. 'I can usually rely on my backhand, but today you would hit it in one place and the ball would be in another, and out before you knew what was happening') and Mrs Jones was back on level terms at 2-2. It was, however, in that fourth game that the injury occurred. She tried to smash, and slipped. By the sixth game, she was still hitting well, but the limp was noticeable. Some people remembered last year's Wightman Cup match at Wimbledon, when Mrs King had cramp in the final set against the British player, and went on to win. Then, Mrs Jones's concentration was broken. Today, as Mrs Jones ran for some shots, and hit others hard when the slightest chance of a winner presented itself, it was Mrs King who found it difficult to deal with the situation. 'I thought of that other match a lot', she said. 'An injury like that makes you take chances, and she took hers well today.'

If Mrs Jones hit more winners than usual, and served better, she also used her strategy of frustration with all her normal skill. Mrs King found it difficult to get to the net, and she was given fewer chances of scoring than she had been at Wimbledon. She led 5-3, but then Mrs Jones's dogged streak showed itself. The British player saved one set-point at 5-6, and no fewer than eight at 7-8. The break finally came in the twentieth game, after a bad bounce and a gust of wind had spoiled Mrs Jones's last shot in a rally. She might have even taken the lead in the second set. She had five points to break service for 2-1, and failed. Then, after the fourth game had gone to deuce six times, and she had failed five times at game-point, she turned for a backhand, and collapsed. Immediately the court was full of officials, but she insisted on continuing. Mrs King broke for 3-1, led 5-2, found herself under pressure again as Mrs Jones counter-attacked, then needed four match-points before the British player finally presented her with the title with a double-fault.

It had been a fine match. All that it had lacked was the spice of uncertainty. From the moment when Mrs Jones began to limp, Mrs King had always seemed assured of victory.

* * *

Virginia Breaks Through

Virginia Wade was already a seasoned competitor when the game became Open in 1968. With her bold shot-making she had promised much but had won no major title when she challenged for the first US Open at Forest Hills. She was seeded sixth, behind Billie Jean King, Ann Jones, Judy Tegart, Margaret Court and Maria Bueno. Virginia began her victory crescendo when she beat Miss Tegart 6-3 6-2 in the quarter-final, going on to beat Mrs Jones 7-5 6-1 in the semi-final. In the last match she faced Mrs King, who was not only the American National title-holder but three times victor at Wimbledon. Virginia was 23, her opponent 24.

Virginia Wade's victory in the United States Open Championships – the best thing that has happened for British lawn tennis since Angela Mortimer won Wimbledon in 1961 – came at the kind of time when no journalist likes to write. It was growing dark at Forest Hills; in London it was creeping towards midnight. She had been waiting to play all day, looking caged and impatient, sometimes reading Kingsley Amis's *Take a Girl Like You*, sometimes watching Ashe and Graebner or Okker and Rosewall, who were occupying the court that she wanted to command, but mostly talking about tennis.

It had been an odd decision to play the final at five o'clock in the evening. Larry King, Billie Jean's husband, complaining on her behalf, said that only a 'rinky-dink tournament' would play a match with a $6,000 first prize depending on it as late as that. When Virginia heard the timetable the previous night, she had been gloomy at the prospect of having to wait through a long afternoon before going on to court. There had been all kinds of official apologies. The men's programme had fallen behind. If necessary, the women's final could always be played the next day. Everyone was flustered about the kind of television coverage that we take for granted at Wimbledon, and the referee's box buzzed with anxiety.

The British did their best to try to make things easy for her. On this kind of trip there is a nice *esprit de corps*. Once there had been eight players from home at this tournament; now only Ann Jones remained in the doubles and everyone else had gone. The journalists remained, making polite conversation. By the middle of the afternoon she had seen Ann Jones and Françoise Durr disappear quickly from the doubles and the strain was beginning to tell. 'I wish people wouldn't keep wishing me luck. It makes me nervous. They're always doing that at Wimbledon.' She herself had made an offering to fortune by wearing the dress that had carried her safely through the early rounds. It was elegant and tingling – someone said it made her look as though she had been carved in wood by a Japanese.

Up to then, this had been the best tournament of her career. Stephanie De Fina, a little left-hander from Florida, had taken a set off her in the first round, but since then she had beaten two professionals, Rosemary Casals (now, by the way, the owner of a horse called 'Wimbledon') and Ann Jones, and the Wimbledon runner-up, Judy Tegart, all without the loss of a set. Four of the games she had played against Tegart had been devastating in a way that one does not expect from a woman tennis player. Serve, volley, smash – all the spectacular weapons – plus a new accuracy in returning service and much more use of the lob. 'I have beaten her eight times', said Billie Jean before the final. 'This time I feel I am playing a new woman.'

It was as though Miss Wade had suddenly put together the jigsaw of her temperament and talent. At 23 she has been slower in turning herself into a champion than the Courts, the Buenos, and the Kings had been, but in this second year of full-time world-class play, she has approached her tournament programme with the logic and method that could be expected from a mathematician. She has resisted the temptation to play too much, because she realises that with her powerful game – which strains emotion as well as body and energy – she must have at least one week's rest a month.

She made only one bad mistake. After the long haul of South Africa and Bournemouth, she agreed to play at Hurlingham, where she reached the final and lost to Margaret Court. That upset her confidence. She went to Rome, where she lost badly because she was tired and had not given herself time to get used to Italian conditions. After the Federation Cup she resisted a great many persuasions to play in the French Championships but went to Berlin, where she played a restful tournament which enabled her to reach a peak both of mood and form in time for the Wightman Cup. 'If I play on hard courts it is very good for me because it means that I have some groundstrokes when I go on to grass.'

She could not maintain that peak at Wimbledon. There were too many distractions for her to practise properly during Queen's week and then she had to wait – as she did here – until early evening before she played

Christina Sandberg. She was nervous because she thought that too much was expected of her and the court was damp – and she has not yet learned how to play on a slippery court. After Wimbledon she went back to hard courts and lost in the semi-finals at Munich and Hamburg.

In some ways she did not really want to come to America this year. She would have liked to have won Boston, but mostly regarded it as a training tournament for Forest Hills and lost to Bueno in the semi-finals. She was a little worried about her service and discussed it with Doris Hart. Afterwards she felt that she was getting 30 per cent more first services in.

Here she thought her draw was ideal. She was seeded sixth, but she had only one easy match to play and she had beaten all her other likely opponents on the way to the final. The first match in which she looked like a champion was against Casals. The American professional had beaten her in the final of the Federation Cup in Berlin last year and always plays a kind of bear-baiting match against her. She had been nervous in her final set against De Fina, who had lobbed well into the sun, and the uncertainty persisted for half a dozen games against Casals, but suddenly her service began to work and she began to hit her forehand in the way that she had done against Nancy Richey in the Wightman Cup. The path ahead suddenly began to look clearer. No one thought it would be quite as free from trouble as it was.

Tegart, Jones, and King were all beaten in the same way. She asserted her supremacy at the start and kept on hitting fierce shots until the opposition crumbled. It was like watching a heavy gun blow down walls. Every game destroyed a little more of the enemy's will and stamina. Ann Jones nearly held her, but the eleventh game of the first set was decisive and her victory by 6-4 6-2 over Billie Jean King, the Wimbledon champion, [was executed efficiently] enough to send cold shivers down most British spines.

Even she could not believe that she could have played so well. When she talked about it afterwards over champagne to a little knot of British reporters, she analysed almost every point in the match. Not a fluke, not the day of the lucky streak, but a calculated victory against the best match-player in the world. It had also been coolly accomplished – a sign that she has really grown up as a competitor. For years it used to be one of the regular parrot-cries that her real battles were not against her opponents but against her own temperament. She can still react with undue passion to the small rubs of the game on odd days, but these are getting fewer. Her concentration has improved; she is beginning to learn how to accept the blindness of a linesman and while outright gamesmanship can still provoke her – as it did in a match in England recently – she can even counter that now.

This effort to eradicate a weakness made her particularly angry about a report in a sedate British newspaper – which was not represented at the tournament – about her allegedly bad behaviour in her semi-final against Bueno at Boston. It had been sportingly played without incident and yet she was criticised for shouting at television cameramen, who were not in fact within shouting range. This plunged her into a depth of depression for two days. 'In England they will just say that I am behaving badly again', she said. Once again she made the effort to discipline herself this week and she was rewarded by her second victory in an Open tournament. There was never a hint of temper and at the end she laughed all the way to the bank.

* * *

Chris Evert is Controversial

Were an award to be given for consistently good sportsmanship and behaviour, Chris Evert would be one of the first nominations. None the less she was human when she played the quarter-final round in the US Open at Forest Hills in 1974. She was currently Italian, French and Wimbledon champion, but did not then take the US title, losing in the semi-final to Evonne Goolagong. Her first American success came a year later.

There was a leaden echo of Wimbledon in the US Open Championships today. Chris Evert beat Lesley Hunt, the athletic Australian, who gave her her closest match of the Championships in July, 7-6 6-3, and once again there was a tense, dramatic battle on a damp court under dark skies. Considering the conditions, it was another fine contest. . .but the wretched court on which the ball seldom bounced truly, indifferent umpiring and the 'sudden death' tie-break reduced its quality.

The difference between Wimbledon and Forest Hills is that the British tournament offers the grass-court player a test of nerve and skill, while Forest Hills merely tests the ability to survive in a confused and totally hostile environment. They met twice before this season and at both Dallas and Wimbledon Miss Evert has won in three sets. The Wimbledon score, in a second-round match, had been 8-6 5-7 11-9. Miss Evert has not lost a set since then. Today the odds were against a repetition of that high excitement. Three inches of rain had fallen during the night and it was a miracle that the courts were dry enough for play. By a strange piece of scheduling, the match had been put on to the Grandstand Court, a kind of swamp on the edge of the Long Island Railroad, instead of on the main Stadium, where the grass is still reasonably flat and where it would have attracted the audience it deserved.

The small stands were packed, and throughout the match other spectators kept trying to force their way in. There was never a moment when the crowd was still or the tennis was easy. 'The courts were worse than ever. We were both trying to play good tennis, but were thwarted by a bad bounce every second ball', said Miss Hunt at the end. Even the umpire called Miss Evert – surely the best-known woman player in American tennis – 'Miss Everitt' until he was corrected by another official.

In the end everything was settled by the lottery of this absurd tie-break. The first set fluctuated, with Miss Hunt struggling back to take the initiative after losing the first two games. Miss Evert, poised at the start, began to look increasingly anguished and flustered. After holding two points for 3-1 and attempting more volleying and smashing than usual, she dropped her service in the long fourth game and then lost the lead again at 5-4 – a game which ended with an incident which clearly cost Miss Evert a good deal of public sympathy.

At 15-40 she served a second ball, which seemed long. The line judge did not call, but someone in the crowd behind him cried: 'Double-fault.' They played on and at the end of a rally Miss Evert netted a backhand. She hesitated and the umpire asked her whether the spectator's cry had upset her. She said that it had and he asked them to play the point again. Miss Hunt protested and the referee, Mike Blanchard, who was summoned, upheld her protest and awarded her the game. 'That happened to me in reverse in a Team Tennis match and I lost the point then. I was not going to give it up here. In any case we played through the point. If she had wanted a let she should have asked for one immediately', said the Australian.

In the tie-break, Miss Hunt, leading 4-1, held four set-points and the crowd made all kinds of obituary noises about the Wimbledon champion. But then Miss Hunt played two weak shots ('I ran so much to get to 4-1 that I felt ill and it took me the next two points to get a hold of myself') and then lost a long rally for 4-4. She played for safety there ('I was afraid of another bad bounce') and missed a forehand. On the ninth point there was another agonised rally and somehow Miss Evert launched herself into an off-balance, mid-court smash to win the set.

Against the odds, she had pulled herself out of difficulty and taken the points that mattered. That is the kind of tennis that wins championships. There was never much hope for Miss Hunt in the second set, particularly when a series of bad bounces cost her her first service-game. It seemed a pity that everything had hung on the risks of the tie-break. This was a match which died of 'sudden death' and it was Miss Evert's 55th consecutive victory.

THE FRENCH CHAMPIONSHIPS

The Stade Roland Garros

The French Championship inspired the following essay, taken from David's papers. It was written in the spring of 1978, then revised.

For any Englishman, the quintessential story of the Stade Roland Garros belongs not to the French Championships but to the great (as far as the British are concerned) Davis Cup final of 1933. It was the fifth and decisive rubber. Fred Perry, leading André Merlin by two sets to one, had held a point for 5-1 and had seen his lead slip away.

The crowd was tense and nervous. When they changed after the eleventh game of the set, Roper Barrett, the British captain, took Perry by the arm. What kind of advice was he giving? What would be the new British strategy in this crisis? Roper Barrett, two decades earlier the hero of so many shrewdly played matches at Wimbledon, and his player looked at the spectators on the other side of the court. 'Do you see that pretty girl over there? If you win this match, I'll introduce you to her afterwards', said Roper Barrett. Perry smiled, relaxed, broke service and won by 4-6 8-6 6-2 7-5. Britain won the Davis Cup. 'A man less resolute might easily have surrendered to the physical and psychological forces opposed to him', wrote Arthur Wallis Myers, the greatest of all English tennis writers, at the end of the match. The only sad part of the story, so Perry says, was that no one ever saw the beautiful girl again.

That catches it all in a moment. Anyone who knows the Centre Court at Stade Roland Garros, that stage for so much tennis theatre, that cockpit of the emotions, particularly in the crisis of a French defence of the Davis

Cup, can imagine the scene. Roper Barrett, with his walking stick and his trilby, and Perry, with even his marvellous self-confidence sagging under the weight of France's tremendous support for his young opponent. What else could a British captain do in Paris but look for a pretty face in the crowd? At Roland Garros French crowds can achieve wonders for their players. In 1958 Budge Patty was leading Robert Haillet by 5-0 and 40-love in the final set of the French Championships. Patty hesitated a little. Haillet, on the utmost edge of the precipice of defeat, hit some desperate, bold and lucky shots, which pulled him back some of the way to safety. The crowd, suddenly believing that a miracle was possible, came to his help and the match swung dramatically away from the old champion. Patty the imperturbable had been caught in one of the familiar ambushes of Roland Garros.

It was a victory to remember. So was Pierre Darmon's victory over Manuel Santana from two-sets-to-one down in 1963. Santana was always one of the greatest of favourites here. Artists speak a universal language and our enthusiasm for those who use a racket with grace and imagination crosses all boundaries. When he gained his revenge against the Frenchman the following year, there was some national lamentation, but all tears were soon dried at the thought of a repetition of the classic 1961 final. For who should have come through on the other side of the draw but Manuel's great friend and rival, the decade's other great European master, Nicola Pietrangeli, the champion in 1959 and 1960 and the runner-up to Santana, then aged 23, in the 1961 final. Santana spoilt the Italian's chance of winning the title for three years in succession, but it was a classic final ending with tears and embraces at the net. The second viewing in 1964 was slightly less dramatic. Pietrangeli's tennis had become a little autumnal, but he still took a set from the Spaniard.

Six years later there was another French occasion and again, as he had been against Darmon, Santana was the victim. By this time he had added the Wimbledon and US titles to his French Championship and his game had lost a little of its ambition and its disconcerting speed. Georges Goven, aided by half the population of Paris, beat him 3-6 6-4 6-3 1-6 6-0 in the fourth round and then accounted for François Jauffret in the quarter-finals. Jan Kodes, that most industrious of champions, an apostle of the gospel of hard labour in tennis, finally ended Goven's run in the semi-finals and won the first of his titles here.

The next year he beat the young Nastase in the final and then in 1972 the French crowd had another hero, Patrick Proisy, their first finalist since Darmon in 1963, to cheer. He had been seeded ninth, but on a damp evening he defeated Kodes by the astonishingly simple score of 6-4 6-2 6-4 and then was an equally convincing winner in straight sets against [Manuel] Orantes in the semi-finals. The weather was dark and menacing for the final. It turned out to be a Spanish revenge, by the senior man from

Barcelona, Andres Gimeno, a veteran of Jack Kramer's old tour, 4-6 6-3 6-1 6-1 in the final. The crowd shivered underneath their raincoats and umbrellas. There was no great tidal wave of support for Proisy. Everyone was too cold to cheer. It was a bleak result for a bleak day. Proisy had played beautifully to reach the final, but his sparkle dimmed and the end was miserable for him.

Since then Nastase, Borg, Panatta and Vilas have all commanded the loyalty and affection of the crowd. It is good to feel that the techniques of clay-court tennis have ruled in the stadium which is the very heart of the clay-court game. There was a period in the 1960s when it seemed that any Australian could adjust his fast-court tennis to win here. Roy Emerson, lean and keen and trained to the last kilo, Fred Stolle and Tony Roche – all great players, but not exactly clay-court specialists – conquered at Roland Garros. They were respected champions, but they weren't the most popular of our winners. Perhaps because they didn't quite bring off victory in the way that Drobny, Patty, Santana and Pietrangeli had taught us to expect. Or in the way that Nastase and those who followed him showed us how to achieve spectacular effects on clay. The Centre Court at Roland Garros requires the generation of that kind of excitement and it may be that the new group of French players, with Yannick Noah and Pascal Portes at the head, will play a major part in entertaining the crowd here in the near future. The stadium is being rebuilt. It would be fitting if, as a part of that change, home victories could be a part of the celebrations of that reconstruction.

[Yannick Noah did indeed bring to the new Centre Court that partisan excitement when he beat Mats Wilander for the title in 1983.]

* * *

Christine Truman Wins

In modern times the Grand Slam title most often won by British players is the women's singles in the French Championships. The first winner in post-war years was Angela Mortimer in 1955, followed by Shirley Bloomer in 1957. Two years later in 1959 Christine Truman, approaching the peak of her tremendous popularity, again emphasised British power when, at eighteen, she became the youngest woman ever to win that title – a record she held until 1987, when Steffi Graf won eight days before her eighteenth birthday.

Today the tumult and the shouting about the latest lawn tennis crown that Miss Truman has captured have died away. She has dealt with the cameras and the journalists as cheerfully and sensibly as she accounted for Mrs Kormoczy, the clever little Hungarian, who had not been beaten on a hard court for two years, and she has gone back home to Woodford in Essex for a week's rest after a month of successes that has been spectacular enough to satisfy the hopes of even her most wildly optimistic admirers. Paris, Rome, and Lugano are safely behind her. Only the greatest of the European titles is still to come, and if she can produce yesterday's confident, aggressive form at Wimbledon she will not fail there.

What was most exciting about the 6-4 7-5 victory that brought her the French title was not so much that Miss Truman won – although that was a major achievement – but that she won in such a splendid fashion. The crowd at the Stade Roland Garros are not usually great admirers of women's lawn tennis but by the end they managed to summon up quite a considerable quantity of interest and applause for what turned out to be a very fine final. To say that is, indeed, to say something.

In the last few weeks, Miss Truman suddenly seems to have become conscious of her power. For some years almost everyone has been telling her that she is a champion in the making. Now, at last, it seems that she has realised what a fine, fierce player she is, but it takes more than reputation, skill, and years of experience to stand up against her systematic application of speed and power. After the first two or three rallies yesterday, those in the press box who have steadily watched her lawn tennis education were proclaiming loudly that she would win. All the signs were there. She was hitting the ball hard and firmly and, perhaps the greatest of this year's improvements, she was thinking quickly and responding splendidly to the challenge of tough competition. There used to be a time when she only seemed to produce her best form if she was a set and a half down. She always fought back well from a tight corner, but she found it difficult to impose her own pattern upon a match from the start. Yesterday she attacked at once and set a pace that was much too fast for Mrs Kormoczy. She was hitting hard and neatly and coming in quickly to the net, and this policy brought her success.

Early on there was a certain danger. Miss Truman's first journey to the net resulted in quick low shots to the line from Mrs Kormoczy. Last year Miss Truman might have been disheartened by these initial set-backs, but yesterday she maintained her attack and courage paid its proper dividends. As the games mounted up her overhead play improved and by midway through the first set she was smashing so accurately that Mrs Kormoczy seldom dared to use a lob.

If a great many service games were lost it was because both players returned service well. A break at 5-4 gave Miss Truman the first set and she might well have finished off the second more quickly if she could have put a whole series of smashes into court instead of over the base-line. A few touches of nervousness on the brink allowed Mrs Kormoczy to come up from 3-5 to 5-5, but then there were several long exchanges in which

Miss Truman successfully out-rallied the best hard-court rallier in Europe. Such was the measure of her ascendancy at the end.

*   *   *

Maria Bueno Sparkles

The greatest success enjoyed by Maria Bueno in Paris came in 1964. She was less successful there than at Wimbledon or in New York and, though five times a semi-finalist, only once went further. This is the record of that happening, before she went down in the final to Margaret Smith by 5-7 6-1 6-2.

How lucky the French have been this year! They could not have asked for a better end for the fortnight at the Stade Roland Garros. It was settled today that Miss Smith (Australia), the reigning champion at Wimbledon, and Miss Bueno (Brazil), the greatest rivals in women's lawn tennis, will meet in the women's singles final of the French Championships. This will be Miss Bueno's first final here, and she reached it by beating Miss Turner, the Australian No. 2, 3-6 6-2 6-0, winning the last eleven games in a majestic surge towards victory. Miss Smith, ruffled and anxious, dropped her first set of the tournament before she defeated Miss Schultze, Germany's leading player, 6-3 4-6 6-2. Miss Bueno and Miss Smith last met at Forest Hills in September when Miss Bueno came up from 1-4 to win. Their last encounter in a major hard-court tournament was in the Italian Championships two years ago, when Miss Smith won in three sets.

As Pietrangeli and Santana, the most graceful masters of the art of lawn tennis in Europe, meet in the men's final today, this ought to be the most exciting lawn tennis weekend that Paris has known for years. No wonder the French federation served champagne in the press room tonight.

The hint must have been given to them by the manner of Miss Bueno's performance on court. This was intoxicating stuff, light, graceful and sparkling, poured out sometimes carefully, sometimes carelessly, but filling poor Miss Turner's cup to the brim. For the first three games, Miss Turner dominated the court, allowing Miss Bueno only three points. This was a splendid start, and it proved enough to gain her the first set – but soon afterwards, it became clear that Miss Turner had begun too well. She never hit the lines or passed Miss Bueno with the same kind of authority again.

Miss Bueno, starting with shots that fell out by small fractions of inches and sighs of exasperation, improved; Miss Turner, unable to maintain the cruel standard of accuracy that she had set for herself, deteriorated. But who could have lived on the same rare heights as Miss Bueno today? In the heat, with the court so fast that it could hardly be recognised as the same soggy red ground upon which Pietrangeli had played Lundquist yesterday, her pace became faster and fiercer. As she groped at the start, there were those in the press box who started talking of her as a mere ghost of the slim, dark fury who ruled Wimbledon in 1959 and 1960. The first sign of substance and resistance came in the fourth game, which she lost eventually after holding five points for it. That loss proved to be her *de profundis*.

It was followed by a sudden, swift counter-attack. Miss Turner, who had given out a great deal, suddenly found herself receiving punishment. Under fire, she won only two points in the three games which took Miss Bueno to 3-4. Miss Turner held service for 5-3 with difficulty, and then, lobbing twice and passing twice, took the set. Some of us, who remembered her sad match against Miss Ebbern in Rome three weeks ago, were glad that there had been at least a flash of the old Bueno in Paris, even though she had seemed slower in getting to the net than she used to be, and even though she had been highly vulnerable to wide shots on the back hand. If Miss Turner, relentless and inexorable, went on to victory, at least it would not have been a complete massacre.

Three games [of] the second set passed without incident, and then, without any great explosion of emotion, Miss Turner found herself left behind. Miss Bueno began to make the business of scoring points look easy. She stopped making unnecessary mistakes – occasionally she was guilty of too much ambition, but in the last two sets of this match, that was almost her only sin. It was a beautiful execution. One had the feeling that even the victim of the block understood the splendid ceremony of it all. From 1-2 in the second set to the end, Miss Bueno rarely allowed Miss Turner to do much more than serve and rally. The deciding of points belonged to her alone.

THE ITALIAN CHAMPIONSHIPS

Drobny's Day in Rome

The former Czech, Jaroslav Drobny, who won Wimbledon in 1954, was held in deep affection by both British and Italian crowds. This is an evocative account of his progress in Rome in 1963 when he was 41, against the flamboyant Willy Alvarez, who will be remembered for having been disqualified in the French Championships in the middle of a match long before any code of discipline was promulgated.

The letter 'D', as Harry Hopman once remarked, stands for both Drama and Drobny. In the third round of the Italian Lawn Tennis Championships today, thirteen years after he took the men's singles title here for the first time, with the sun fiercer than ever and the emotional temperature rising, the old champion won one more dramatic match.

In the noisy, marbled Centre Court, 10,000 miles in spirit from Wimbledon, he recovered after losing the first two sets and beat Alvarez (Colombia), his junior by sixteen years and one of the most tenacious players on the hard-court circuit, 4-6 2-6 6-3 6-3 6-3. J. G. Fraser, the promising Roche, and Alvarez have been his victims in the four days of the Championship so far. Jovanovic (Yugoslavia), the sixth seed, whom he challenges for a place in the quarter-finals, had better take care. This has been Drobny's week, and Rome is loudly enjoying the sentimental occasion.

Drobny and Alvarez had to play for three hours in the blazing sunlight. The Centre Court was two-thirds full, a compliment which Rome only pays to its particular favourites, and for the second half of the match the

Colombian must have known exactly what it was like to be a tormented lion in an arena 2000 years ago. Drobny may be a naturalised Briton, but, as the director of Italy's Davis Cup successes in recent years, he is also an adopted Roman. Every point that Drobny won, whether deliberately or inadvertently, was cheered; every Colombian mistake was applauded; every time that Alvarez gave a visible sign of his frustration – and this happened frequently – by dropping his racket on the ground, there were jeers. Drobny stayed inscrutable behind his dark glasses. He can hardly have played before such a partisan crowd since he beat Rosewall in the final at Wimbledon in 1954.

It was a genuine five-set victory. At the start, Alvarez scampered forward to pick up Drobny's drop shots and beat the older man with counter-drop shots that Drobny, plump and stolid, never had any hope of reaching. There was a swagger in the way that Alvarez walked. This was youth flourishing its speed in the face of experience. Then Alvarez failed with four game-points for a lead of 3-0 in the third set, and before he had recovered from this frustration, which left him grimacing like a demon king in pantomime, a lead of 3-2 had melted away into a lost set.

After the interval, the Colombian's frustrations grew worse. The fact that Alvarez's racket survived being bounced angrily on the court so fiercely and frequently was a wonderful advertisement to the strength of its frame. In the fourth set, Alvarez showed signs of tiring. He found it more difficult to reach the drop shots. His lobs lost their length. The swagger disappeared. Drobny, the old man of lawn tennis, he suddenly realised, was outlasting him. He had spent his energy, whereas Drobny had economised and waited for the proper moment to counter-attack.

Alvarez led 2-0 in the final set and there was some anxiety in the Drobny-Italian camp, but that lead was soon wiped out. As it went, Alvarez banged furiously on the net. Then, in the middle of the set, Alvarez fell heavily. He dusted himself, but it was plain that he was suffering from cramp. Once he went rigid, like one of the twenty marble statues that surround the court, in the act of serving, and Drobny found it easy to finish off his success. It was a wonderful victory. As Alvarez limped forward to shake hands Drobny stood and acknowledged the applause, a champion who had shown that his long-learned and carefully acquired skill was still potent.

* * *

Emotion in Rome

This is David's report covering activity at the Italian Championships at the Foro Italico in Rome on Wednesday, 6 May 1964. At that time the meeting had the reputation of being one of the most joyous if not the most efficient of tournaments. The Californian Karen Susman, formerly Miss Hantze, had won Wimbledon in 1962, but her opponent, the notably charming Lea Pericoli, although a most efficient hard-court player, had not had like success. The eventual winner in Rome this year was Margaret Smith.

The sun blazed down in Rome and, in the heat, the Italian Lawn Tennis Championships came to life, vigorously and vividly. A Wimbledon champion, Mrs Susman (United States), who won the women's title in 1962, was beaten – by Miss Pericoli, to the delight of the home crowd – and several other distinguished players drifted perilously close to defeat. The women suffered worse than the men. They have now played through to the last sixteen and, with the women's game at its present high standard, it is no mean achievement for a player to reach the third round here.

Mrs Susman's downfall overshadowed everything, but in the course of the morning Miss Lehane had to save five match-points against Miss Durr the French No. 1; Miss Richey, the US No. 3, only just survived against that tireless defender, Miss Rees-Lewis (France), and Miss Catt, one of the two British survivors, dropped a set to Miss Lesh (Australia), her flat-mate in London, before winning 6-2 2-6 6-1. It was all highly emotional, and at the end there were several players who could have sat down by the banks of the Tiber and wept about chances that had been missed.

Mrs Susman, who lost 6-4 0-6 8-6, held a match-point at 5-4 in the final set, but wasted it with an indifferent return of service. This is her first tournament in Europe since her Wimbledon year, and in the interval she has had a baby. Her results in America this season have been poor and, for her first difficult match in Rome, she could scarcely have faced a more dangerous opponent than Miss Pericoli. The Italian No. 1 is one of the cleverest lobbers in the world, and Mrs Susman won her Wimbledon on the power of her service, volley and, most of all, her smash.

The battle yesterday was between the smash and the lob. When Mrs Susman was smashing well, Miss Pericoli could only lob defensively, but, luckily for her, the American's instinct for the kill is not quite as sharp as it was. She missed some easy smashes and Miss Pericoli's remarkable anticipation prevented her from putting away others. She was also slow in spotting and going forward for the drop-shot.

Miss Pericoli took the first set because Mrs Susman missed a great many shots of the kind that she would have snapped up efficiently two years ago. 'Nothing in life is so exhilarating as being shot at without result', Sir Winston Churchill once remarked. Miss Pericoli gracefully ducked out of the way of the wilder smashes and watched others trickle into the bottom of the net. Occasionally she adjusted her purple chiffon bandeau and indulged in small conversation with her nearest supporters. Mrs Susman merely looked dour.

The second set was different. Mrs Susman's eye and arm worked together, Miss Pericoli found that anything less than a perfect lob was suicidal, and the American did not drop a game. And so to the third, with Miss Pericoli now trying to lure her in and pass, and Mrs Susman trying to force mistakes and chances to punish. Miss Pericoli led 4-3 and then the storm broke. A return from Miss Pericoli fell near a line. The umpire judged it good. Mrs Susman did not and said something harsh about Italian umpiring. Miss Pericoli suggested that as they had an umpire they ought to accept his decisions. Mrs Susman replied, 'Have you two eyes? Have you a brain? Have you a conscience?' Miss Pericoli ignored this rhetoric, lost the game, saved her match-point and won. Mrs Susman made no secret of her discontent and Miss Pericoli, always a graceful competitor, rather enjoyed it all. This match was one more demonstration of the fact that it is difficult for a champion, after an interval, to make the long journey back to the top.

* * *

Pietrangeli in the Hunt

Nicola Pietrangeli, a player of fine touch and arguably the best Italian of all time, was involved in many exciting contests round the world and not least in front of his own supporters at the Foro Italico in Rome. In 1966 he beat the Australian, Roy Emerson, in the semi-final. He was not, though, destined to take the title, as he had done in 1957 and 1961, for in the final another Australian, Tony Roche, beat him 11-9 6-1 6-2.

The Centre Court at the Foro Italico suddenly became full of noise, passion and drama, and, at the end, full of the wildest jubilation as Pietrangeli, the best of all post-war Italian players, completed the destruction of Emerson, the Wimbledon champion, after being twice within two points of defeat. This was the victory that all Rome had been hoping for. The day was cold and wet but there was not an empty space on the terraces and for two and a half hours the lawn tennis generated its own blazing excitement as Pietrangeli advanced through a perilous fourth set to win by 3-6 6-1 3-6 8-6 6-1 against an opponent who visibly grew more and more depressed about the chances he had missed and about the burden of playing against an opponent with 10,000 supporters in this men's singles semi-final.

Pietrangeli's inspiration deserted him at times in the course of this absorbing, fluctuating match, but whenever he showed signs of faltering a great flood of optimism, enthusiasm and encouragement would thunder out from the terraces. Emerson, who played wonderfully well at times, must have felt horribly lonely. His ordeal was less gruelling than Okker's last year. Then, with the Dutchman in command, Pietrangeli behaved badly and the crowd took their cue from him. Today, Pietrangeli controlled himself and the line-judges were on their best behaviour. Emerson was simply drowned in a great sea of patriotic fervour.

His disappointment must have been all the more intense because for four fifths of the match the Australian seemed to have a firm grip upon events. Early on Pietrangeli busily tried to undermine both the Australian's backhand and his patience. Pietrangeli, however, missed a great many shots himself and Emerson, moving as quickly as ever but choosing mainly to rally from the base-line, took a disappointing first set without much difficulty.

In the second Pietrangeli became the king of Rome again, hitting majestically and ruling the groundstroke battle. Emerson realised that it was essential for him to go in and take the risk of volleying even if it meant that from time to time Pietrangeli would pass him. He now hit some shots and Pietrangeli's splendid strut declined into plump and troubled agitation. Although he wiped out Emerson's lead of 3-1 in the third set, another Australian acceleration left him far behind. At set-point he hit a ball which was plainly going out. As it went low into the net he looked at it with a resigned shrug. Very definitely Emerson was on top, both in mind and in stroke-play, when they walked out down the long tunnel for the interval.

They came back to chants of 'Nic-o-la, Nic-o-la' and Pietrangeli responded by winning three games superbly. There were memorable backhand drives and artful Italian dropshots, but then suddenly Emerson awoke and won five successive games. Some of the volleys and smashes which he produced at this time were the result of his own quite remarkable combination of strength and speed. This was a Wimbledon champion demonstrating the art of playing attacking lawn tennis. He was two points from the final at 5-3, a game which Pietrangeli won from love-30 and at 5-4 and 30-all, the net cord thwarted him. He would have been even sharper if he had realised that the whole match was about to melt away from him.

Certainly one felt that he allowed himself to be outwitted in the last few games of the fourth set. Pietrangeli seemed to be flagging and Emerson, growing tired, yielded to the temptation to relax. There were a few rather passive exchanges and then suddenly Pietrangeli struck and captured the set. It was a perfect psychological ambush.

The first two games of the fifth set were close. Both Emerson and Pietrangeli were clearly taking part in the battle. Then it began to seem as though Pietrangeli was there all alone. He lost only three points as he moved from 1-1 to 5-1, for Emerson, his face leaner and more drawn than ever, was utterly dejected. He did lead 40-15 on Pietrangeli's service in the last game, but that was only because the Italian had become over-excited. It was that same patriotic Roman net cord which helped Piet-rangeli to match-point. Emerson gave it the kind of dark look that the camel must have given the last straw. He has never won the Italian title and if, as he has said so often, he makes a shorter tour next year he may have missed his last chance of gaining it.

* * *

Chris Humbles Martina

In May 1974 Chris Evert, who was nineteen and yet to win a Grand Slam title, met Martina Navratilova, aged seventeen, in the final of the Italian Championships in Rome. It ranked as no more than a clash between two young and promising players with the weight of experience, such as it was, belonging to Miss Evert. The meeting presaged what was to be the basic rivalry in the women's game for the next decade and more.

The women's final was not the most distinguished of the Italian Champ-ionships, but at the end Chris Evert, the runner-up at Paris, Rome, and Wimbledon last year, won her first major European title. She defeated Martina Navratilova, the seventeen-year-old Czechoslovakian champ-ion, an imaginative, athletic left-hander, 6-3 6-3, in an hour and 27 minutes.

More than anything, it was an endurance test, which Miss Evert won because she was almost the only person who kept cool and alert in the heat of a long afternoon at the Foro Italico. In the Centre Court the temperature was only just below a hundred. It was so hot that one could hardly sit on the marbled terraces as the sun blazed down.

The stadium was full, but after an erratic start in which both players presented each other with sequences of service-games the crowd watched it sleepily, applauding respectfully but not becoming really excited until Miss Navratilova, trailing 1-4 in the second set, staged a later counter-attack. They cheered her then, but it was much too late.

Throughout the match she had been the more ambitious player, attempting spectacular shots which looked fine when they worked but which often went to waste and relieved the pressure on the precise Miss Evert. If Miss Navratilova sometimes won points that any woman in the world would have been proud to win, there were other moments when she looked exactly like a kid from Prague playing in her first major final. She had done well here, defeating Helga Masthoff and Pat Walkden

[Pretorius], Virginia Wade's conqueror, by the sheer strength and determination of her attack, but she made too many mistakes against Miss Evert, who has never played like a junior at any time in her life. According to the record books there is only a year and ten months' difference in their ages. There is at least ten years' difference in their approach to match-play.

Miss Evert, staying back and seeking and eventually finding an admirable length, tried to keep her away from the net. Sometimes the Czech got there and wrenched points from her, making Miss Evert shake that old head which sits on her shoulders. There were long games with plenty of deuces, but Miss Evert ruled most of them, even if she did sometimes have to stretch and run more than usual. It was noticeable too, that extra-special efforts invariably helped her to capture extra-special points.

When Miss Navratilova slipped to 1-4 and 0-30 in the second set, everything seemed to be over. On the terraces the ice cream men and the beer sellers (more beer than coke at the Foro Italico this year ... is that a sign of diminishing American influence?) did a tremendous trade. There was a sense of fiesta everywhere. Miss Navratilova looked agonised whenever she missed a shot, but seemed resigned to failure.

Suddenly, however, she began thundering back to the net again, smashing and grabbing. Miss Evert was jerked out of her rhythm and Miss Navratilova had won a couple of games before she found it again. Her particularly good lobs helped to smooth her way through the last games, but although she won the title it would be wrong to say that this match showed that she had extended the range of her talents greatly in the past year. She may win Paris, but on today's showing it is hard to think of her as a Wimbledon champion – even in a year without Margaret Court.

THE BRITISH HARD COURT CHAMPIONSHIPS

Misery in the Rain

R eporting tennis was not always stimulating. On this occasion David writes from the Hard Court Championships at Bournemouth in 1966 when the meeting was drawing towards the final stages.

This article is written in a leaking tent, set on a flooded lawn, in a gale by a disenchanted, miserable reporter and it is supposed to be about lawn tennis, a summer game. It rained all morning at Bournemouth; there was then a short interval and two semi-finals of the men's singles of the British Hard Court Championships were played. Since then the rain has swept down for four hours. The courts are flooded; the spectators may well have been drowned; the competitors, broken and dejected, are forced to watch television; and although there was once some wildly optimistic talk about playing doubles by floodlight, no one really cares. The whole history of this tournament has been written in water. Tomorrow may be another day, but at the moment *'il pleut dans mon coeur comme il pleut dans la ville'*. Verlaine, who taught here, certainly knew a thing or two about Bournemouth.

If anything could have made matters worse, it was the fact that the small amount of play that the weather allowed resulted in the complete overthrow of the British. From the two matches Wilson and Sangster collected exactly seven games; and the final, which is alleged to have been arranged for today, will be between Fletcher (Australia), who beat Wilson 6-1 6-1 and Okker (Holland), who defeated Sangster by 6-3 6-2.

The scores, in fact, look slightly more depressing to British eyes than the matches actually were. It has to be said that Fletcher and Okker both hit and moved with a great deal of skill and confidence, considering the slipperiness of the soggy courts and the force of the seaside wind. Wilson, lobbing slowly to mid-court and showing a marked distaste for the whole affair, was never allowed the faintest hope of success. Fletcher took the match by the scruff of its neck at once and found himself able to force it into any shape that he wanted. It was a tough, determined and efficient performance. Against Matthews and Stilwell, earlier in the week, Wilson had escaped somewhat luckily from perilous positions. Fletcher made absolutely certain of success. This disappointing showing may have cost Wilson a singles place in next week's Davis Cup match against New Zealand.

Sangster's resistance was sterner. He was unlucky enough to be up against the fastest and most graceful mover in European lawn tennis and while he tended to find himself stuck in the mud, Okker ran and hit as easily and, it seemed, as happily as if the match had been played in dry and blazing midsummer. In both sets the Dutchman sprinted away with an early break of service and although Sangster pursued him from a distance – and even gained a little lost ground in the first set – Okker was always too quick for him. Sangster hit one or two handsome drives, but his service is still less accurate than it used to be and several times he fell into the temptation of attempting delicate little volleys and these were usually disastrous – as they were against Holmberg at Connaught. Sangster really ought to keep a sharp curb upon his artistic instincts until his game is a little sharper.

Fletcher and Okker met once on grass in Australia during the winter and then Fletcher won. As for the British, this whole sodden week has upset the Davis Cup team's planning. They, like the New Zealanders, will go into the match at Queen's Club without having had any play over five sets. That probably does not matter too much in this case. What is important, however, is that they should have some arduous match play before their probable second-round meeting with Hungary in Budapest.

*   *   *

Amateurs Hold their Heads High

The British Hard Court Championships at Bournemouth, which opened on Monday, 22 April, 1968, were of great significance in the history of tennis. For the first time all classes of player, amateur or professional, were free to meet in open competition, with total prize-money of £5,440. It was generally assumed before the start that the amateurs would be no match for the acknowledged masters who had been professionals for many years. No professional had so high a reputation as the brawny Pancho Gonzales, and the news of his defeat by Mark Cox rang round the world. At that time Cox was ranked third in Great Britain.

The third day of the British Hard Court Championships was the day when Open tennis really became Open. The first of the great professionals was beaten – Mark Cox, Britain's No. 3, defeated Pancho Gonzales by 0-6 6-2 4-6 6-3 6-3; Keith Wooldridge, tenth on the ranking list, led Fred Stolle, three times a runner-up at Wimbledon, by two sets to one before going down by 8-6 5-7 5-7 6-2 6-0; and even David Lloyd, the junior champion of 1965, took a set from Roy Emerson.

For almost the whole afternoon Bournemouth was in a state of lawn tennis earthquake and the tremors of the day's events will be felt at tournaments all through this year of transition in the game. Cox's deserved and spectacular victory will be regarded everywhere as chipping away at the legend of professional invincibility. If a Briton, who until yesterday can scarcely have been considered to be among the best twenty hard-court players in the world, can beat Gonzales, what might the Santanas and Lundquists have achieved? One of the great arguments inside the ILTF against opening the game was that the professionals would beat the amateurs every time, and some of the best of the so-called amateurs in Europe decided not to risk their reputations at Bournemouth this week. Cox showed them what they were missing. It was no wonder that an Italian journalist began his story last night by asking: 'Nicola Pietrangeli, where are you?'

At the end Gonzales said ruefully: 'Someone had to lose through an amateur some time, so it might as well have been me.' It was the first time that he had been beaten by an amateur since 1949 and it meant that his prize-money from the singles here amounted to no more than a second-round loser's £40. Time helped to beat him – Gonzales, at 40, is no longer the old sharp-toothed tiger who ruled the professional world. He still hits beautiful shots, but it had been five years since he last played a five-set match of any kind (that was on wood against Rosewall) and probably twice as long since he went the full distance on clay. Cox, fifteen years his junior and absolutely fit after a long tour on the South African and Caribbean circuits, ran faster and longer, and at the end he had a far greater reserve of strength.

The British victory was all the more remarkable because the match began so badly for Cox. He lost the first set without winning a game. Gonzales toyed with him, teasing and punishing. The tiger was at play, scratching deeply when it pleased him. Cox, who had only seen him play on television, had been 'very impressed' then. As the points mounted against him yesterday, he thought he was going to be 'humiliated'. He made the mistake of trying to play too well too soon. 'At one stage I thought that I was not going to win a game at all', Cox said. 'But once I got the first game of the second set I knew that I had a chance, and as the match went on he became less and less sharp and made more and more errors.'

Cox had one ragged period at the end of the third set, but apart from that he can never have played so coolly, strongly and sensibly on a hard court. Nor has he ever moved so well. Certainly, he was far sharper in mind and movement yesterday than he was when he left England in December for South Africa; his big, swinging left-handed service kept Gonzales under continuous pressure and there was more touch and daring in his volleying than one had ever seen from him. He missed some smashes, but that was because Gonzales lobbed well. The American seldom hit hard, but he never stopped struggling. In the fourth set he changed his shoes, after sending Laver with a message to the pavilion, and he promptly lost five games in succession. The only blemish on the way he accepted the disappointment of defeat was an argument about a service of Cox's, which he thought to be a let, just before the end. It seemed that he used the crowd to force the umpire to change his mind. Cox might have exploded then. It was a sign of maturity that he did not.

*　*　*

Nastase in Generous Mood

Although the Rumanian genius, Ilie Nastase, was on one occasion disqualified from the Hard Court Championships at Bournemouth because of his behaviour, he also delighted spectators by his sense of fun and generosity of spirit. This report recalls such an occasion in 1974, when he was playing Martin Robinson, who, despite his gawky style recommended by no coach, had recently won grudging acceptance as a junior of merit from the powers-that-be. His good results demanded such acceptance. Later he took up a tennis scholarship to an American college, but having reached the foothills of the top-class game he did not progress much further.

The Bournemouth crowd have seen Ilie Nastase in all kinds of moods. They do not often see him amusing himself by educating the young, but in the Rothmans Hard Court Championships yesterday he spent an hour on extending the lawn tennis horizons of Martin Robinson, an eighteen-year-old bank clerk from Bolton, pale, slightly built and left-handed, a player who sometimes seems to have stepped straight from a Lowry landscape.

He beat him 6-3 6-1 – and in a stricter mood he might have won without losing a game – demonstrating the width of the gap between the greatest of post-war clay-court players and a boy from the north, whose best virtues were industry, fitness, doggedness, and a complete refusal to surrender. But he paid Robinson the compliment of taking the earnest boy seriously both during and after the match. 'He has not many shots, but he is brave and he always runs', he said at the end. And that was no bad summary of Robinson's talent and diligence. The Lancashire player, using his double-handed backhand shrewdly, chased every ball. Sometimes Nastase, using him as a sparring partner for the sterner tests that are to come, made him play rallies of as many as 60 strokes; but he came out of the ordeal well, showing that he could concentrate, defend resolutely, and occasionally hit more winners of his own than might have been expected against Nastase.

Perhaps the most impressive part of Robinson's game was his return of service. In the two sets he did not miss more than half a dozen returns and two of those were aces. Robinson has not been one of the LTA's fashionable youngsters – they added him to their BP Junior International squad only on Tuesday – but by the end of the match yesterday there were plenty of spectators who were wondering whether the British had not at last found a clay-court specialist. 'A British Merlo', said someone. 'Another Howard Walton', was another verdict. Certainly, he looks like a competitor who will find it easy to play for hours at the Foro Italico or the Stade Roland Garros and, since we play most of our Davis Cup matches on clay, it says much about the LTA's attitude to potential clay-court players that he has not had over-much official help in making his way from Bolton to the Centre Court at Bournemouth.

Perhaps only a very determined traveller could have made as much progress as he has done in such a short time. He struggled to the very end yesterday, leaping to hit a remarkable forehand volley at the start of the sixth game of the second set and then breaking Nastase's service. Most British players would have been preparing to bow out gracefuly at that stage. 'I hate losing, even if it is to Nastase', he said.

THE DAVIS CUP

When the British were Giants

A delightful Davis Cup tie was enjoyed by the British team in 1959 when they overwhelmed Luxembourg at Mondorf-les-Bains, playing in a public park a few yards from the border with France. Their hosts were charming, hospitable, but not very expert.

The official literature about this small spa, which is about ten miles from the capital city of Luxembourg and ten yards from France, says that the mineral quality of the water causes it to be 'laxative, purgative, cholagoguic, sedative, anti-haemorrhagic, diuretic, stimulating, tonic, anti-anaphylactic, anti-anaemic, and recalcifying'. In this healthy atmosphere, Great Britain finished the first day of her first Davis Cup tie against Luxembourg with her anticipated lead of 2-0. A. R. Mills (Lancashire), making his first Davis Cup appearance, beat J. Offenheim 6-0 6-0 6-0 and then W. A. Knight (Northamptonshire) beat F. Baden, the nineteen-year-old Luxembourg champion, 6-1 6-2 2-6 6-3.

There was not much for local pride to feed upon in the first match. Offenheim, a railway engineer with a stiff-looking collection of strokes, offered no real resistance to Mills and in 32 minutes he became the eighth player in the history of the competition to end with a blank score. He won the first two points and then, with Mills growing more and more confident and finishing off rallies swiftly and tidily, he won only twenty more in the whole of the match. The first set lasted ten minutes, the second thirteen – the last game went twice to deuce and Offenheim had two game-points – and the third, in which Offenheim won only four points, was all over in nine, which must be nearly a Davis Cup record.

It soon was obvious that Knight faced a much tougher task. Baden, a tall law student, who moved easily and hit a firm and graceful backhand, contested every point and surrendered nothing. He rarely let the former British hard-court champion win a game without taking him to deuce, and he gave Luxembourg her first success one hour and 23 minutes after the start of the afternoon's play by taking the sixth game of the first set. He collected two more games in the second and in the third, as Knight's service began to lose its edge, he counter-attacked so boldly that he broke the Northamptonshire left-hander's service for 4-2 and won the next two games for the set. Baden led 3-2 in the fourth, and Knight, who was making a number of unnecessary errors, was 15-40 down on his own service in the sixth game. He fought his way out of that tight corner and somewhat uneasily finished off the rubber.

*

Britain gained her expected 5-0 Davis Cup victory over Luxembourg here this evening, but F. Baden, the home champion, gave an unexpectedly uncomfortable twist to the tail-end of the success. In the final rubber he led Mills by two sets to one, after coming within a point of taking the first set which Mills won, and it was only after a great deal of British head-shaking that Mills scrambled home with a victory that kept the Luxembourg score-sheet blank.

Everything else had happened exactly as it should have done. The doubles were won yesterday by Knight and R. K. Wilson (Middlesex), who beat Baden and G. Wampach, 6-1 6-1 6-2, in a match that lasted only 39 minutes. There the British success was interrupted only by occasional flourishes of fierce but uncontrolled power from Wampach.

Then Knight beat the hapless Offenheim – the man who was 'whitewashed' by Mills on Friday – 6-0 6-1 6-1. In the first set he allowed Offenheim only five points, and Offenheim's first score came on the eleventh point of the match when Knight served a double-fault. After that he won one or two good rallies, but mostly Knight hit as he wanted and there scarcely seemed to be anyone on the other side of the net.

For Mills and Baden, there was a complete change of mood. Against Knight, from whom he took a set, the nineteen-year-old Luxembourg champion had shown that he was a capable player, who might achieve much if he could get more tournament competition. In today's 'dead' match, he had nothing to lose – if he could win only one set all Luxembourg would applaud him – but Mills, fighting for a place in the British team for the next tie which will probably be against Sweden at Eastbourne, could lose everything.

Baden chose the wise course of giving him as little pace as possible on the slow court and it was soon obvious that Mills, who likes the other man to do the hitting, was going to be in trouble. After surviving a set-point at

4-5, Mills managed to take the next three games for the first set. But then the command changed. Baden, an easy mover with a kick-service that Mills found difficult to return, began to rule the rallies. With a little firmness, Mills should have won the third set, for he came up from 0-4 to 5-4 but lost it in the eighteenth game. Luckily for him, Baden is as yet so unused to success that he cannot grasp it securely when it comes to him and he was not the same man after the interval, whereas Mills was much stronger.

Amid the crying of the peacocks (Mondorf like Valmouth, that other spa, has its store of these), the strains of 'Colonel Bogey' from a military band, the lowing of cattle, the shouts of children playing among the trees in the park and all the other noises-off that have given the minor drama of this Davis Cup tie its own special atmosphere, Mills finally won 7-5 4-6 8-10 6-2 6-2. The match lasted two and a half hours, far longer than the live rubbers of the tie, which were all over in 112 minutes.

*   *   *

Davis Cup Doldrums

Having won two Davis Cup ties by 5-0 the British were outplayed by Italy on the grass at Wimbledon in 1960. It was felt by some that the best use was not being made of the talent available, and Great Britain did not win more than two rounds in the Davis Cup until 1963.

Nicola Pietrangeli, who led the visitors, was already an experienced Davis Cup man and he continued to play until 1972, by which time he had taken part in a record 163 rubbers. Italy's 4-1 defeat of Great Britain was in the semi-final of the European Zone, not then divided into sections. Italy went on to beat the United States before losing the Challenge Round 4-1 to Australia.

The European zone Davis Cup semi-final at Wimbledon ended lamely and quietly. The dead rubbers were shared. Wilson beat Tacchini, an Italian reserve, 3-6 6-3 8-6 6-2, and Davies, listless and casual, playing as though lawn tennis was not a game but an act of self-mortification, went down 4-6 3-6 4-6 to Pietrangeli, who really did not have to try very hard. This gave the Italians a deserved 4-1 victory. They move on to a zone final against Sweden, and Britain is left lamenting and wondering what can happen next. Only once since the war has her side reached the zone final.

The home team's performance in this tie must have been an unpleasant surprise for those who rule British lawn tennis. In 1955, when they took over from Paish and Mottram, Davies, Knight, Wilson, and Becker seemed full of promise and talent. Where other countries had to work with two or, at the most, three players of Davis Cup quality, Britain had four good youngsters and, in addition, could always call upon the hard-working Mills or the spectacularly erratic Pickard.

When they ran Italy so close in the final at Milan in 1958 it looked as though the major prize of an inter-zone appearance was near. Now that kind of success is as far away as ever. The team, if it is a team, is not fulfilling its promise. No one can have any illusions about that. Somewhere something is going wrong. The fact is that British lawn tennis always seems to lose its psychological wars. Nobody seems to expect success any more or to be bold and optimistic enough to take a chance when it comes. The long-term planning that produces discipline and the proper frame of mind for a confident attack is missing. Training for a Davis Cup campaign does not just mean a few hours of practice with Worthington, the coach to the All-England Club, in the week before a tie. Worthington works hard, but he cannot be expected to bring off miracles at short notice.

The fault lies, one thinks, not so much with the players as with the organisation of the Lawn Tennis Association. Strong, knowledgeable leadership has been needed and this has not been forthcoming. This is no criticism of J. E. Barrett, the present captain, or of H. F. David, his predecessor, both of whom have used limited power as well as possible. Most decisions of importance are in the hands of the selection committee, which has S. H. Hawkins (Surrey) as chairman. And well-intentioned though Hawkins and his colleagues may be, not one of them has had any active experience of international play since the war, and, as busy men, they obviously find it difficult to spare the time necessary for the job. Decisions taken in Barons Court might be different if the selectors were able to travel to tournaments in say Rome or Paris where they could see matters for themselves.

What is needed is the appointment of a team manager (Drobny, who helped the Italians in this way, would have been an ideal man) who could take over full responsibility for selection and training, and at least two more coaches, players of international reputation, to be added to the LTA's training staff. At the moment Maskell and Worthington are forced to carry a tremendous amount of responsibility. Two additional coaches of the right quality would enable a great deal more junior training to be done. This is obviously necessary, for when one looks beyond the present side, one cannot feel very optimistic about Britain's prospects in five years' time.

A strong team manager would certainly say something harsh about the way that Wilson and Davies played their matches on Saturday. Wilson began by underestimating Tacchini (in his present form he ought not to underestimate anyone) and lost the first set. After that shock he improved, but it was only occasionally that he played decisive lawn tennis. Davies obviously hates to play in a dead rubber, and against Pietrangeli – who had given the afternoon one of its few cheerful moments by appearing with Drobny and Sirola before the start in British national costume (bowler, dark suit, and umbrella) – he really wasted everyone's time. One sympathised with those people who had paid for admission, and those of us who were paid for watching the match felt that we were earning our money the hard way.

*   *   *

Trials and Triumph in Copenhagen

With Mike Sangster joined by Roger Taylor in the van of the British side, and with Bobby Wilson in the doubles, the Davis Cup adventure in 1965 included a trip to Copenhagen. There, in the second round – the first having been a win against Israel at the Chandos Club in Hampstead – Sangster showed some nerves, looking at one stage as though he might lose from a winning position.

After the successes in Denmark, Great Britain lost to South Africa at Eastbourne. Spain won the European Zone that year, going on to reach the Challenge Round which Australia won 4-1.

After eight hours and five minutes on court (the equivalent of playing Hamlet two and a half times) in three days, M. J. Sangster gained Britain a winning lead of 3-1 against Denmark in the second round of the European Zone of the Davis Cup here this evening. By the time that he had made victory certain by beating T. Ulrich, the elder and cleverer of the Danish brothers, 9-11 6-4 6-4 6-4 in his second singles rubber, he had been playing for longer than any other British Davis Cup player in any tie since the war and he had won the three rubbers which take Britain into a quarter-final against South Africa at Eastbourne next month. For a player who was out of form when he arrived in Copenhagen, this was a splendidly tough and resolute performance and it was all the more commendable because Sangster's short ration of match-play this season (a Davis Cup match against Israel and one round of men's singles in Rome) had done little to prepare him for all the rigours and ordeals of this tie.

The odd thing about the contest was that as long as Denmark were winning the weather was perfect. For T. Ulrich's successful first rubber against R. Taylor on Friday, there was blissful sunshine and a Danish blue sky, but later that afternoon as Sangster and J. Ulrich fought out a long battle the clouds gathered and the temperature dropped. When darkness stopped them at 5-5 in the final set, it was a time for overcoats and the bleak cold which began then persisted for the rest of the tie.

Sangster, after three hours and 22 minutes of play, took only eight more minutes to complete his victory over the younger Ulrich yesterday. In three of the five sets, Ulrich had been the slower starter and he was left behind again when the game of sudden death began yesterday. Sangster quickly broke service and, after a slight faltering on the brink of victory and some wastage of match-points, won the rubber 5-7 8-6 6-0 4-6 7-5.

Then came the doubles – Sangster and R. K. Wilson against the two Ulrichs – and once the first set had been gained, there was never much doubt about which was the stronger pair. T. Ulrich again smashed superbly and played with a good deal of wit and sophistication, but J. Ulrich, obviously suffering from the disappointment of losing in the singles, made too many mistakes. Alas, poor Jorgen! Towards the end his forehand betrayed him completely and Sangster and Wilson won 10-8 6-0 6-3 in one hour and 25 minutes. It was their seventh victory in nine doubles rubbers they have played together for Britain and Wilson's 50th Davis Cup appearance. He is now within striking distance of the records set up by A. J. Mottram and F. J. Perry.

And so to today's slow march to victory, with the weather colder, damper and drearier than ever. There was heavy rain during the morning, but the court was covered and the start was delayed for only half an hour. For the first half of the match T. Ulrich and Sangster exchanged shots gracefully and elegantly. If the end had come after an hour and a half instead of after three hours and ten minutes as the players were exhausted and bludgeoned into inaccuracies, this would probably have been generally acclaimed as one of the best Davis Cup rubbers of the year. Some of the rallying was delightful and the players so different in character – Sangster stern and strong and Ulrich shrewd and deft – were closely matched, so closely, in fact, that the first three games lasted sixteen minutes and contained eight deuces and no fewer than 38 points. As the cleverly constructed stalemate continued, there were terrible visions that the tie would stretch over and beyond the start of the French Championships. Breaks of service were plentiful and both players held four setpoints before Ulrich finally captured the set in the twentieth game after one hour and eighteen minutes.

That victory turned out to be pyrrhic. Ulrich is 36 and twelve years older than Sangster and the effort of concentrating so hard, running so swiftly and enduring so many crises for so long gradually wore him down. He led 2-0 in the second set, but then Sangster overtook him and when the Dane was leading 3-1 in the third set Ulrich was stricken with cramp in one thigh. Sangster ought to have profited more from this handicap than he did. But he seemed to grow tired at this time. This was the seventh hour of play for him and his inspiration deserted him. Instead of producing drop-shots, he tended to hit the ball to Ulrich, allowing the Dane to rally.

Time and again Sangster was to be heard chattering to himself. Once when a net cord went against him he said fatalistically 'somebody up there doesn't want me to win', but gradually he struggled out of this despond. Towards the end Ulrich could do no more than stay passively on the base-line, but although he delayed Britain's victory he could not prevent it. In the last dead rubber J. Ulrich was leading Taylor 8-6 6-5 when it was decided that it was too dark for this exhausting tie to be completed.

*   *   *

Taylor's Last Match

Italy beat Great Britain 4-1 at Wimbledon in 1976 in the final of the European Zone B, clinching the tie when Adriano Panatta beat Roger Taylor in the first rubber of the third day. It was Taylor's 41st Davis Cup match since 1964 and his last. The curtain came down on a distinguished career in which he won 26 singles, a tally which, at that time, only three British men had bettered – Bunny Austin with 36, Fred Perry with 34 and Mike Sangster with 29. Buster Mottram subsequently won 27.

This was the last report by David for *The Guardian* as a staff writer. He left to become General Secretary of the International Tennis Federation.

The sad aspect of Britain's Davis Cup European Zone final against Italy was that Roger Taylor, the toughest competitor we have produced since the war, was four years past his best. At 34, after three Wimbledon semi-finals and 41 matches for Britain in a Davis Cup career dating back to 1964, he was presented with the chance of saving the tie by beating Adriano Panatta, eight years his junior, and the most successful player in Europe this year. It was the classic sporting situation. The old hero answering the trumpet call. Italy were leading 2-1. The Lloyd brothers had kept the match alive on Friday by saving five match-points in that astonishing and dramatic doubles against Panatta and Paolo Bertolucci. Taylor had failed on the first day against Antonio Zugarelli, but here was his second opportunity in what may well prove to have been his last Davis Cup match.

'Roger has been the mainstay of the team. We have relied enormously on him', Paul Hutchins, the British captain, had said at every one of the press conferences that he gave after the matches in the earlier weeks of the competition. The value of his presence in the team was obvious. Sure, he is slower and heavier now than he used to be, later in making his volleys and missing a little of the old snap of pace in that swinging left-handed service, which he has always used to bludgeon his opponents. But he was still as keen as ever, as amused by being part of a team, and compensating for loss of sharpness by depth of experience. He was one of the first of the new generation of professionals, an original member of the World Championship Tennis group, living for a long time in the best company, playing against all the great champions and enjoying a fair measure of success against them.

Stubbornness has been one of the keynotes of his lawn tennis. He has been a fighter for his rights, an exponent of the theory that you won in tennis if you kept slugging longer than the other guy. He has covered his weaknesses – notably that backhand which everyone used to try to attack – and he has made the most of his physical strength. 'Dogged', 'determined' and 'rugged' were words that we used about him all the time as we respected the effort involved in his steady climb to the top. But this hasn't been an easy season for him. He hasn't won many matches in major championships and his confidence has suffered. On Thursday he was uneasy from the start against Zugarelli and he never settled down. Perhaps he was disconcerted by the volume of support that flooded down from the terraces for the Italian. As an ex-Boston Lobster, he ought to have been used to that kind of noise.

The chanting Italians who came to Wimbledon were simply turning the Davis Cup into the highest possible form of World Team Tennis, and in any case he has played some of his best matches in front of hostile crowds. His first important success in the Davis Cup was against Hungary in 1966 when he quietened the stadium in Budapest by beating Istvan Gulyas, then one of the best clay-court players on the Continent.

Character and experience were thus the two greatest qualities that he brought to his match against Panatta. He knew that he had to stop the stylish Italian champion from making full use of his skill – and for an hour and a half it looked as though he might succeed. Panatta was slightly ruffled. The Lloyds' victory had shifted the psychological balance. Panatta had now played ten sets in two days, and had been on court for nearly seven hours. That could not have done much to help his injured arm.

The mood at Wimbledon was different, too. Something was stirring in the sedate suburbs. The British were counter-attacking and learning how to cheer like the opposition. David Lloyd and Roger Becker, the British coach, were not the only ones who came to Court One with Union Jacks on Saturday.

Panatta's edginess was apparent in the first game when he argued two line-calls (one without any justification), and in the second Taylor held service from love-40. The Italian hit every ball possible to the Yorkshireman's backhand. And, in fact, the contest gradually developed into a battle of cross-court backhands. There was a great deal of shrewd think-ing. Panatta was faster and more flexible, but Taylor punished him whenever his concentration flickered or whenever he attempted a short cut and broke him in the seventh game. Helped by the gift of three Italian double-faults, he won the first set 6-3.

Taylor lost the initiative immediately in the second, in which Panatta broke him for 2-0 and 5-2, but the third was close and absorbing until it became obvious that Taylor was tiring. Winning a protracted fifth game seemed to sap his energy and soon afterwards he lost his service for 3-4. He led 30-love on Panatta's serve at 4-5, and produced a backhand down the line at 30-all, which caused a major dispute. The line-judge signalled out, the referee asked for the point to be played again because he was by no means certain that Taylor's shot had been wide, and Panatta won the replay. Afterwards Hutchins felt that that call had been crucial: 'Roger had been trying that shot all afternoon and just missing. Then when he got one in at an important moment, it was called out.' Taylor lost the set and struggled through the fourth until Panatta finished him with a final flourish of ten straight points. Taylor looked quite bewildered at the end. It was the triumph of time as well as the victory of the Italians. Panatta won 3-6 6-2 6-4 6-4.

The last rubber was also disappointing. John Lloyd took the first two sets from Zugarelli and then, tired, irritable and complaining of a strained thigh muscle, went down by 4-6 6-8 6-1 6-1 6-1.

In spite of the anticlimax of that dead rubber, Hutchins can still regard this as a satisfactory year. He has built a team; he has reawakened public interest in Britain's performances in international competitions; and he led us to a zone final again after seven lean years. Some of us who were sceptical about the wide-ranging powers given to him at the start might end by admitting we were wrong.

● An end, indeed, it is. After twenty years of writing on lawn tennis for this newspaper, this will be the last of my regular pieces. When I was a small boy, my grandmother took me to see George Robey appear for the last time at Wolverhampton Hippodrome. At the end he made a long, rambling speech in which he said that after 40 years as a red-nosed comic he was now regretfully taking his leave: 'He's drunk, of course', said my grandmother. I think that after all these years I beg leave to differ with her ghost. I now know how hard it is to say farewell to an audience.

THE WIGHTMAN CUP

Great Britain Win

V ictories for Great Britain against the United States in the Wightman Cup have been rare. In 1960, at Wimbledon on Court One, a week before the start of the Championships, the home side achieved an enthralling last-minute win by 4-3. When, two years before in 1958, the British had achieved their first success since 1930, Christine Truman had been the outstanding British heroine. Again she filled that role.

Just before eight o'clock at Wimbledon on Saturday, with the shadows long and the sun low behind the scoreboard, Miss Hopps, the United States captain, who had chosen to bear every burden possible in the tie, hit a ball from Mrs Brasher over the base-line. Everybody suddenly burst out cheering. The long torture was at an end. For the sixth time in 32 meetings and by four rubbers to three the British women, coming out of darkness into light in the last two matches, had won the Wightman Cup.

That was the end of a grandstand finish. Victory depended upon the last doubles, in which Miss Truman and Mrs Brasher beat Miss Hopps and Mrs Knode 6-4 9-7, after being down 0-4 in the first set and 2-5 in the second. When Britain won last – in 1958 after 28 blank years – the contest was safe by the late afternoon, but on Saturday there was no relief. It was doubt and anxiety all the time. In the sixth rubber, the singles in which Miss Mortimer, after a disastrous first set, suddenly found the length and the touch to beat Miss Hopps, the Americans were within two games of total success, and when their pair left the court after the decider it was in a blaze of saved match-points. For Britain, the business of winning was agonisingly drawn-out. Mrs Walter, sitting in her captain's chair by the side of the umpire, grew perceptibly older between the beginning and the end.

The day started well. Miss Truman, nineteen years old and playing in her fourth tie, made the score 2-2 by firmly disposing of America's seventeen-year-old newcomer, Miss Hantze, 7-5 6-3. Service ruled the first set until Miss Truman, heralding her attack with a battering ram of a cross-court forehand drive, broke through in the twelfth game. After that breach, the elegant Miss Hantze was never quite the same again. Self-possession went, and with it control. She slipped out of the match in exactly the same way that she had done against Miss Haydon on Friday, and Miss Truman's single-minded attack upon her forehand paid dividends. The gaps appeared and Miss Truman volleyed into them. It was rather like watching a heavy hammer on a piece of light, bright metal. The blows kept falling on one weak spot until at last the metal broke.

Miss Hopps had gambled twice in selecting her team for the match. Miss Hantze's second defeat meant that one of her chances had gone. It had been a bold risk, and it came within two points of success against Miss Haydon. Another time Miss Hantze will know how to stop a victory from getting away, and she will have learned that on a lawn tennis court it is not always the clever-looking moves that bring the important points.

Then came Miss Hard's 5-7 6-2 6-1 victory over Miss Haydon to give the United States a 3-2 lead. The British player had beaten last year's Wimbledon runner-up four times on the Caribbean circuit in the spring, and it seemed at first that she was going to contain her once again. The good-length ball down the middle of the court kept Miss Hard away from the net. When Miss Haydon gave her an angled shot, she was dangerous, but in the straight test of patience from the back of the court Miss Haydon ruled and Miss Hard, an extrovert in chains, was unable to settle down. The first set went to Britain and Miss Haydon broke to lead 2-0 in the second. Then, suddenly, it seemed that the effort of imposing so much discipline upon herself, of playing so cannily for so long, overwhelmed her.

She missed a series of easy chances and found herself 2-3 down instead of, as she might well have been, 4-1 up. Miss Hard, seeing that the cork was out of the bottle, attacked and effervesced. Miss Haydon won only one more game. This was her first defeat in a Wightman Cup singles and she had defended her record gallantly, but whereas she began the match at full pressure, Miss Hard had kept some of her skill and strength in reserve for the end. Undoubtedly the American must now be favourite for the women's title at Wimbledon.

Britain now was one down and two to play, but it was time for the second of Miss Hopps's risks to come to the test. By nominating herself for the last singles and for the second doubles, she was deliberately plunging herself straight into crisis, but here again the gamble nearly succeeded. Britain had regarded a victory by Miss Mortimer as a certainty, but soon she was a set and 2-4 down and Miss Hopps, valiantly assaulting the net, was sweeping her out of the match. It was neck or nothing and in the gusty wind Miss Mortimer's small, calculated accuracies were going astray. The transformation came after one of the worst winning strokes of the match. Miss Mortimer was given an easy smash. She made a late, desperate, cliff-hanging lunge at the ball and hit it halfway up the racket handle. It fell slowly into Miss Hopps's court. Even Mrs Walter laughed. This somehow seemed to take the nervous tension out of Miss Mortimer's game. Afterwards she played serenely and easily and Miss Hopps, limping just before the end with cramp, never looked like a winner again.

There was some doubt about whether she would play in the doubles, but out she came and soon she and Mrs Knode were ahead. They attacked Mrs Brasher successfully at first, but then overplayed this winning strategy by giving her so much of the ball that she found her confidence and her volleying touch. Once the first United States advance had been checked at 4-0, the match proceeded like a four-handed singles with the British pair combining better than the Americans. Miss Hopps, obviously determined to settle the matter herself, charged everywhere and was spectacular when she hit and when she missed. Mrs Knode, playing what seemed to be a solitary game on the wing, can never have known where her partner was going to appear next. Britain made up the lost ground in both sets, but it needed six match-points (one of them, a return from Mrs Knode, must have bruised Miss Truman considerably) before Mrs Brasher stuck out her chin and said: 'This time' to Miss Truman. That time they did indeed finish off the victory.

* * *

Virginia in Top Form

G reat Britain's next Wightman Cup win, their seventh, came in 1968, again on Court One at Wimbledon. The mainstay of the home side were Christine Janes, the former Miss Truman, and Virginia Wade, still nine years away from her triumph in the Championships in 1977.

At 7.52 on Saturday evening – eight minutes before play was due to end – in the final set of the last rubber Nell Truman, who believes in getting them in boundaries rather than in singles, put a backhand volley in between Miss De Fina, a left-hander from Florida, and Miss Harter, a stately Californian. There was a large gap on the American side of the court of a kind that is not usually visible in doubles of the highest quality.

Miss De Fina and Miss Harter could only watch the ball ruefully and the Wimbledon crowd did not so much cheer as sigh with relief. A harrowing day was over; Britain had won the Wightman Cup for the first time since 1960, for the third time since the war, and for the seventh time since the first competition in 1923.

Our other postwar victories and some of our narrow defeats have seemed agonising enough, but nothing really compared with this year's long weekend of uncertainty. You have to be strong to watch women's tennis at this level, ready for splendours and miseries, most of them unexpected. By the end most spectators had been drained of emotion and the players paralysed by nervousness.

On Friday night, with a lead of 2-1, it had looked as though Britain was going to win. By tea, on Saturday, the Americans were 3-2 up with two to play and Nancy Richey, who had not lost for months, was about to go on court against Virginia Wade. Winnie Shaw had not been able to upset Peaches Bartkowicz's steady base-line rhythm and had lost 7-5 3-6 6-4, and a revived Mary Ann Eisel had beaten Mrs Janes 6-4 6-3. Then Miss Wade won the finest and most important match of her career so far and the Truman sisters made everything safe, justifying Angela Barrett's four years of dedicated captaincy.

The chief glory belongs to Miss Wade. On Friday she demoralised Miss Eisel, the second American, allowing her only one game – the heaviest defeat suffered by an American in the history of the Wightman Cup. She and Miss Shaw beat Miss Richey and Miss Eisel in the doubles and on Saturday, with Britain's situation utterly desperate, she exorcised all ghosts and beat Miss Richey by 6-4 2-6 6-3.

In the two previous Wightman Cup matches she had served for victory against the American and failed, beaten by the situation rather than the opponent. This time, disciplined, relaxed, and determined, she broke down the Texan stone wall, and all the benefits of a year of world-class play showed themselves. She captured Miss Richey's service for 5-3 in the final set, faltered a little in the next game but at 15-30 she produced two superb service winners to carry her to match-point – 'if you can serve like that in this situation you can do anything', said the wise old tennis player who was sitting next to me.

The Wightman Cup, full of red roses, was by the side of the court. 'I looked at it this time, before I served', said Miss Wade afterwards. By then the trophy had a decidedly British appearance. Miss Richey, who won the French title last week, had been as relentlessly accurate as ever and she is a better volleyer now than she used to be. But she could not withstand the British player's power and versatility.

That would have been a wonderfully good women's match in any circumstances. The fact that it played the major part in winning the trophy for Britain added an extra dimension to the crowd's pleasure and excitement. Then came the Trumans – the most typically British players of their generation – to face the classic British situation. The deathly hush in the close; ten to make and the match to win; the light fading; the sky full of rain and the grass growing soggy.

They, of course, attacked at once. Neither has ever believed in anything but direct action. As they loomed out of the darkness, hitting and mis-hitting volleys and smashes, Miss Harter and Miss De Fina, representing the US for the first time, looked increasingly bewildered. They must have felt that they were fighting an army in a fog. The first set went to the British. Miss Truman was the liveliest player on the court and Mrs Janes contributed some forthright winners. The British rackets had wooden frames and the Americans' were steel. Even if you could not see who had hit the ball you could usually hear. Steel won the second set, but in the nervous crisis of the third the greater experience of the British pair told.

Mrs Janes had been in the same position in 1960 and she and Shirley Brasher had won the deciding rubber then. The sisters lost a couple of games at 5-1, but then Miss De Fina's service wobbled again, the British advanced (Mrs Janes fell twice in the process) and suddenly the ordeal was over.

BRITISH JUNIORS

When British Juniors Sparkled

The mid-1950s were halcyon years for the British women's game with high talent among the juniors. David, as enthusiastic a supporter of the juniors as any tennis writer, reports on the girls' final of the 1956 British Junior Championships, played on the hard courts at Wimbledon. It was contested between Christine Truman and Ann Haydon, both of whom rose to great heights. Each won the French singles; five years after her junior title Christine was in the all-British women's final at Wimbledon against Angela Mortimer; and eight years after that, thirteen years after her junior loss, Ann, now Mrs Pip Jones, took the Wimbledon crown.

For those who like to look into the future the match in which C. C. Truman (Essex) beat the holder, A. S. Haydon (Warwickshire), 1-6 8-6 6-4, in the final of the girls' singles at the Junior Lawn Tennis Championships was one of the most gratifying occasions that British lawn tennis has known since the war. There have been odd single encouraging events – Mottram beating Drobny, Wilson beating Patty, Miss Buxton (a year or so before the time was ripe) reaching a Wimbledon final – but never before have the prospects of future success seemed so solidly laid and firmly founded as in this match.

To produce one young player of the promise of either Truman or Haydon is a piece of fortune that might hearten any country, but to produce two – and S. M. Armstrong, if she can remedy her forehand weakness, and V. A. Pitt are not so far behind – is to plant the hope of a large gathering of laurels. With every set today, as new perils were countered with new skills and as the game became sharper and fiercer, the Wightman Cup seemed to come a little nearer to Britain.

The quality of the match – afterwards strong men who do not usually waste superlatives on women's lawn tennis were to be heard talking in hushed voices about the beauty of the strokeplay – was the more remarkable because it was played in a sharp gusty wind, and Haydon took the first set because she accustomed herself more quickly to this disadvantage. It was, however, a much closer thing than a 6-1 score suggests. Indeed, everything in this match was close and bitterly fought for. At this time Haydon was imperturbable and relentless, maintaining an admirable length and floating the ball skilfully into the wind. Truman, with her long-armed grace, hit some hard and beautiful winners, but Haydon, who was less spectacular, won all the points she needed.

After this Truman made a new beginning in force and Haydon's accuracy wilted under so much power. The certainty left her forehand drives and once she completely missed a smash. At 5-2, however, Truman relaxed a little and this small respite gave Haydon a chance to recover control. She won four games in a row and came within two points of victory, but Truman hit her way splendidly out of difficulty and at last realised that the way to break up the rhythm of Haydon's steadiness from the base-line was to bring her into the net more often.

The final set was won when she took Haydon's service in the ninth game. And the last shot of all contained the spirit of the whole game. This was a backhand volley from Truman, desperately made and desperately taken, which went into a foot of space between Haydon and the side-line. It was unanswerable. ('A d'Alvarez touch', said someone afterwards.) Haydon, who had tried everything always, lunged at it but could make no return. There was a silence, and then as the applause came Haydon, who had come so very close to equalling B. Nuthall's record of winning three junior titles in a row, ran to the net to congratulate the winner with a smile as brave as the game she had played. This had been the kind of play that puts heart into those who play, those who coach, and those who watch.

* * *

Discovering Young Talent

A t the National Junior Championships, held annually at Wimbledon, promising young players could be observed and selected for special assistance to develop their tennis. In this article David reviews the system through which young players reach this stage.

The National siftings are the '11-plus' of lawn tennis. So, as soon as the Junior Championships end, the Lawn Tennis Association begins to look forward once again and to put its youngest players under scrutiny. This year's examination ended at the All England Club yesterday and there were seventeen candidates, boys and girls ranging in age from eleven to fifteen.

The idea is that promising young players are sent to Wimbledon from all over the country. There, for two days the material is shaken up in match play and everyone looks for talent that is strong enough to survive the test. On the whole it is a time to watch and hope. The riddle is there, but no one will know whether there are Davis Cup or Wightman Cup answers for at least half a dozen years. All that the LTA can offer the youngsters who come through the siftings is a certain amount of lawn tennis education – residential schools for young players are held in the Christmas and Easter holidays each year – and the hope at some time in the future of a place on the nominated young players list, which means free access to the courts at Queen's Club and certain other training privileges.

For most candidates, sifting begins at home. County associations send promising youngsters to preliminary siftings, which are held at seven regional centres, and there the players are studied by local training committees. The best go forward to Wimbledon, where results count but potential ability is said to be all-important. The LTA feels that it is good to use the All-England Club as the main sifting centre. It gives extra prestige to both the siftings and the sifted.

School tournaments like the Youll Cup and the Thomas Bowl are also useful to the official spotter, but for the most part the LTA depends upon the enthusiasm of the counties and local coaches. Each county receives a coaching grant – altogether the Association's direct and indirect expenditure on training is about £6,000 a year – and some effort is now being made to meet the grievances of coaches who used to argue that they were not given sufficient credit for their work. The most common complaint was that once a pupil had shown signs of promise the LTA swept him away and broke up his understanding with his old teacher.

At future training schools the emphasis is likely to be upon play rather than on instruction. Senior players will give the juniors hard match practice and when it is felt that changes are necessary in a young player's technique, the LTA's headquarters staff will discuss the matter with the player's own coach. This, it is felt, is the way to reduce the risks of conflict between teachers and bewilderment among pupils. 'The relationship between our training manager, Dan Maskell, and our coach, George Worthington, and the local coach will be rather like that of specialist and general practitioner', said W. E. Ramsden, the chairman of the LTA.

The LTA's junior training scheme is now eleven years old. It has received a certain amount of criticism – a great deal of which has been unjust – but it has achieved some sound results. Junior Wimbledon has been steadily improving in quality, and, except for Miss Mortimer and Mrs Hales, all Britain's best international players have passed through LTA schools. Equally important is the improvement in the general standard of coaching, which was low in 1949. No one, however, can be complacent about the present position, and in the next few years one of the LTA's most important tasks will be to make the best possible use of the great flow of young players who are learning the game in the secondary modern schools.

Once upon a time lawn tennis was a game for the upper class. Now, thanks to a great deal of publicity and to the help of the Ministry of Education, more and more schoolchildren are being given the chance to play. The LTA's job must be to keep them interested and to give them targets to reach. If one motto is 'Catch them young', then there should be a national under-fifteen championship as a supplement to Junior Wimbledon, and if another is 'Keep them playing' – so that they do not fall away in the years after eighteen as so many good players have done in recent seasons – then an under-21 event of proper importance might help to do this. National competitions are always tests of nerve and it is nerve that tells in international play. New events for players under fifteen and under 21 would be useful end-of-season attractions and they would also be valuable to those who are looking for youngsters with spirit enough to come out on top in the major crises of the senior game.

A MISCELLANY

A Bright Year for Britain

In summarising the British game for 1958, David presented a cheerful picture. With hindsight one may reflect on 'Laver and Mark, who have had three world tours, have not so far measured to the standards of their predecessors'. Laver was destined to do so!

In a year when the lawn tennis market generally has been falling it is pleasant to report a steady rise in British stock. Old stumbling blocks have gone and with them it seems that at long last some of the old inferiority complexes have been rooted out.

The Wightman Cup, United States' property for 28 years, has been won and, without the loss of a rubber, the men reached the European zone final of the Davis Cup for the first time since 1933. In 1958 it seemed as though quite suddenly British lawn tennis grew up, asserted itself, and became accustomed to the face of victory. Success breeds more success and in sport the habit of winning and expecting to win is as easy to fall into as that of being a game loser and always failing at the last fence. This increase in British confidence has not really been much more than the realisation that there are no such creatures as lawn tennis supermen and superwomen, that even Wimbledon champions are mortal. But it is the year's most significant sign of progress. 'You play against them and you go on losing, but then one day you suddenly realise that they are not as good as all that and that you have got a chance of beating them. Once you begin to think that you start winning', said one British player, who had just emerged from several lean years, at the end-of-season tournament.

Because of this encouraging cultivation of proper frames of mind, the season's honours list is the most impressive since the war. Thanks to Davies and Knight the men's covered- and hard-court singles titles stayed at home – the one for the first time since 1951 and the other after a four years' absence. As Miss Bloomer won the women's singles at Bournemouth for the second year in succession, Knight's victory in a good final against Merlo meant that Britain provided both hard-court champions for the first time since Perry and Miss Stammers brought off the 'double' in 1936.

At Wimbledon Wilson, after a fine victory against Pietrangeli, became the first English quarter-finalist in the men's singles since Mottram in 1948. Miss Mortimer made the most of a good draw to reach the women's final and Miss Haydon, defeating Miss Bueno on the way, came through to the semi-finals. In the quarter-finals Miss Bloomer took from Miss Gibson the only set that the American lost on her journey to the title.

Abroad, Miss Bloomer assembled a remarkable collection of near-misses. Her Italian title went when she lost to Miss Bueno in the semi-finals (she avenged this defeat in Paris and Hamburg), her French Championship when she fell in the final to Mrs Kormoczy, and she was beaten by the long-playing Miss Coghlan in the German final. The Italian doubles title, which she won with Miss Truman, and a cluster of mixed doubles successes can hardly have been adequate compensation for the other disappointments. Miss Haydon and Miss Truman, both of whom are beginning to spread their wings, reached the French quarter-finals and they both fell to finalists in the United States Championships. Miss Haydon lost to Miss Hard and Miss Truman was forced to allow a 'nervous' Miss Gibson to avenge her Wightman Cup defeat.

Among the men Knight, who has done most travelling, began the season well on the Riviera. He became the first English player to defeat Drobny (another familiar stumbling block) on a hard court – his regular doubles partner, Pickard, later followed suit most brilliantly at Shirley Park – and at Bournemouth he pioneered his way to the first British win over Patty on the same surface. He went out in Rome to Ayala, whom he later beat in Toronto, to Gimeno in Paris, and to Davidson, the eventual winner, in Hamburg after gaining revenge for his Davis Cup defeat by Sirola in the previous round. Davies did not regard journeys to Rome or Paris as necessary and he was beaten early on in Hamburg by the exiled Hungarian, Jancso, who defeated Wilson in the French Championships. At Forest Hills Davies lost to Fraser and Knight was beaten by Anderson.

In international play the fortune that gave the British women the chance to play against an American Wightman Cup side that did not include Miss Hard and Mrs Fleitz played the nasty trick of striking down Knight and Wilson with influenza a few days before the Davis Cup zone final with Italy in Milan. Knight sweated himself back into something like fitness by practising in the blazing heat, but it may have been that his poor showing in his singles against Sirola on the first day was partly due to the after effects of illness. Wilson felt that he could do nothing more than stay lugubriously in his hotel room until the last day of the tie. It will be some time, one thinks, before he is chosen again for a Davis Cup match abroad. The burden that Knight and Davies bore in this tie was enormous and Pickard, a newcomer to the team who was not given a match, supported them admirably.

The bold manner in which Britain travelled through this year's competition makes a zone victory next year seem a considerable possibility. Italy will have to play on grass in this country next time. Sweden, as strong an enemy as Italy this year, has now lost Davidson, who says that he has 'retired' from major tournament play, and must now rely upon Schmidt and Lundquist, two rather chancey players. Brichant is the only player in Belgium's one-man band and this year's defeat by Germany demonstrated that he cannot carry a whole team.

The Danish side of Nielsen and T. Ulrich has a poor Davis Cup record and France, now without Remy, who has turned professional, is left with Darmon, Haillet, Molinari, and Grinda, men who have still to prove themselves in Davis Cup play. The rising nation is Spain. With Gimeno and the Arilla brothers – the younger may well be the most promising youngster in Europe – they should soon be a most difficult country to beat.

Outside Europe, the season has left both the United States and Australia with considerable problems. Several of America's best players have refused the USLTA's Davis Cup invitations and the selection committee cannot really be happy about the form of the men who are willing to play. Mackay, a lanky player with a violent service but little more, did not seem to have improved at all when he reappeared at Wimbledon after a year's absence. Of those who stayed at home, players like Holmberg, Crawford, and Douglas (who was summoned from near-obscurity to join the Cup squad) have all won occasional victories, but not one of them has played with the kind of consistency that wins Davis Cups.

No one doubts that Australia will again finish the year as top nation, but what is doubtful – and what must be causing considerable anxiety to the ALTA – is the strength behind the lines if any of the present crop of leading players turn professional. Kramer has made no secret of his plans for expansion and the Wembley tournament showed plainly that he and Segura are coming to the end of their first-rank touring days. Replacements will have to be found and Cooper and Anderson seem obvious choices. If they were lured from the amateur game, Australian supremacy would be seriously endangered.

Laver and Mark, who have had three world tours, have not so far measured to the standards of their predecessors, but, of course, further losses to professionalism would not be a matter for Australia alone. Every major world tournament would complain about the absence of the players who draw crowds. It may be that the volume of their protest will be loud enough to force the International Federation into taking something other than an ostrich's-eye view of the amateur-professional question.

* * *

Majestic Frank Sedgman

The wooden court at Wembley was a shop window of the professional game for many years, and in 1958 it provided the setting for the Australian, Frank Sedgman, to display the fluency and majesty of his compelling game. Former Wimbledon champions, no longer amateur, were thick on the ground.

For those who had endured two long nights of wonderful, nerve-racking excitement it was just as well that this year's professional lawn tennis championships at Wembley ended with a swift and straightforward triumph for Sedgman. Another great match like the semi-final in which the Australian beat Gonzales, the world champion, or Trabert's desperate struggle with Rosewall, might have been too much to bear. How would it have been possible to go back to the plain amateur life of the mere Wimbledons and days in Paris or at Queen's Club or Budleigh Salterton if there had been yet another evening to be spent in gazing at lawn tennis of the first quality?

It is true to say that on Thursday and Friday nights the press room seemed to be full of journalists humbly wondering how they could possibly pay sufficient tribute to the sustained brilliance of the play that Kramer's men produced on the wooden court at the Empire Pool. Superlatives were not enough and the ordinary jargon of the game was quite useless. It is easy to write about bad lawn tennis, but such stuff as was seen in the last days of last week deserves only the finest phrases. When Sedgman played Gonzales no one wanted to take out a book and make notes, because every time one looked away one was likely to miss some flashing beauty of stroke, and the moment of high art would be gone for ever. The players wasted nothing; every stroke was a positive attempt to score, and the match turned on the merest trifles of accuracy.

In point of fact, when Sedgman won that match, he really won the tournament. Trabert, whom he beat 6-4 6-3 6-4 for the £1,000 prize on Saturday, is a brave fighter who strikes hard and never surrenders, but he is two or three classes below Sedgman, an absolute lawn tennis thoroughbred. It was a match between a player who gathered points with stylish ease and one who had always to labour to score. Where Trabert laboured Sedgman would cover the same ground lightly and swiftly. When Trabert hit a fine winner, as he did often enough, the shot was usually stamped with effort, but when Sedgman scored the ball and racket seemed by a kind of magic to do all the work for themselves. There is nothing in lawn tennis today quite so majestic as Sedgman's forehand volley.

With both men coming in hard for the net, the first set went with service until Sedgman broke in the tenth game, giving a fine demonstration of how to score points in a crucial game by hitting three deadly shots which Trabert, lawn tennis optimist though he may be, can never have hoped to return. This exhibition, and all that it portended, was so unnerving that Trabert wasted the final point of the set with a double-fault. He took the Australian's service to lead 2-1 in the second, but Sedgman resolutely and confidently swept him aside for 3-3, broke again, and collected the set at 6-3. At 4-1 in the third it looked as though Trabert had been completely extinguished, but with him it is difficult for the light of battle to go out. Sedgman hit an easy volley over the side-line instead of into an empty court, and the shock of this bad stroke seemed to disturb him so much that for two or three games his touch deserted him. Trabert, seizing upon his errors, came up to 3-4 and then had a point for 4-4, but by cruel luck a passing-shot fell inches out. Sedgman, thus reprieved, took the game for 5-3 and never allowed Trabert another chance of prolonging matters. The final was not so good as the semi-finals because there was never any doubt that Sedgman would win, and Trabert was never able to force the best out of him.

In the match for third place Gonzales, who had been best man at a wedding in the afternoon, played like a man who had been best man at a wedding in the afternoon: but eventually he showed that he was a better man on court than a rather stale Rosewall, winning 10-8 0-6 7-5. Trabert earned £750, Gonzales £500, and Rosewall £400. Altogether £7,500 is said to have been given out in prize-money during the week. Good value has been given.

* * *

Anguish in Torquay

I n the 1950s and 1960s the indoor tournament at the Palace Hotel, Torquay, provided halcyon days (and nights) for tennis enthusiasts. The tennis on very fast wooden courts had its own standards, on this occasion featuring only one official line-judge – although many spectators were only too ready to express their own views. This story relates the events of 1960, when Angela Mortimer, still a year away from her Wimbledon singles title, competed on her own territory. Bobby Wilson and Ann Haydon went on to become the singles winners that year.

Old battles will be fought again in the singles final of the Palace Hotel lawn tennis tournament at Torquay. Becker will try to take the men's title from Wilson, the winner for the last three years and his rival since their junior days, and Miss Haydon will go into battle against Miss Mortimer for the third year in succession. If history be any guide, she faces a considerable task. Miss Mortimer has not lost a match on the wooden courts of the Palace – where she learnt the game – since she won the event for the first time in 1952. In all, she has taken the title six times. In the two years when she did not compete – 1956 and 1957 – Mrs Long and Miss Curry were given short leases upon the trophy. Miss Haydon's singles final today will be her 26th of the year, and she has won thirteen different titles in different parts of Europe, Africa, and America.

Becker last played Wilson at the Connaught tournament in April when he lost, giving the Middlesex man revenge for a beating the previous year. Yesterday he had to struggle hardest of all for his place in the final. In the end and after the most dramatic match of the week, he beat Pickard 6-4 8-10 8-6. It was notable for the closeness of the challenge, for the quality of many of the exchanges (in particular for the fashion in which Becker drove home his passing shots in the first set), and for the unhappy arguments about line-decisions which disturbed both players and spectators.

The umpire was working with only one line-judge and that, of course, was insufficient assistance for a two-hour match played at a fast pace on wood between two Davis Cup men. At any time, it is a difficult job to take the chair and pass judgment on a tense and passionate match, and the major piece of entertainment yesterday was stormier than most. Several times Becker and the umpire were involved in terse exchanges about disputed points, and Becker was distracted further by a woman spectator, who appointed herself judge of the official judge. Then, worst of all, at 5-4 and 30-30, Pickard, who once again had played with what was for him surprising control, was robbed of what would have been a match-point. Becker tried to hit a backhand down the line and, to some onlookers who were perfectly placed to judge, it clearly fell out of court. The umpire thought otherwise, and Pickard, bleak and bitter, lost the game when he served again. He had another chance of the match, at 6-5, but Becker, sounder in a crisis, took his service without losing a point, and broke him finally in the fourteenth game. It was noticeable that neither player thanked the umpire at the end.

All through the season, there have been rumblings of discontent about the quality of present-day umpiring, and the fault does not lie entirely with the officials. The only solution is for more players to assist by taking lines and chairs. The Umpires' Association says that volunteers are hard to find, but almost every tournament entry-form stipulates that players must, if asked, take a match a day. If this were enforced by tournament committees, the difficulty might be eased.

* * *

The LTA Looks Ahead

A lways on the side of reformers, David reported on moves by the British Lawn Tennis Association in 1960 to improve its administration. The domestic scene was still the heart and soul of the game in Britain, and the broad horizons engendered by the Open game and the Grand Prix were in the future.

The Lawn Tennis Association has decided to carry out an investigation into the state of lawn tennis tournaments in Britain. Representatives of tournament committees have been invited to a meeting in London next month, and among the questions that will be discussed are general finance, the effects of television, and the possibility of holding more events for players in the under-15 and under-21 age groups. This is an attempt to step forward from a position which has remained more or less constant for the last ten years. In 1934 in the days when British lawn tennis, led by Perry and company, ruled the world, the LTA gave permission for 155 senior tournaments to be played in England and Wales. Since 1950 the average number of clubs wanting to hold tournaments has been about 80.

For most delegates finance will be the major question, but the answers there lie not so much with the LTA as with tournaments themselves. Talking to a tournament treasurer is rather like talking to a farmer. Times never seem to be good, and yet somehow the books balance in the end. It is a general rule that, given ordinary luck with the weather, tournaments make the profit or loss, in both cash and prestige, that they deserve. The tournament that complains about the poverty of its entry and the empty seats on finals day ought to take a careful look at its methods of publicity and organisation. In nine cases out of ten the remedy lies in hard work and enthusiasm. Good tournament committees make good tournaments.

Some ways of raising money do not seem to be used as effectively as they might be. It is surprising that more clubs do not guarantee their security by the 'subsidy-by-vice-president' method. The club which canvasses a town and enrols a hundred or so vice-presidents at a guinea a head, offering in return the right to a reserved seat every day, gives itself a valuable working fund. From that kind of foundation facilities can be built up and hospitality offered to players. More use might also be made of local industry. Lawn tennis seems to have lagged behind other sports in interesting large firms in the possibilities of prestige advertisement through the game. If Open lawn tennis is approved in the next few years and British tournaments are to hold any place in the market for players, clubs will need every possible source of revenue.

On the Continent the situation looks happier. It is not uncommon for a resort – Baden-Baden, perhaps, or Gstaad – to regard a tournament week as a major tourist attraction and to subsidise it accordingly. It draws support from the whole town. Hotels give free accommodation to competitors and shops put up valuable prizes to ensure that the best players, bringing with them, of course, maximum publicity, take part. Among the English resorts only Eastbourne, with the great broad stretch of Devonshire Park, Bournemouth, and, thanks to the Palace Hotel, Torquay, make proper use of the publicity that can be gained by a small investment in lawn tennis. With so much attractive opposition abroad, it is no wonder that, once Wimbledon is over, British tournaments, working on thin budgets, find it difficult to keep leading players in this country. This year only a few New Zealanders remained behind to give a little international spice to the August and September tournaments, and very few ranked British players were to be found competing at home. Expenses, prizes, and the weather are all better abroad.

One matter which the LTA ought to be considering is the fall in the number of clubs holding tournaments in May and September, both usually good weather months. In 1934 the pattern of senior tournaments was: March, six; April, ten; May, fifteen; June, 25; July, 31; August, 54; September, sixteen; October, six; and November, one. This year the picture had changed to: February, one; March, one; April, six; May, five; June, seventeen; July, twenty; August, 27; September, five; and November, one.

Two-thirds of these tournaments are to the South – lawn tennis leagues occupy a great deal of competitive energy in the North – but there are large areas of the country where room might be found for additional senior tournaments. Leicestershire, Derbyshire, Oxfordshire, Cambridgeshire, North Staffordshire, and North Wales are among these. Tournament entries, according to Slazengers, have been well up to average this year in senior events, and the number of junior competitors and junior tournaments improves every year.

That is the most hopeful aspect of the situation, and it offers the greatest opportunity for the game to advance. One hundred and twenty junior tournaments were on this year's list, and there will be at least two newcomers next season. Now that National Service has ended, it should be easier for boys to keep the habit of playing in tournaments, and more under-21 events will help both boys and girls through that discouraging time which comes when they reach eighteen and plunge into the swifter, more difficult waters of the senior game.

* * *

Kramer Voices a Grievance

The autumn professional tournament at Wembley took place in 1960 under the shadow of the rejection of Open tennis in the summer. Jack Kramer, Wimbledon champion of 1947, was the leading impresario of the professional game which, despite its playing standards and the obvious merits of its players, failed to enjoy full 'respectability'.

Talking to Kramer usually means listening to Kramer, but recently he asked a question: 'My players are the best in the world, and they play the best matches. Why don't I get more publicity? You press boys travel all over the world to see Ayala playing Candy in some amateur tournament, but when I put on a show in Paris with five Wimbledon champions, all it rates in the British papers is a few lines of results at the bottom of a column. It is the same in America. You can't tell me that people aren't interested in us.'

The night before, the first round of the London indoor professional lawn tennis championships had been played at the Empire Pool (capacity 8,000). Some of the circus's top-line acts had been on show – Sedgman and Trabert, two of the best of the post-war winners at Wimbledon, Segura, probably the best player who never got past a second round there, Nielsen, twice runner-up, and Gimeno, who might have been the first Spaniard to take the title if only he had stayed amateur a little longer. All these, together with Haillet and Remy, two of France's post-war Davis Cup stalwarts, played in the singles, and in a fine doubles, Olmedo, the 1959 Wimbledon champion, and Segura beat Davies and Gimeno. On paper, all those matches would have been worth Centre Court space at Wimbledon, but the programme attracted fewer than 500 people to Wembley. As the umpire's voice echoed dismally through the empty hall, Kramer, the entertainer, listened to the thin applause, and said encouraging things to himself and to the people around him. Sometimes he looked like the manager of a dying hippodrome.

The next night for Davies's first professional solo performance in Britain, for Cooper (Wimbledon, 1958), for Anderson, lean and quick as a greyhound, for Olmedo, for Rosewall and Cawthorn, and for a blazing meeting between Hoad and Segura, the attendance was 1,200. The Pool was half full on the Wednesday, and afterwards there were not many empty seats. The end of the week hardly could have been more success-ful, and as far as publicity was concerned, most newspapers and the BBC did Kramer proud.

Kramer made a profit at Wembley. But he must have found the week disappointing, and he cannot be regarding the future with absolute confidence. He is determined to go forward. His organisation is expand-ing – there is now to be an office in Paris as well as an American base – and he has captured some new players of rather mixed quality, and he talks about fresh conquests. In spite of all this fighting conversation, however, there is still no sign that professional lawn tennis is attracting a new audience, or winning back its old lost customers.

At the moment his new policy of putting more players into the ring is on trial. The argument for it was that with regular annual tours the established professionals were losing their curiosity value for the ordi-nary spectator; new faces, bigger tournaments, and a spice of national interest would, it was felt, mean larger crowds. The new theory was tested first in Paris at the Stade Roland Garros, where there were appar-ently small audiences early in the week and good attendances on the last two days. Wembley, which is financially one of the most successful tournaments in the world, amateur or professional, suffered from the same slack beginning. These two events are Kramer's brightest shop windows in Europe, yet even at these he was not able to attract the number of customers that his players deserve. It may be that the new formula will work in time, but so far the experiments have not been encouraging. One reason for this, even with its new recruits, is that the world of professional lawn tennis is too small. The real fascination of the great amateur tournaments – Wimbledon, Paris, Rome, or Forest Hills – lies in the variety and the size of the tasks they set, their full-scale tests of stamina, concentration, and determination. The man who wins at Wimbledon has jumped seven hurdles, and left behind 127 other com-petitors, and for those whom he beats the chance of the prize has gone for a year. Professional lawn tennis never has such great occasions. The players travel together. They are playing against or practising with each other constantly – since Sedgman turned professional, it is estimated that he must have played Segura 200 times – and they are completely familiar with each other's strength and weaknesses. This is one reason why the professional game so often looks so good.

For every defeat there is a speedy chance of revenge. Amateurs like Pietrangeli and Mackay may meet two or three times a year, and when they do the results will be interesting because of their bearing upon the great individual championships, and because of the Davis Cup. If, how-ever, Cooper meets Anderson ten times out of seventeen in a Kramer competition, all that it means is that Cooper's bank balance gets a certain amount of extra reinforcement, and one can hardly imagine that even in

Australia anyone outside the Cooper household will work up much passion or enthusiasm about that. That kind of thing is nice for Cooper but Kramer must not expect it to make headlines. It may be that the new inter-zonal Kramer Cup will catch the public imagination. There the players will be playing not for self, but for zone.

Next month a sub-committee of the International Lawn Tennis Federation will begin to discuss the question of 'Open tournaments' again. Its recommendation will go forward to the annual meeting at Stockholm in July. The Lawn Tennis Association of Great Britain will be forced to express some kind of opinion. At the moment its advisers on the matter seem to be divided into three groups, one for, one against, and one that wants to play for time in the hope that Kramer will run out of money or enthusiasm. There also are those who regard Kramer's recent signings with what seems to be undue pessimism. Certainly, the amateur game will be poorer for the loss of Gimeno, but for the last two years Davies and Nielsen have not been happy players to watch, and Haillet never achieved much outside France.

*　*　*

When Roger Taylor Became a Pro

Skilled, handsome and popular, Roger Taylor was the top British player when the British revolution was taking place. He was in fact a key figure, for complaints about his intention to break what amounted to a professional contract so shocked the LTA that its leaders were constrained to support a revolution that would end 'shamateurism'. The vital step came early in 1968, when Taylor signed a contract with World Championship Tennis to become part of the 'Handsome Eight'. His guarantee of £41,000 over three years was enough to make a headline.

Roger Taylor, the 26-year-old Yorkshire left-hander, who has been Britain's leading lawn tennis player for the last two seasons, yesterday became the first British player to join a major professional group since Mike Davies signed for Jack Kramer in 1962. His agreement with Dave Dixon, the new American promoter, will give him just over £41,000 in the next three years.

Most of the tournaments that he will play in will be in the United States, and the other players who will travel with him will be three of the younger members of the old pro group – Dennis Ralston, Earl Buchholz, and Pierre Barthes – and four recent amateurs, John Newcombe, Tony Roche, Cliff Drysdale and Nicola Pilic. Taylor will travel to Australia on 15th January for a television tournament and then the tour will begin in Kansas City on

1st February. He will be playing most nights for 40 weeks a year – 'a tough schedule and a big challenge', he called it yesterday – but he will be taking part in the first serious attempt to present professional tennis to the American public. Professional tennis under Kramer, Trabert, and then under the players' own association was successful enough, but it never made full use of personality and publicity. No one doubted that the best players in the world were on the old tour, but no one beat the big drums loudly enough for them and in the end the public began to tire of seeing the same players beat the same rivals in the same places and for the same prizes.

They forgot the elementary rules of publicity. It was difficult for the public to find out minor points of interest like how many times X had beaten Y or how much Z had won in the first twelve weeks of their season. In the end, after Gonzales, Hoad and Segura went into semi-retirement, most of the life went out of their tournaments. Laver and Rosewall began to look like match-winning automatons and the others looked more and more tired and depressed. Dixon and his supporters have gone for personality first: the group is to be known as the 'Handsome Eight', all of them are supposed to be crowd-pleasers. Dixon may have less talent at his command (although with the passing of time this will become debatable), but at least he will have the best-looking and the most dramatic competitors.

All this is part of his campaign to make professional tennis popular with the masses. Some of their innovations which they are supposed to be contemplating will cause some raising of eyebrows among the traditionalists – each player will have his personal colour ('And that is Roger Taylor in green coming out to meet Nikki Pilic in blue') and it is rumoured the Van Alen Simplified Scoring System, which is based on table tennis scoring, will be used frequently. The argument is that VASSS stops audiences that are not initiated into the finer arts of tennis from growing bored with long bouts of serving and volleying and, with its strict limit of points, it is easier to package matches for television. Whether they will stick to VASSS when they play before better-educated tennis audiences is another matter. Certainly, the public reaction in Britain to the VASSS experiments that have been held so far here has been unfavourable.

Taylor, rugged, easy-going, amiable, should fit into this new world happily enough. In his last amateur matches he has found it difficult to play well until the challenge was sharp enough to stir him. Even so, 1967 was a memorable season for him. Against Canada at Bournemouth last May, he saved nine match-points and only enjoyed the match when he was living dangerously; he beat Cliff Drysdale, an old enemy, on the Centre Court at Wimbledon in June, and then lost in the semi-finals to Bungert; in his last amateur appearance for Britain he beat Santana in the semi-finals of the King's Cup at Stockholm and then, in a match which he ought to have won easily, had to save a match-point against the less highly rated Bengtson to give Britain the title.

Another King's Cup match gave him the record of having played the longest three-set singles in the history of the game – 126 games – against Gasiorek in Warsaw three years ago. He has always been at his best in endurance tests and when crowds have been against him. His mother taught him to play in a Sheffield park and his Junior Wimbledon [National Junior Championships] final at sixteen, when he lost to Michael Harvey, was one of the worst and most nervous on record.

If one had to choose his four most interesting matches, two of them would be indoor victories in the King's Cup: that grand finale against Santana and a match against Jorgen Ulrich in Copenhagen in 1963. Denmark needed that rubber to be sure of winning and Ulrich, slightly supercilious, was leading by a set and 5-2 before Taylor overtook him. His finest defeat came in his Wimbledon semi-final against Bungert and his best Davis Cup match was that noisy, memorable piece of resistance against Gulyas on a slow hard court at Budapest last year. He is certain that he will be back to play at Wimbledon next year.

* * *

The Experiment in Kansas City

In 1968, Open tennis made the status of players, however designated by their national associations, irrelevant, and at the same time World Championship Tennis inaugurated a new commercial approach to the game. This Dallas-based organisation, later controlled by Lamar Hunt, opened in Kansas City with an attempt to bring tennis to the masses as pure entertainment, although its move towards spectator participation and general razzmatazz did not get far.

David was the only British writer to report on the opening scene.

From the beginning Kansas City, which makes Wolverhampton look like Athens, had seemed a strange starting point for the first world tour of the 'Handsome Eight', the newest of the professional lawn tennis groups. At the American Royal Arena, an ice-rink in a corner of the stockyards on the bank of the river Kaw, it seemed odder than ever.

The first week of the tour is being devoted to what David Dixon, the promoter, describes as his World Cup competition: Newcombe and Roche represent Australia; Pilic and Barthes, Europe; Ralston and Buchholz, the United States; and Taylor and Drysdale, 'England and South Africa'. (They wanted to call themselves the 'British Commonwealth' – but that was rejected on political grounds.) It was not quite hinted that this competition would be as important one day as the Davis Cup, but there was the promise that it would be a regular feature of future tours.

The hall, which holds 6,000, was one-sixth full; the temperature outside was two degrees below zero; inside, with the players walking over ice to reach the synthetic grass in the middle of the arena, it was colder. There was an awful hint of frost in the air. For a long time it didn't seem like a tennis tournament – Van Alen scoring and no rallying because the astro-turf was too fast and needed spraying – and yet, in spite of the privations, the seats at the end were not much emptier than they were at the beginning and a good deal of noise and excitement was generated. It was not a triumphant start, but at least it was not a failure and the things that were good about it were the things that are always good about lawn tennis. 'You should have seen us in Australia last week in 100 degrees of heat', said John Newcombe sadly. 'It was quite different.'

Barthes had it all explained to him and then went out and lost 31-27 31-29 to Ralston to give the Americans a 1-0 lead over Europe. Ralston was rewarded with $620 and Barthes with $380. Afterwards Barthes sat wistfully in the dressing-room. Then he said: 'Of course, I don't care about the money, I'm just desolated that Europe should have lost. I speak as a true European patriot.'

There were, in fact, prizes for everyone. Newcombe got $582.40 for beating Drysdale ($417.60), 31-30 25-31 5-2; all the children in the audience got vouchers for free tennis rackets. 'We want to popularise the game and we know that the kids are the paying customers of the future', says Dixon; the ball-boys got boxes of balls, and for shouting encouragement to selected players all the women in the crowd were given skin lotion by Revlon and all the men cologne. (On perspiring days at the Foro Italico, where there is a much greater need for cologne, everyone shouts their heads off free of charge.)

There was even a lawn tennis dance during one of the intervals. This was called 'The Serve' and it was a rock and roll routine with boys and girls either hitting ambidextrous forehands or volleying spasmodically with the same action and slight air of surprise that Françoise Durr always assumes when she accidentally finds herself at the net. It wasn't an evening for traditionalists; it wasn't white flannel stuff – but Dixon, the Barnum of tennis, cannot be dissatisfied with the quality of the entertainment. Before the evening started, he said: 'I know that tonight isn't going to be the success that every promoter hopes for and it isn't going to be the kind of flop you always fear, it will be something in between.'

The important thing was that tennis won. At the moment Dixon is experimenting wildly in the attempt to attract a mass audience to the game. There wasn't anything particularly new about last night's spectators. They were the usual solid, middle-class American tennis crowd and they like the things that American and any other lawn tennis audiences always like, the moments of tension, high skill and drama, which came over in spite of the scoring system and the state of the court. When the tennis was indifferent, you thought about the surroundings and the cold. When it was good – as it was for most of the Newcombe–Drysdale match – you forgot everything else. When at the end Drysdale was robbed of a key point in the best-of-nine-points third set by the decision of a linesman, the whole place erupted and Dixon got the kind of crowd reaction that he has been longing for.

At other times when spectators were simply shouting for one side or the other in the hope of winning skin lotion or cologne, the noise sounded artificial. Newcombe said that Drysdale's shot had been good (they had agreed beforehand not to correct calls) and Drysdale said bitterly: 'That linesman owes me $200.' There was more emotion when Ralston skidded off the court, crashed into a linesman's chair and then skidded dangerously on the ice.

The question of colour and uniform is still under continuous scrutiny. All the players went to the arena yesterday in blazers with the 'World Championship Tennis' emblem, which owes a little to the Pan American Airways badge, but Ralston began the day by refusing to wear any sort of colour on court because he was under contract to a manufacturer to wear only a certain type of clothing. Eventually he compromised by wearing one of Dixon's sea-green shirts and his manufacturer's trousers. The general opinion seems to be that dark shirts and white trousers give the players the best of all worlds. Newcombe wore brown trousers yesterday and looked as though he had just strolled in from the beach.

* * *

The Magic of Hoylake

Open tennis came about in 1968 and brought many changes, not least of which was the falling away of 'fun' tournaments. Among the most striking was the tournament at Hoylake, staged soon after Wimbledon, where play did not start until early evening and took place on public courts. There even the most hard-boiled of 'shamateurs' entered into the universal jollity. The story concerns Hoylake's last venture in the world of the old amateur game.

Britain's all too brief post-Wimbledon international lawn tennis came to a grand climax at Hoylake on Saturday. Five thousand spectators for the finals, more than 20,000 for the week, wild enthusiasm, record profits, John Newcombe, the best amateur in the world, triumphant in the men's singles, Roger Taylor almost overtaking him, a bold, disciplined victory for Virginia Wade in the women's singles, blazing sunshine all the week, and autograph hunters, ice-cream, and beer everywhere.

Can it ever be so good again? Will there be another summer when Wimbledon erupts, and the British surprise the world? At Newport the previous week, the Welsh Championships had been more uproariously popular than ever, but even their bustling life could not be compared to what happened in the Wirral. 'There is nothing like this tournament anywhere in the world', said Newcombe, thanking the chairman of the local urban council, who had been serving tea and sandwiches all through the week in the refreshment tent, on the day when she put on her chain of office and received us formally. You had to be there to appreciate the unique quality of Hoylake's tennisomania.

Middle-aged enthusiasts would walk up to strange players and ask them to pose for snapshots for the family album. Souvenir hunters queued to buy the balls used by Newcombe and Taylor in the men's final. People were asked for autographs as far away as Chester, and, as one left the ground at ten o'clock one night, a man loomed up in the darkness and asked plaintively: 'Do you know whether Mr Sangster's gone? I've been waiting here for two hours for him to sign my book.' And the great thing for lawn tennis was that no one can possibly have been disappointed by the quality of the matches on Saturday. First, Miss Wade, darkly concentrating, repeated her Beckenham victory over Judy Tegart (Australia) 6-3 6-4 in threequarters of an hour of highly efficient serving and volleying. There is never much rallying when these two meet and, with so much powerful serving, the ball was difficult to return on the bone-dry (almost bone-coloured) court.

The exchanges were short, sharp and spectacular. Maybe Miss Tegart helped Miss Wade by always serving to her forehand, which the British player now hits more soundly and effectively than she did a season ago, and whenever Miss Wade was in danger she could always put a bit more flash and zoom into her service and pull herself out of trouble.

That match was played at a fine speed, but it merely whetted the appetite for the crushing pace of Newcombe's 7-5 3-6 6-3 victory over Taylor, who tested him and challenged in a way that Bungert had never managed in the Wimbledon final. These are the two most improved men of 1967. Both have gained the confidence to attempt bold strokes. Newcombe was always sound. Now, since Wimbledon, he has become sound and exciting. He misses little and, unlike some recent major figures at Wimbledon, he does not seem to regard minor tournaments more as an opportunity for collecting money than for victories. It is nice to find that this champion is a 100 per center.

The difference between him and Taylor was that he was rather better at playing the big shot on the important point. Taylor always looked more secure than the champion when he served in the first set, and yet Newcombe, coming up from 15-40 to break for 6-5, thwarted him. The York-shireman well deserved the second, but started the third badly. Even so, he might have caught up. On three or four crucial occasions he tried to play for a safe winner when a bold shot might have brought its dividend. This is an old failing with him, but he has almost conquered it. Only in the tensest moments of all does he slip back again. It is good that he has decided to go to the US Championships at Forest Hills next month. Newcombe will find him even more difficult to beat on those uneven courts.

* * *

Women's Lib Makes a Gesture

Events in Great Britain in the weeks before the first Open tournament at Bournemouth in 1968 were stormy. Ann Jones, who had been the top-ranked British player for the six previous years and was to become the Wimbledon singles champion a year later, took exception to the disparity of prize-money between men and women and did not compete there.

Ann Jones, Britain's leading woman player, has asked the Lawn Tennis Association for permission to play in a tournament in Texas during the period of the British Hard Court Championships, the first Open event held in this country, which begin at Bournemouth on 22nd April. This is one more move in her campaign of protest about what she and several other prominent British players regard as the unfairness of the way in which the prizes have been distributed at Bournemouth. The winner of the men's singles will receive £1,000 and the runner-up £500 with £250 each for the losing semi-finalists and £100 for the losing quarter-finalists. The winner of the women's title will get only £300 and the runner-up £150, and other women's prizes – particularly in the doubles – fall away heavily by comparison with the men.

During the last few weeks Mrs Jones, who is supported by Angela Barrett, the Wightman Cup captain, Christine Janes and Virginia Wade, has been discussing the situation with officials of the Lawn Tennis Association, but she does not think that the LTA have yet come to understand the women's point of view on the matter. The allocation of the prize-money at Wimbledon caused considerable dissatisfaction, but in spite of considerable public support for the women the LTA have treated them even less generously at Bournemouth.

The women are anxious that their point of principle should be under-stood. As far as the British public is concerned, women tennis players are almost as well known and as frequently watched as men and for years

Bournemouth has depended on the top women for its best entertainment. Apart from Roger Taylor, who is now a professional, Mrs Jones and her group are the only home players of world class and they are annoyed that, after so many years of struggling in wind and rain at the West Hampshire Club, the LTA should have chosen to present the bulk of the prize-money to the professionals.

They know, of course, that the professionals will be an enormous attraction, but they believe that the LTA are underestimating the popularity of Britain's own players. Is an ageing Pancho Gonzales a much greater draw than Christine Janes, who has been a national heroine for years? Could any men's final between Rod Laver and Ken Rosewall be three-and-a-third times as exciting as last year's battle for the women's title between Mrs Jones and Miss Wade? The men deserve their high prizes, but the gulf between their rewards and those of the women ought not to be so great. The discussions have proceeded along those lines and Mrs Jones, after achieving nothing, now feels that she wants to make her protest more strongly.

She wants to play at Bournemouth and regain a title, which she has won three times, but she feels that if no one takes action, the LTA and other tournaments, who may take the official championships as their pattern, will get used to paying considerably smaller prizes to the women and this may do considerable harm to the women's game in this country. She is not only concerned about the top prizes. A man who is beaten in the first round at Bournemouth will get £20 and a second-round loser £40. Some provision may still be made for losers in the first round of the women's singles, but second-round losers will only be given £10.

That, she thinks, may discourage young players from competing. Tennis is an expensive game to play if you are not in the higher income bracket and Bournemouth has never been a cheap tournament for competitors. The LTA point out that much more money is being given to competitors this year than in the past – but that, says Mrs Jones, does not prevent the women from feeling aggrieved that there has been such heavy discrimination against them.

Something may be done to remedy the situation tomorrow when representatives of the organising committee at Bournemouth meet W. D. and H. O. Wills, the sponsors. The LTA laid down the proportions into which the prize-money was divided, but Wills, who will be spending more than £5,000 on the event, are very conscious of the public reaction to the points which Mrs Jones has raised. Although more money may be available, the LTA committee don't feel that they can change their decision, but one answer may be to make the trophy that Wills will present to the winners of the women's singles into something so attractive that any woman, no matter how militant, would be happy to possess it.

* * *

Women in the World Game

No one was less a male chauvinist in his regard for women's tennis than David. Here he follows its progress ten years after the open tournament reform of 1968.

Three months ago, on a cold afternoon in New York, Chris Evert won the Virginia Slims Championship for the fourth time since 1972. Her victory over Sue Barker by 2-6 6-1 6-1 was watched by a crowd of 11,651 at Madison Square Garden and her prize for that match alone was $50,000. In the twelve weeks of the tour she played in eight tournaments and won at Hollywood, Florida, Seattle, Chicago, Los Angeles, and Philadelphia. Altogether, she earned $174,500 from Virginia Slims this year. Last year, when Evonne Cawley beat her in the final, her total for the whole season was $343,165, slightly down on 1975's $350,977 but ahead of her $261,460 in 1974. That means that she has won more than a million dollars from match-play alone in the last three and a quarter years – a figure which doesn't take into account the extra money brought in by endorsements and by her Team Tennis contract. Chris is the perfect professional, a model of consistency on a tour full of sharp rivalries as well as a joy to her bank manager. 'You've come a long way, baby' was the slogan Virginia Slims found for Gladys Heldman when the women's tour began seven years ago. In 1971 Billie Jean King, winning $117,000, became the first woman to collect more than $100,000 in a year. Several other babies have travelled a considerable distance since then.

In a way, the development of women's tennis has been the major phenomenon of the 1970s. Once the game was opened to the professionals in 1968, it was predictable that the men would earn huge sums. There had been superb women players – Lenglen, Wills Moody, Connolly – over the years, but the real glory and publicity in tennis had always belonged to the men. For many years, the USTA kept its men's and women's championships separate. The crowds at the French and Italian Championships, some of the most educated tennis spectators on the circuit, are often reluctant to watch women's matches. Only at Wimbledon did the crowds do justice to the goddesses as well as to the gods.

Mrs Heldman's revolt changed that. Pacific South-West at Los Angeles, one of the oldest established of US tournaments, offered the women only 12 per cent of the prize-money they were putting up for the men. Billie Jean King, Rosemary Casals, Françoise Durr and six other leading women refused to compete there and went instead to a rival unsanctioned tournament, promoted by Mrs Heldman, then the publisher of *World Tennis* magazine, at Houston in Texas. Philip Morris, the tobacco company, who were in the process of launching Virginia Slims, a new brand of cigarettes for women, provided the prize-money and a profitable partnership was born. The USTA counter-attacked by staging a rival 'official' tour, with equally high prize-money.

The public showed an unexpected interest in women's tournaments. Billie Jean King proved a remarkable publicist for the cause and, exactly at the right moment, with the perfect timing now expected from her, Chris Evert arrived on the scene. In 1971, aged sixteen and eight months, she reached the semi-finals at Forest Hills. Since then her steady flow of success has gathered pace. Concentrated, dedicated, disciplined and industrious, she has been the ideal model for every young player on court and at her press conferences she is cool, shrewd, candid and witty. With a No. 1 of such quality, the success of the Virginia Slims tour has been assured.

The prize-money available to women has been increased this year by the inauguration of the Colgate International Series, a Grand Prix for women. Originally, the International Lawn Tennis Federation's idea was to promote a Grand Prix on similar lines to the successful jackpot series for men. Commercial Union, the men's sponsors, supported the project, but it died quietly. The hostility between the USTA and the top women, which had caused the original revolt, still smouldered and the arrival on the scene of World Team Tennis in 1974 ended all hopes of staging a women's Grand Prix. Mrs King, enthusiastically supporting the new league, led the way and soon almost all the leading women had signed WTT contracts.

Last year, however, Colgate Palmolive, who had organised the women's professional golf tour with spectacular success, came into tennis. They sponsored the Federation Cup, the women's international team competition, and announced that they were giving a bonus pool of $600,000 for the International Series. At first it seemed that most Colgate International Series tournaments would be in the United States, but gradually Europe rediscovered its interest in women's tennis and began to back it with prize-money. In addition to Wimbledon, Paris, Rome, Hamburg and Kitzbuehel will stage international series events this summer. That is an important development. In the 1973 season notable for a Goolagong–Evert final in Rome, a superb final between Margaret Court and Miss Evert in Paris, and for Mrs King's fifth success in the singles at Wimbledon (yet another failure in that year for the unlucky Miss Evert!), it seemed that women's tennis was booming in Europe. The poor fields of 1974 and 1975 halted that progress and it is only now, with Colgate's help, that the work of restoration has begun.

But it isn't only at the top of the women's game that European tennis is reasserting itself. Until this year it seemed that all the bright young players had to go West into the wilds of the US if they wanted to gain the necessary experience and computer points to play on the major circuit. It was hard to find a place on the top tour and almost as hard to qualify for the Futures tour, sponsored by Avon, the cosmetics firm, for lesser players. Competitors with quite considerable Wimbledon records sometimes found themselves struggling to avoid relegation to the mini-tour. California and Florida produced streams of tenacious, ambitious kids, who came on a production-line straight from high school to frighten established players. Tracy Austin, aged fourteen, from Rolling Hills, California, beat Linda Mottram at Portland and Greer Stevens at Minneapolis before losing by 6-3 6-3 to Rosemary Casals. Stacy Margolin, seventeen, from Beverly Hills, defeated Lindsey Beaven and Laura DuPont at Portland and then lost in a final-set tie-break to Natasha Chmyreva at Minneapolis.

The Europeans have taken note of this American concentration on cultivating the talents of the young. Team competitions like the under-21 Annie Soisbault and the under-18 Princess Sofia are useful preparations for the major circuit. But now the European Tennis Association, a representative organisation based in Basle and supported by the strongest national associations on the Continent, is building a series of satellite circuits for women. The tournament structure of girls' tennis in Europe has been haphazard up to now. This is a welcome step towards order and rationalisation.

Here, too, the British Women's Tennis Association, with Susan Mappin, the former Wightman Cup player as its chairman, and Shirley Brasher and Winnie Wooldridge, two of the most successful of post-war British competitors on the international circuit, among its advisers, has played a large part in organising and encouraging the young. With holiday tournaments at such centres as Queen's Club and Beaconsfield, they have provided opportunities for competition at times when there were blanks in the LTA's official calendar. Michele Tyler, Jo Durie, Anne Hobbs, Cathy Drury and Kate Brasher are among the players who have profited from this kind of enterprise. The BWTA was formed in response to the decision of the British men players to form a union three years ago. The men's union died quickly from lack of organisation and division of interest. The BWTA has turned itself into one of the liveliest forces in British tennis.

But one of the oddities of the women's international game is that most of the talent still comes from the countries that have traditionally done best in women's tennis. On the Virginia Slims tour the leaders came from the United States, Britain, Czechoslovakia and Australia. The United States hold the Federation Cup. Australia are usually their closest rivals. In Europe, Britain and Czechoslovakia invariably share the control of team competitions and now both have reinforcements waiting in the wings. The French haven't managed to produce a young player to take over from Françoise Durr in the aristocracy of the game and the Dutch have no obvious successor to Betty Stove. Mima Jausovec, from Yugos-lavia, and Regina Marsikova, from Czechoslovakia, look the best young players on the Continent. South Africa's hope, Greer Stevens, has been disappointing of late and the South Americans look sadly short of prom-ise. If only Brazil could find another Maria Bueno!

* * *

The Start of the Tie-break

The Philadelphia indoor tournament in January was attended by most leading British writers. In 1970 it brought an experiment in scoring which was to have far-reaching effects on the game. This was the tie-break, albeit in a different form from that in current use.

The first time I came to Philadelphia I marched through the centre of the city in a Republican parade with Gloria Steinem. We were covering the 1968 Nixon campaign and we had to march because the press-bus moved away while we were interviewing a man dressed as an elephant.

Tennis at The Spectrum hit me six months later. Marilyn Fernberger wrote and said: 'Come to the first tournament with revolutionary scoring changes.' That year it was called the ITPA – International Tennis Players' Association – Championships. Tie-breaks had been under discussion for six months; the USLTA was enthusiastic ... but scoring changes weren't then a part of the policy of the International Lawn Tennis Federation.

The management committee here never made any secret about what they planned to do. Philadelphia's tie-breaks and the idea of recognition at last for Jimmy Van Alen, the Maecenas of VASSS (the Van Alen Simplified Scoring System) filled the gossip columns on both sides of the Atlantic. Officially, of course, the whole idea was illegal. If the ILTF had been asked they would have said: 'If you have an Open tournament, it has to be played according to the rules and if Marty Riessen and Arthur Ashe play a 24-22 set, that is just too bad for the schedule.' But the USLTA, about to persuade the rest of the world to experiment, benevol-ently turned a deaf ear and blind eye (or maybe they didn't read the tennis magazines). The only doubtful point was the exact form that a tie-break should take. As I remember, the twelve-point tie-break, ultimately used for the singles, was suggested by Rod Laver and slightly modified after-wards. For the doubles Mr Van Alen presided over another experimental form of scoring and Tony Roche and John Newcombe, the reigning Wimbledon champions, lost their first match.

Everybody at The Spectrum scrutinised what happened calmly. The co-chairmen of the tournament felt like pioneers but didn't really think of themselves as rebels. Nothing was heard from the USLTA in New York, but on the third day a cable arrived from the ILTF in London, saying that the tournament must revert to normal scoring at once. Apparently, no one on the ILTF's management committee could understand why sets kept ending at 7-6.

There was a hasty conference. In the end, Philadelphia was forced into a new Declaration of Independence. Ed Fernberger wrote a polite reply, outlining the case for shortening sets in an expensive stadium with only two courts, but it fell on stony ground. Later, the composers of this reply realised that instead of a cable back directly to the ILTF they ought to have replied to the USLTA as their own governing body. That would have forced the USLTA to take a stand of some kind on the matter and the delay (perhaps three weeks or a month) would have given Philadelphia time to finish the tournament without confronting the rulers of the international game. As it was, defiance was the only course and afterwards they were penalised for being ahead of their time. Actually, apart from saving valuable time, the first tie-breaks weren't a tremendous success. It took a long time to get used to the form and player reactions were pretty mixed. It was not until Margaret Court and Billie Jean King played a tense tie-break at the end of the women's final that the possibilities of the idea were fully revealed.

Still, that was one example of The Spectrum tradition of showing off all the smart notions of modern lawn tennis in their best colours. I have to make a confession. In some ways, it isn't my favourite tournament. You can't sit at an open-air restaurant, looking down at the play and eating lasagne and drinking Frascati, like you can in Rome. The sweep of the wine-dark Mediterranean doesn't lie beyond the far stop-netting as it does at Monte Carlo. The crowd aren't such noisily excited partisans as they are in Paris. You don't feel that every rally is a part of the history of the game like you do at Wimbledon.

But when you rate indoor tournaments, Philadelphia is in a class by itself. It is unique. 'If you have a better-organised event than anyone else, the world will make a beaten path to your door', Roy Emerson's uncle, Ralph Waldo, almost remarked. It has better international coverage than any American tournament except for Forest Hills. And as far as the people who work for it and contribute to it are concerned, there is a wonderful sense of involvement.

Too many events drift out of the calendar or lazily rely on the goodwill of their sponsors. Philadelphia sets an example to the rest of the tennis world by the business-like way in which it has created an international reputation for itself. If you want a pattern for the development of modern lawn tennis, look at the way the US Professional Indoor Championships are being staged at The Spectrum this week. Forest Hills is a century behind it.

Billie Jean King Humbles Riggs

In September 1973 in Houston, Texas, Billie Jean King was matched against Bobby Riggs, the 1939 Wimbledon champion, in a woman v man challenge that was probably the most publicised contest in the history of the game.

It was not an ordinary lawn tennis match at Houston, but it was won by the exercise of the traditional lawn tennis virtues. Anyone who looks at BBC television today will see Billie Jean King gaining the kind of crushing tactical, technical and psychological victory over Bobby Riggs that ought to keep the male chauvinists quiet for a long time. The score of 6-4 6-3 6-3 leaves no room for argument. Riggs, who called his autobiography *Court Hustler*, was himself hustled to defeat.

Unlike Margaret Court, whom he beat 6-2 6-1 in the first of the 'unisex' matches in May, Mrs King enjoyed the razzmatazz of the evening. She has always been a player for brass bands and showbiz tennis and once Riggs lost the psychological advantage, once he discovered that he could not dominate by force of personality, it simply became a straight match between Wimbledon's most successful postwar woman player and a 55-year-old former men's champion, who was giving away 26 years and began to suffer from cramp before the end.

Riggs learnt that man could not live by wit alone. In California he had played Mrs Court on slow cement, which had suited his versatility of shot. Lobbing and slow-balling had been highly profitable. At Houston, Mrs King knew what to expect and she had taken warning from Mrs Court's mistakes. The plastic court was faster and so were the balls. She insisted on playing over five sets – backing her own fitness against that of the man on the other side of the net – and let it be known that she was going to volley her way to victory. In spite of Riggs's skill in verbal warfare the pressure was always on him. He had taken up an extreme position and had made the most of a bright idea but, as a man, he was expected to win on court as well as in the off-court battle of words. In the end Benedick was put down by Beatrice. The pressure of asserting the superiority of his sex proved a little too much. 'I think he was nervous. Any great athlete has to be nervous before a match. I think he was', said the formidable, voluble woman.

Considering the circumstances, it was a match of some quality. Once the pre-match jokes were over, they settled down to a hard, fierce match, full of shrewdly played rallies. Once Riggs had been left behind in the first set, it seemed certain that Mrs King would win. Afterwards he said: 'I have nothing to be sorry about. She played too well, too good. Girls her age are tough on 55-year-old guys. I have to eat a lot of crow. I said a lot of things and I have to take them all back. Billie Jean deserved to win, but I would like a re-match within six months if possible.'

Mrs King regarded her victory as 'the culmination of my nineteen years of playing tennis'. It was a vindication of her campaign for equal status and prize-money for women's tennis and it had also popularised the game in a way that no ordinary match could have done. The match was televised nationally in the United States and it will be shown in twelve countries. Mrs King said: 'Tonight a lot of people saw tennis for the first time. Nothing could be greater for tennis. I love it. I love people screaming in spectator sports. I have wanted tennis to change. This has made a lot of dreams come true for me and for tennis. This is a delight.'

It has been one of the few occasions that woman has beaten man in a public lawn tennis match. Suzanne Lenglen was once easily beaten by Bill Tilden, who also defeated Pauline Betz when he was 50, only to lose a return match to that aggressive Californian five years later. Mrs King herself, in spite of the gift of ten points, lost to Eugene Scott 21-17 in an experimental match some time ago.

* * *

Masters in Melbourne

B efore the Grand Prix Masters' Tournament was established at Madison Square Garden, New York, its venue was peripatetic and in 1974 it was staged in the southern hemisphere, at the Kooyong Stadium in Melbourne. The Argentinian Guillermo Vilas was an unexpected winner on the Australian turf.

It is late to be writing about grass-court tennis, but if this year's Commercial Union Masters taught the Australians anything, it is that the rest of the world now knows how to play on grass. Tennis in Melbourne, where so many of the great Davis Cup Challenge Rounds were played, used to be a matter of Australia first, the United States second and the rest nowhere. Australia used to beat the Indians comfortably, and when the Europeans came, they were usually languid, pessimistic and desperate to return home. Australia ruled the world (what was clay, anyway?) and the others were people you tried to persuade to stay on for the Nationals. It was a sign of the shift in the balance of power – and of the way that so many leading Australians arranged their playing schedules in 1974 – that no Australian was in the top eight of the Grand Prix.

Rod Laver was hardly seen after the WCT tour ended; Ken Rosewall saved himself for Wimbledon, Forest Hills and the Pittsburgh Triangles; and John Newcombe finished twelfth and was invited to take the place reserved for the home country's representative in the tournament. Immediately, he became the favourite because he was the player with the best record on grass. Jimmy Connors was staying away with a toothache and Onny Parun was the only other player who could be regarded as a grass-court specialist.

Of the other would-be Masters, Ilie Nastase, the winner for the three previous years, had played in Australia for only half a week in 1969. He had won Forest Hills in 1972, but had not played much on grass since then and had always been disappointed at Wimbledon. ('You need luck to win on grass. I never have luck at Wimbledon', he said before the start at Kooyong.) Manuel Orantes plays on grass with genial resignation. Harold Solomon, America's answer to Beppe Merlo, is rightly depressed about the way his neat little shots stand up for punishment. 'Why did you come here?' asked a belligerent journalist after he had finished by winning only eleven games in three matches in the qualifying round-robin. 'I have worked for a whole year to get into the top eight, and so I had a responsibility to come to Melbourne. Some people seem to dodge those responsibilities. It is just my bad luck that the Masters was on grass this year', he replied.

Bjorn Borg went to Australia three weeks early. He won Adelaide, defeating Parun in the final, and came to Melbourne with a retinue of eighteen Swedish journalists who dictated stories about him which gurgled into telephones like disappearing bathwater. The rise of Borg has created an entirely new Swedish industry. Time was when you only saw Swedish journalists at Davis Cup matches and at Wimbledon. Now they fly all over the world.

Borg was confident and optimistic. And so was Raul Ramirez, who told everyone that he regarded grass as his best surface. That left Guillermo Vilas, the winner of the $100,000 first prize in the Grand Prix and the player whom no one in Australia knew. Vilas arrived five days before the Masters, practised with great seriousness on the outside courts, consulted Neale Fraser, another distinguished left-hander, about his service and with Argentina's Davis Cup trainer about the best way to keep fit after so many weeks of match-play. Newcombe told everyone what a good match-player the Argentinian was, but how could anyone have anticipated that a player who lost to Erik Van Dillen at Wimbledon would sweep through the Masters?

'You have to be very good to win both the Masters and the Grand Prix in a year. Only one other player in the history of the game has done that', said Nastase, who brought off that double in 1972 and 1973, with a straight Rumanian face. He explained Vilas's swift adjustment to the Kooyong grass by saying that it was a matter of confidence: 'When you win the Grand Prix, you have so much confidence that you don't think that you can lose in the Masters.' But all the other virtues that carried him through the Grand Prix helped Vilas to this last victory. He was superbly fit. He played the longest matches of the week and finished by beating Ramirez in a four-set, two-and-a-half-hour semi-final (when the heat on court was said to be 125 degrees) and then Nastase by 7-6 6-2 3-6 3-6 6-4 in a two hour 49 minute final the following day.

His stamina was remarkable. His ability to sprint and scramble surprised even those players who compete against him regularly. The accuracy of his groundstrokes and the weight of his topspin disconcerted everyone. And if he served a great many double-faults, he also produced plenty of aces and good, testing second services. Nastase returned superbly in his semi-final against Newcombe. Of the final, he said: 'By the time I had got used to Vilas's service, I was down by two sets to love.'

Vilas began by beating Newcombe 6-4 7-6. For a few days before the start there had been some doubt about the Australian's fitness. But he practised so formidably on the Sunday before the tournament began that Nastase wondered whether Newcombe had been injured at all. That was the mood of Newcombe's beginning against Vilas. There were thunderous flourishes, and he won the first three games at a cost of four points, making Vilas look merely a runner. The crowd sat back to watch a familiar performance, Newcombe steamrolling his way to victory in one of the best Australian acts in the business.

But suddenly the steamroller stopped. Vilas found his length on his groundstrokes and began to time his passing shots properly. There was Argentinian topspin everywhere. Newcombe's 3-0 slipped to 3-4 and, when the Australian broke back in the eighth game, Vilas captured his service for 5-4 and finished the set with an ace which left Newcombe looking like a tractor overtaken by a racing car. ... 'I was landing my volleys two or three feet short, and he could pass me', said the Australian. 'There aren't many players who can pass me if I volley a little too short, but he did.'

Vilas's next match ended Borg's chance of a place in the semi-finals. The Swede had lost to Newcombe by two tie-breaks, mainly because he missed far too many low volleys and forehand returns of service on a damp day. Vilas v Borg, the winner of the Grand Prix versus the hero of Rome and Paris, wasn't a perfect contest. There were too many mistakes – missed volleys by Borg and double-faults by Vilas – but there was also a huge ration of flair, pace and imagination in the first set. Vilas won 7-5 6-1, and if Borg faded towards the end, his falling away was typical of the normal pattern of their matches. 'This was our sixth match and now we have each won three. Almost always there has been a long first set and the winner of that takes the second set easily', said Vilas. In the first set he held two points for a lead of 4-0 and then Borg caught him at 4-4. He won the ninth game in spite of three double-faults ('I had to take risks with my second service because Bjorn returns so well'), and then served superbly for 6-5. A wonderful topspin lob and a flat backhand return broke Borg for the set and the rest was easy.

He was still experimenting with the new challenge of grass; Parun, who had nearly beaten Borg and played with vain solidity against Newcombe, extended his education the following day in a match which went to 7-5 3-6 11-9. Parun served for the match at 6-5 in the third set but lost his service to love. 'How can I lose my serve to love on grass?', he asked miserably after Vilas had won a contest which had kept him on court longer than he wanted on the day before the semi-finals.

By topping his group, he earned a match against Ramirez, who had taken a set from Nastase on the first day and beaten Orantes and Solomon. Nastase, who had cruised through, spending longer at his press conferences than on court, played Newcombe. Nastase won 6-3 7-6 6-2 in two hours of strict, disciplined play. He had won their three previous meetings, but this was the first time that he had beaten Newcombe on grass and in front of an Australian crowd. Even in his Forest Hills year he did not play with as much touch and confidence as on this blazing afternoon. He survived Melbourne's fiery furnace. Newcombe wilted. At the end he said, 'I am beginning to believe that I was born on grass'. Yet another of the clay-court players had won away from home.

Newcombe's only chance came in the second set. Then he led 4-0, only to see his volleying betray him again. Nastase overtook him and won the tie-break, and afterwards there was no hope for the Australian. 'That set was a disaster for me. It turned the match around', he said. He felt he had not been fast enough or fit enough to do himself justice, and he withdrew from the third place play-off against Ramirez, complaining of a sore toe and a blistered hand.

The afternoon had been fiercely hot for that match. For Vilas v Ramirez, Latin America's occupation of the court where Sedgman, Rosewall, Hoad and Laver ruled, the heat was so fierce that 50 spectators fainted. Vilas won 4-6 6-3 6-2 7-5, but in the fourth set Ramirez, always accurate and economical, never hitting with Vilas's urgency or impulsively chasing so many half-chances, came back from 1-5 to hold a point for 6-5. As Vilas's lead melted, he began to show signs of distress. He asked for a hat and complained of dizziness, saying, 'Everything turned yellow'. Somehow he summoned up the strength to break back in the eleventh game and another huge effort of will – the sort of determination that wins the Grand Prix – enabled him to hold service from 15-40 for the match. 'I should have won if it had gone to a fifth set', said Ramirez.

Vilas looked exhausted then, but he was helped the next day by the fact the sun disappeared. There was rain in the morning before he and Nastase went out for the final. The wind never stopped (John Newcombe says that it blows in four directions at once at Kooyong) and at regular intervals large blobs of rain fell slowly. Would Vilas be tired? He answered the question immediately with a series of disconcerting dashes to pick up points from shots which would have beaten anyone else. They moved each other about the court cleverly, but the wind and Vilas's speed spoiled some of Nastase's defter moves. Part of the reason why Vilas won the Grand Prix is that he is the best athlete in tennis, a sprinter who can keep on running through long matches. No one who saw him against Nastase would have believed that he had played to the limit of his stamina against Ramirez.

He was always determined and concentrated, even when the third and fourth sets slipped away. Nastase attacked intermittently. He had played his match of the week against Newcombe. He did not hit as hard or as purposefully against Vilas. There were moments of brilliance. There were periods of utter waste when his volleys fell harmlessly in mid-court waiting for Vilas, who was merciless on anything short, to punish them, when his returns of service floated away, when his judgment of the bounce disappeared completely.

Nastase said afterwards that he could not understand how anyone could hit so many shots with so much heavy topspin as Vilas had done. 'I could not see which direction the ball was coming from. I wish I had a backhand like his. Every shot came differently.' The keynote of Nastase's press conference was respect. He almost forgot to make jokes when he talked about Vilas's talent. He thought, too, that he had played some of the crucial points badly. He held two points for a lead of 3-1 in the first set and then came back from 3-5 to 5-5. In the tie-break he caught up from 2-6 to 6-6, only to be thwarted by a bad bounce for 6-7 ('You have to have luck if you play on grass') and an injudicious drop shot ('That was stupid. If I had hit a long ball, I had a 95 per cent chance of winning the point').

Vilas dominated the second set, but then the wind died and Nastase, finding it easier to take the kind of risks that he likes, took charge of the third and fourth. At two sets-all he seemed in command, but he started the fifth badly, losing his service in the first game. 'I was stupid on the first two points. I had been going in, but I stayed back and lost them. Then I went in and was passed twice.'

He was broken again for 1-4, and although he won Vilas's service in the next game, he wasn't allowed to make up the lost ground. Vilas's final set was a champion's finish, sharp, tough, resolute and with few errors. He had served twelve double-faults in the first four sets, but not a one in the fifth. 'I realised that I was doing something wrong with my feet and corrected it. After that I served better', he said. At the end a small group of Argentinians at the back of the court waved flags and sang a football song adapted into a message of support for Vilas. Gordon Dunlop, Commercial Union's boss, handed him the prize and said that in the course of the week Vilas had collected $140,000 for the Grand Prix and the Masters. 'I came here to play tennis and not to collect that money', said Vilas. 'I use money like everybody else, but if there wasn't any money in the game I would still care about tennis and want to play every day.'

About his conquest of grass, he said: 'I was like a schoolboy when I first came here, learning how to move, and I thought to myself, "Isn't it stupid? I have been playing well all the year and now I have to start all over again".'

It began to rain during the presentation speeches. In the middle of the ceremony Vilas suddenly turned and spoke to an official. He asked him to cover his rackets with a towel to protect them. After that piece of professionalism, he turned back to listen to Wayne Reid, the president of the LTAA.

* * *

The Whisky Circuit

The Dewar Cup series was prominent from 1968 to 1976. All its indoor tournaments achieved a light-hearted joyousness among both spectators and, frequently, players. It attracted wide interest when it was played at the Royal Albert Hall in London. This is the story of the semi-finals there in 1975, when Eddie Dibbs was to beat Jimmy Connors in the last match and Virginia Wade became the women's winner.

Send in the clowns. After all the missed cues at the start of the Dewar Cup, the penultimate act at the Royal Albert Hall last night was broad and sometimes brilliant comedy. In the semi-final that everyone wanted to see Jimmy Connors beat his doubles partner, Ilie Nastase, 6-3 4-6 6-1 and now plays another American with a double-handed backhand, Eddie Dibbs, in the final. It was another version of their famous (or deplorable according to your taste) double act. Nastase always used to win. Now Connors, six years his junior, stronger and quicker but less subtle and less imaginative, has taken command. The rivalry is a matter of shots, strategy and gamesmanship.

Last night they volleyed and lobbed jokes at each other. Some of these were winners. Others were nicely timed to break concentration at moments when the other man was getting ascendancy. The American, whose asides were broadsides, won all the battles in the end. 'Carry On Serving' might have been the title of the evening's entertainment. Sometimes Nastase laughed so much that you might have thought that Sydney Smith, Sheridan, Ben Travers and the Marx Brothers were on the other side of the net. 'Get on with it, Connors', shouted a basso profundo from the boxes after one inordinate delay. 'Yes, ma'am', said Jim. Nastase laughed and lost the next point. Everyone else had to laugh, too. 'I don't like playing him because he is my friend. One half of my head wants to concentrate and the other half wants to clown, but it is no good saying that it hurt me to win because that is my job', said Connors at the end.

Nastase, who has reached quarter-finals and semi-finals all over the world this year but won only one Commercial Union Grand Prix tournament, began by looking as serious as Matthew Arnold. There were no frills about his early stuff. With a funeral face, he told off a latecomer and glowered at a photographer, but then he made Connors run from the base-line to the net for a drop-shot and still beat him. Connors threw a playful steel racket at him and cheerfulness broke in. Afterwards Nastase could not resist the temptation to try and win the contest for laughs and the quality of his tennis slipped.

Connors won the first set. Nastase ran and worked mightily to take the second in spite of a flood of quips, pranks, wanton wiles and heavy passing shots from the other end. The set-point was farcial. Connors moved up to volley, turned to try and deceive Nastase, misjudged the shot and missed the ball altogether, finishing on his knees. Then Nastase pretended that he did not want to serve at the start of the third, lost his service (perhaps he was not pretending after all), and then was never in the match. He sat in the dressing-room muttering gloomily. The comedy was over and he knew as well as anyone that he had been beaten because he had lost some of his old determination to win.

The other semi-final was a British anticlimax. Buster Mottram, who had been so brilliant in beating Jan Kodes, the 1973 Wimbledon champion, 6-0 6-1 on Thursday, fell by 6-3 6-3 to Dibbs, the 24-year-old US number eleven. Against Kodes, hitting streams of winners, he had looked like a potential world champion. Yesterday he looked like one of the game's apprentices again. After intoxication – sober reality again. That's the way it goes on the Whisky circuit.

Mottram blasted away at him, trying to recover the careless rapture of his match against Kodes. Once again he hit a great many powerful shots, but Dibbs, stocky and sturdy, scuttled about the court, defending too well. He hit hard – this was a match between a strong little man and a 6 ft 3 in boy – and that double-handed backhand produced some quite remarkable angles. Lobbing and drop-shotting, he exploited Mottram's weaknesses and made few mistakes himself. The British player could never keep him under consistent pressure. Continually he tried to out-manoeuvre the American by hitting wide to that backhand. The angles were extravagant and the results were often disastrous. Invariably Dibbs directed vigorous returns to the wide open spaces that he left. Mottram's best spell came at the end of the first set when he caught Dibbs at the net several times. Not even the American's closest friends would regard him as one of the great close volleyers.

Mottram lost his service for 3-1 and although he broke back in the next game he immediately fell behind again. Dibbs held a set-point at 5-2 and hit a backhand down the line. The line-judge ruled against him. He walked belligerently to the middle of the court and said: 'It fell smack on the line.' His next shot fell equally close to the same line. Again Mottram was given the point. He won the game and held three points for 4-5. Dibbs was volleying angrily rather than accurately, but the American served his way to safety. When Dibbs had won the game and the set, he made a gesture of rather vulgar dissent to the man on the line. He was still flustered at the start of the second, but it did not take him long to wipe out Mottram's lead of 3-1. Experience, concentration, determination and basic accuracy – these were the virtues which brought him victory. Mottram hit some spectacular shots, but he lacks Dibbs's solidity – both off the ground and in his approach to match-play. He is wonderfully hungry when he has nothing to lose, but he is nervous when he has a chance of victory. It ought to be the other way round. On form.

Evonne Cawley quickly reached the women's final. There was another of the Dewar Disasters. (One day someone is going to write a history of this week, entitled 'The Ill-luck of the House of Dewar'.) Renata Tomanova, the Czech who beat Rosemary Casals in the quarter-finals, injured her neck dancing at the house where she was staying at Epsom on Thursday night. She had treatment before she went on court yesterday, but never moved easily, and Mrs Cawley won 6-2 6-1. This evening she will play the holder, Virginia Wade, who beat Mima Jausovec 6-3 7-5.

*   *   *

Philadelphia Storms

The most notable of indoor tournaments in the US is that held at the impressive Spectrum Stadium in Philadelphia early in the year. It was 1975 when tennis form seemed turned upside down by the defeats, right and left, of established favourites. Here David weaves the strands of the surprise happenings of that year.

To Philadelphia for a cataclysm. The US Professional Indoor Championships, the start of this year's World Championship Tennis tour, was notable for so many eruptions of form that The Spectrum, the city's huge indoor arena, felt like Pompeii in the middle of its last days. At the beginning there were fifteen seeds (Guillermo Vilas, the winner of the Grand Prix and the Commercial Union Master, was too ill to play), but only five reached the last sixteen and Marty Riessen, the winner, was the only seeded semi-finalist.

There has never been such a week in the short but spectacular history of the tournament. It was like Haydn's Farewell Symphony. The elegant strings would play for a while, then bow, put out their candles and leave, unbalancing the draw and furrowing the promoters' brows. The final should have been Borg versus Laver – but the Swede, the runner-up to Newcombe at the WCT Finals in Dallas, lost to Bob Lutz in his second match and Laver, who needed match-play for his contest with Jimmy Connors at Las Vegas, did not even survive a round. Phil Dent beat him 7-6 5-7 7-6.

The process of chopping and guillotining was continuous and so much of the top people's blood was spilt that in the press box we began to understand what it must have been like to have a good week at the French Revolution. We listened to the tumbrels, watched the baskets fill and knitted phrases. At some other stadiums, they quote to players that hack sentence about meeting triumph and disaster and treating the imposters the same. The text for Philadelphia came later in the poem: 'If you can keep your head when all about you others are losing theirs and blaming it on fatigue, lack of match-play and intensity of competition, then you'll win the US Professional Indoor title with its first prize of $15,000, my son.'

Riessen understood that message. While the wind of change was blowing, while players like Vitas Gerulaitis (reaching the final in his first WCT tournament), John Alexander, Jaime Fillol and Paul Gerken were upsetting form, while the pillars of the professional establishment were trying to find excuses for the general uncertainty ('Yes, I still believe in the ATP computer', said Arthur Ashe), Riessen advanced steadily. This was one of Marty's iron-clad weeks, like the wonderful time at the Albert Hall five years ago when he beat Cox, Newcombe, Okker and Rosewall to win the prize and convince himself that he wasn't just a doubles player. His success at Philadelphia wasn't quite so spectacular because he was able to cruise until he reached the final, but from the point of view of reward and publicity it was the best of his career and he won the title coolly and easily.

His statistics were impressive. Normally, he wins one WCT tournament a year. The Albert Hall was followed by Teheran in 1971, Quebec in 1972 and Milan in 1973. Nothing last year. Not even a second place. And now, here he was loping through WCT's biggest tournament, with his H. F. Lawford moustache and a gait like the Pink Panther, and winning the race by sound, solid serving and volleying while the other leaders of the circuit sputtered and misfired.

On his way to the final he lost only 24 games in five matches, defeating Anand Amritraj 6-1 6-3, the improved Dick Dell 6-1 6-4, Syd Ball (Roscoe Tanner's conqueror) 6-3 6-2, Tony Roche (who beat Dent and then fell a victim to the combination of Riessen's persistent aggression and a damaged Achilles' tendon, which put him out for two months) 7-5 6-0 and Jaime Fillol (who won a dramatic match against Ashe and then had all the drama knocked out of him) 6-1 6-4 6-0. As his victories piled up, Riessen sounded slightly puzzled. 'I keep saying to myself day after day that it isn't going to be like that tomorrow', he said at one press conference. 'My scores have been pretty decisive. I have beaten players whom I ought to have beaten, but I wouldn't have expected to win by such huge margins', he remarked at another.

What happened to the perpetual quarter-finalist, to the doubles player whose serve so often shortened and whose volleying stiffened in the crisis of an important singles? Here he was in Philadelphia's revolutionary year, surviving by the simple process of methodically continuing to do all those things that we have been watching him do for years slightly better than usual. He is 33 now and he has been a tournament player for sixteen years, the sort of competitor that it is easy to refer to with words like 'honest', 'rugged', 'straightforward' and 'journeyman'. John Newcombe once played him at Forest Hills and alluded to Marty's tendency to choke when a match became tight.

It has taken a long time for the cannon fodder to turn into a cannon. His tennis has always seemed 99.984375 per cent perspiration and 0.015625 per cent inspiration. But this time there was less perspiration than usual, less strain. The effort was less obvious. The Riessen who won Ed and Marilyn Fernberger's remarkable tournament was more relaxed than usual. Fate had given him a promising draw. He was confident and he was making the most of it.

One of his texts for the week was: 'Those who are lucky and in good shape win.' He played so well that he scarcely needed luck in the early part of the tournament. When his left leg began to trouble him in the final, when a string went in his favourite racket in the crisis of the fourth set, when Gerulaitis took him to a fifth, he still played with total assurance. He never looked or sounded as though he doubted the inevitability of victory. If ever there was a man in his hour it was Marty Riessen, only the second American player to win the US Pro Indoor title, at Philadelphia in January, 1975. By comparison, that earlier victory at the Albert Hall was heady stuff, a first success for a player who was celebrating the discovery that he was better than he had thought himself. Philadelphia was a prize gained by an assured competitor who saw his chance and took it, directly and purposefully. No aching joys or dizzy raptures. No frills or detours. Just a straightforward advance to victory. Art concealed art. Riessen had never served and volleyed so efficiently for a whole tournament, never attacked so consistently. Journeymen don't win titles in that way. Only craftsmen.

He won his matches so comfortably that he was almost unobtrusive, one of the quieter shades of The Spectrum. The headlines were stolen by the seed-scatterers. When he played against Japan at Adelaide, Phil Dent was so uncertain that his performance left Neale Fraser, Australia's Davis Cup captain, loudly demanding the recall of his veterans. At Philadelphia

Dent had to play Laver, the arch-hero of that old brigade, for whom he had ball-boyed at White City in Sydney when he was thirteen. ('Do you remember him?' someone asked Rocket. He looked blank: 'There were a lot of those kids. . . .')

Laver had come to the tournament after a long rest. The previous week he had won the CBS Classic at Palmas del Mar in Puerto Rico and the return to The Spectrum must have seemed like a homecoming. In six years he had won the title four times and only once had he failed to reach the final. Dent, who always tends to play better when he has nothing to lose, looked an awkward first opponent for him, and on the 'horses for courses' principle you had to pick Laver. Except this time the horse wasn't allowed to run in the old way.

Dent, strong, athletic and resolute, held the initiative for most of the match, winning both the tie-break by 7-3 and coming from 1-5 to 5-5 before losing the second set. He missed a few first deliveries when he served for the match at 5-3 in the third, but most of the time Laver could not cope with the pace of his serves. 'I haven't played enough tight matches. I have just had a four-month rest and I was relying more on eyesight than reflexes', he said. 'Flashy' was the word he used to describe his performance and that was accurate. He produced some brilliant shots which made all his old Philadelphia supporters cheer, but there wasn't much of the old depth, weight and consistency. It was a sign of his uneasiness that he looked uncharacteristically anxious in the crises.

The casualty list grew longer. Metreveli, Stockton, Tanner, Stan Smith and Harold Solomon were in the first crop. Lutz, with fewer bandages than usual (there have been times when he has taken the court looking like a brother of Rameses II), beat Borg, who looks like one of the victims of La Belle Dame sans Merci – which is maybe what top tennis is – when he goes on to court, devitalised and palely loitering. He won Rome and Paris last summer by attacking fearlessly when he was in danger, but all that joy in battle now seems to have disappeared. He ought to rest. But perhaps he is now too valuable a property for his commercial advisers to allow him to take that sensible course. 'I didn't know he was the top seed', said Lutz.

Certainly, nothing that Borg did on court could have made the American think that he was playing the favourite. Afterwards Borg talked miserably about his problems with his technique: 'I don't feel the ball. I'm stiff when I hit it. I'm not standing properly. My groundstrokes were the strong point of my game, but now I can't play groundstrokes. I don't feel tired, but at the moment I'm not playing well.' Last year Borg won $206,160 from match-play; he has huge off court contracts with sports manufacturers and other sponsors; and he now lives in Monte Carlo – a move which hasn't been popular in Sweden. He has earned more in the last year than almost any other eighteen-year-old in the history of sport. It seems like the classic case of the boy who gave away his old lamp for a new one.

It was one of the week's ironies that at the start Gerulaitis, the twenty-year-old New Yorker, who took the place in the final reserved for Borg, was continually mistaken for the Swede. Their build is similar and they both have long fair hair, but whereas Borg's tennis conversations are never more than polite apologies for failure or modest acceptances of success, Gerulaitis, a Lithuanian-American from Queens, never stops talking. He exudes vitality, and whenever he looked back over a week in which he beat Ove Bengtson, Tom Okker (who seems to have lost a little of his pace), Raul Ramirez by a surprising 6-3 6-0, Paul Gerken (who survived a match-point against Vijay Amritraj and then defeated Alex [Sandy] Mayer 7-6 6-7 7-6) and John Alexander, he enjoyed his success.

He had a brave tournament, showing himself to be swift, strong and capable of serving consistently ('He served a lot better than I thought he would', said Riessen of the final) and dominating the net when it mattered. When Riessen served, he took the ball early and returned positively and he had far more control of his strokes and his temper than when he played in the BP Cup at Torquay two years ago. His press conferences were long chapters of uninhibited autobiography. He told us in detail about his health – he was particularly moving when he described the stiffness of his neck midway through the tournament and the effects of an Italian meal on his stomach – the way he slept, why he gave up an academic scholarship at Columbia (the combination of playing tennis and reading the *Odyssey* apparently left him 'confused'), his liking for dancing and his dislike of finding sawdust on the court at The Spectrum.

Is he a possible superstar? Certainly, he has personality and he played compelling if not entirely flawless tennis in this tournament. Not every new boy is good enough to brush aside the sixth-formers and the prefects and try to rule the school in the first week of his first term. Riessen, who has seen them all in these first years of Open competition, said of him: 'It takes more than tennis to make a superstar. He is flashy, he is young, he is good copy and he has crowd appeal.'

Bill Riordan came to watch the progress of this graduate from his IPA tour. Gene Scott, another of his advisers, looked in and Harry Hopman telephoned him frequently. Altogether, Gerulaitis seems destined to become the most popular player from the East since Clark Graebner. Riessen beat him 7-6 5-7 6-2 6-7 6-3. He might have won in straight sets, but Gerulaitis counter-attacked stubbornly to take the second from 5-5 and 15-40, and after a string went in Riessen's racket when the older player was two points from victory at 5-4 in the fourth, came back again and won a tie-break to make it two sets-all. Riessen broke at the start of the fifth, led all the time and the only doubt was about the match-point.

Gerulaitis thought there had been a let, but his protest was drowned in the roar of congratulation for Riessen.

There remains only to discuss Arthur Ashe's remarkable failure against Fillol. From Monday to Thursday he played confidently. Brian Gottfried and Jeff Borowiak both took sets from him, but he was strict and steady when it mattered. Against Fillol, he held no fewer than eight match-points in the third set and lost. He missed two at 5-4, two more at 6-5 and then he led 6-3 in the thirteen-point tie-break. He failed narrowly twice. The other times Fillol frustrated him. 'I knew I wasn't going to miss any points. If he hit winners on his match-points there was nothing I could do about it, but I knew that I was playing well enough not to give him anything. Before that he had been hitting winners, but he didn't hit them then', said the Chilean.

Ashe went through the match without losing his service. At the end he sounded as miserable as he had when he lost to Nastase in the 1972 final at Forest Hills. 'I thought that I had won the third set a long time before. I outplayed him in every department. I think that if you added up all the points in the match I would have had a margin of 20-25 points.' Of the double match-point at 6-6 in the tie-break, he said: 'It was a routine forehand. I was trying to get to the net quickly and I mis-hit it. That's all.'

Another major title had escaped him. Why does he miss the prizes he deserves? When you listen to him analysing a match, you feel that he tries to turn tennis into too exact a science. He has too much imagination. Action bothers him in advance. It is the sin which Hamlet called 'thinking too precisely on the event'. He won his Forest Hills in 1968 in the days when he could play by instinct, serving his way serenely through long afternoons. He is too sophisticated a competitor to play by instinct nowadays.

*   *   *

The Uncomfortable High Seat

David reflects on the age-old difficulties of umpiring. It was written before the infra-red ray service machine came into use and before the creation of full-time professional officials. This essay, none the less, is still as valid as when it was written in 1977.

The old prints show Wimbledon's first umpires perched precariously on what look like kitchen chairs and tables. After a hundred years no one can say that the modern umpire's chair is the easiest seat at the Championships. They are all volunteers who are asked to march straight into the firing-line.

From the start of the Championships no one had any great illusions about the possibility of eliminating human error. Henry Jones, the first referee, commented: 'It is hopeless to expect exceptional umpires at Wimbledon. Players must take the chance of a mistake, which, after all, is as fair to one side as to the other.' The only remedy he suggested was that umpires' chairs should be raised two or three feet and today they are nearly twice as high.

For a century players have complained about officials, and line-judges have shrugged off their criticisms with the stoicism of those who are sure that they have done their duty. 'Umpires are like women', wrote a famous Victorian player. 'It is impossible to live with them or to do without them.' Dr James Dwight, one of the first American lawn tennis intellectuals, laid down a rule which still sets the pattern for the manner of umpiring: 'An umpire is an unfortunate necessity and his first object is to make himself as little conspicuous as possible, and to annoy the players as little as he can.'

Of course, the ideal would be to do without umpires and to leave everything to the freemasonry and chivalry that exists among players. There have been a number of experiments of that kind, but usually they have broken down because in the ultimate crises most players prefer not to take the extra responsibility of deciding whether close shots on crucial points are in or out. It is hard enough to play, let alone act as an umpire as well. That is why we need Dr Dwight's 'unfortunate necessities' at Wimbledon. Some are better than others. Most of them have their bad days; many have very good ones and all contribute something very important to the Championships. They are the guardians of order on court.

Some of them tend to be obtrusive, a sin that Dwight criticised, and over-control matches, destroying the confidence of their linesmen, and some allow dissent and gamesmanship to interrupt the pattern of play. But the best umpires we hardly notice. After a good match we normally praise the players and forget about the man who controlled it because his touch on the reins has been so light and easy. Like the perfect butler, the good umpire melts into the background. We don't want histrionics from him. All the drama should be in the play.

One of the problems is that tennis, by its very nature, requires more umpiring than almost any other sport. A football referee is largely a disciplinarian. At the moments when goals are scored, the issue is usually clear cut. Either the ball has crossed the goal-line fairly and squarely or it hasn't. Umpiring at Wimbledon is largely a matter of judgment and concentration, of gauging small accuracies for long periods (think of the test set by three hours of serving by Roscoe Tanner on a summer afternoon). Wimbledon's crowds are quieter than some others, but there are times when the full-blooded passions of SW19 must disturb any linesman.

Governing two players in a packed, excited Centre Court often seems more difficult than controlling 22 on a soccer pitch because in the single combat of tennis the action is magnified. Television cameras relay every gesture, every unguarded moment of anger across the world. We never put footballers under such consistent and intimate scrutiny. And because we are dealing with individuals, rather than teams, at Wimbledon, the noises often sound louder and more distracting. 'I do wish the crowd wouldn't sigh every time I miss a shot. It upsets my judgment and makes me feel they have no confidence in me', Virginia Wade remarked once.

Any Centre Court line-judge, faced with a series of close calls, might echo that *cri de coeur*. For two weeks the All England Club require from him clear sight, alertness, concentration, sound judgment of player and ball, and enough self-confidence to correct obvious mistakes. The linesman who pleads 'unsighted' and defers to his chair-umpire is a far better advertisement for the spirit of the game than the man who sticks stubbornly to an erratic opinion even though both players, all his colleagues and the 14,000 linesmen *manqués* who attend as spectators tell him that he is wrong. Even the best line-judges nod occasionally.

We know that the system is fallible. Perhaps by Wimbledon, 2077, science will have taken over and umpires will be obsolete, but so far no one has produced a perfect electronic device for delivering a verdict on a close ball. At the moment the human eye, plus experience and concentration, is the best that we can offer. It is a pretty good best. The presence of umpires reminds us that this is still a game for men and women and not for computers and statisticians. The line-judges are part of the 'humanity' and uncertainty of tennis. They are actors with parts to play. Sympathy is a key virtue in umpiring. Could a computer, breaking down the mechanics of a rally, have as much rapport with the players and the crowd as, say, Bertie Bowron, the world's most travelled umpire, in the theatre of the Foro Italico during the Italian Championships?

There are moments when Bertie makes mistakes, but no one in Rome – not so long ago one of the dark spots on the umpiring map – regards him as anything but the embodiment of British fair play and good will. He may fracture the Italian language, but he controls the players and the crowds so gently and effectively that when Italy were due to play a Davis Cup semi-final against Australia in Rome last year, the Italians suggested that Bertie should umpire all five rubbers. In the end the captains, Neale Fraser and Nicola Pietrangeli, decided that such a prolonged spell in the chair might prove too much for even his enthusiasm and powers of endurance and compromised by merely giving him the most important matches.

He has devoted himself to tennis since his retirement from the Foreign Office. Most of Wimbledon's umpires are part-timers, snatching odd days at tournaments in the earlier part of the season to keep in practice.

Many are members of the Umpires Association, which trains them and tests their ability to control matches. They all act in an honorary capacity here. That also may have changed by the time Wimbledon reaches its bicentenary. Already there are moves towards increased professionalism in umpiring. The escalation of prize-money has resulted in demands from players, sponsors and tournaments for the highest possible standards of umpiring.

Wimbledon is lucky. Grass may be a difficult surface for line-judges, but, in addition to the British contingent, the All England receives a number of offers of service from umpires from other countries. A visit to Wimbledon can be one of the peaks of an umpire's career and often voices from abroad – particularly from Australia and the US – are heard at the Championships. Exchange visits of that kind may be the beginning of a larger process. Arthur Ashe, the men's champion here in 1975, has produced a scheme for a corps of travelling professional umpires, whose example would, it is hoped, help to improve the general standard of the control of matches and, indeed, Britain saw its first professional umpiring at the Benson and Hedges tournament at Wembley in November when a newly formed group of uniformed umpires officiated, experimenting with the use of high chairs – a memory of Henry Jones – on the lines.

The rules for the Grand Prix have also been tightened and improved by the Men's International Professional Tennis Council, the governing body of the professional game, on which the International Lawn Tennis Federation, the Association of Tennis Professionals, and the tournament directors, are represented. The Council have laid down clearly the arrangements which a tournament must make about such matters as entries, seeding and the draw. They have stated formally a tournament's obligations to its competitors and a player's duties to a tournament, its sponsors and spectators. There is also a graded list of fines for various forms of dissent and misconduct. These are backed by the possibility of suspension for aggravated and persistent breaches of the rules.

The Council have also given their approval to the idea of a limited number of experiments with a penalty points system, which has already been tried in the United States. This would give an umpire the power to punish a player who argues, delays or indulges in any form of gamesmanship, by awarding the point at issue to his opponent. This gives an enormous new responsibility to the man in the chair. If it is universally accepted, what effect will it have on the high dramas of Wimbledon?

* * *

Tennis – Confrontation or Pleasure?

This essay was written for the programme of the Queen's Club tournament of 1977. David was perhaps over-optimistic in the mood of his final sentence.

Whether you like it or not, lawn tennis is a game of confrontation. That is its problem – and its chief pleasure. It is a form of direct competition. At any level, you collide with the opposition and that impact creates excitement. The more skilled the players and the larger their personalities, the more sparks fly.

The biggest stone thrown by critics of the professional game is that standards of behaviour have declined since the game became Open and prize-money escalated. Tennis, it is argued, has become more 'sensational'. The headlines in the newspapers are larger. Television magnifies disputes. An exchange of conversation at the net, which might have been only a few muttered words, becomes an angry quarrel when it is transmitted into eight million homes. The word 'Gamesmanship' is a post-war invention. It wasn't like that in the old days.

Or was it? When I was very young, brushing up on my lawn tennis history, I spent many hours talking to one of the game's elder statesmen. His memory spanned the sixty years from the golden age of Edwardian tennis to the twilight of amateur tennis. I'd read all the best books, most of them interesting but illuminating. The great heroes of the game were about as lively as the figures in the Wimbledon Museum. No one ever spoke anything but good about matches that were dead and buried. Even the legendary pieces of deception – like the identical Allen brothers' habit of trying to ensure that the brother with the better serve served as often as possible – were politely shrouded. You were left to guess whether this ploy was cheating or just a late Victorian joke, designed to amuse spectators before the Allens disappeared into the champagne which they insisted upon as an inducement to appear.

Were the manners of Edwardian lawn tennis quite so perfect as its chroniclers suggest? 'The Dohertys always behaved perfectly', said my old friend. But as for some others – there was a good deal of swearing and some people were notorious for their sharpness on line-calls. It was politer, the pace was slower and more formal. And, of course, early lawn tennis wasn't reported in the same terms as the game today. The press was more respectful. The first tennis writers were journalists who were deeply involved in the game. No one, even in the halfpenny evening papers, ever wrote stories like: 'Mrs Lambert Chambers slams LTA.'

Arthur Gore, Wimbledon's oldest champion, could drink his glass of champagne as he changed ends in difficult matches without comment from the journalists of the day. 'Champagne Arthur bubbles to victory.'

But that has changed as tennis has expanded from an upper middle-class diversion to a world game. Tennis has become 'news'. Our champions aren't just heroes for small boys. They are superstars. Every housewife in Goole and Gloucester now knows Ilie Nastase. Small boys on parks all over Britain try to hit double-handed backhand returns of service like Jimmy Connors. The heavy topspin of Bjorn Borg and Guillermo Vilas has caused a general revolution in style. And as our champions and our tournaments have grown bigger, the pressures and the publicity have increased enormously. The sparks now fly far higher and hotter in the single combat of the topmost reaches of the game. When a point is worth $20,000 to a player, it is not surprising that he reacts angrily if he gets a bad call from a line-judge.

Tournament promoters can protect the leading players from mistakes and aggravations by doing everything possible to improve standards of umpiring. In return, spectators and sponsors . . . require from them strict measures of self-discipline. Tennis is a game of skill. The player who allows his skill to deteriorate through petulance and irritation is failing in his duty as a public entertainer. Most competitors recognise that, in these highly professional days. The game now has a strict conduct code with a graduated system of fines for offences. Tournaments report breaches of the code to the Men's International Professional Tennis Council, a body on which the International Lawn Tennis Federation, players and tournament directors, are represented. It is an encouraging sign that so far there have been comparatively few fines for bad behaviour on court.

* * *

PERSONALITIES

Sangster the Server

Mike Sangster played 65 Davis Cup rubbers for Great Britain in 26 ties between 1960 and 1968, more than any other Briton; he was in the last four of both the Wimbledon and US Championships singles in 1961, and reached the same stage in the French title meeting in 1963. No man did as much for the prestige of the British game in the post-war period. He was born in Torquay on 11 September 1940, and died suddenly, also in Torquay, on 30 April, 1985. This study was written in 1963.

It is one of the curiosities of lawn tennis in Britain that until recently both Angela Mortimer, the only home player to win a singles title at Wimbledon since the war, and Michael Sangster, our best hope this time, lived at Kingskerswell, a suburb of Torquay. They had the same coach, Arthur Roberts, a man with a remarkable flair for bringing the best out of a junior, and they both learned the game on the wooden courts of the Palace Hotel.

Sangster is now 22. This is his fourth year in senior lawn tennis and already he has achieved more than any other British man since the war. At Wimbledon two years ago after one of the best victories of his career – against Dennis Ralston, which he won after losing the first two sets – and a fortunate draw, he became the first British player to reach the semi-finals of the men's singles for 23 years. Soon afterwards he became the first post-war British semi-finalist at Forest Hills.

In 1962 his year of astonishing progress was followed by a gloomy season of anticlimax and ill health. At Bournemouth he had to retire from the Hard Court Championships. In Paris, he disappointed. At Wimbledon, the enormous Orlando Sirola, amusing both himself and the crowd, reduced him first to ill temper and then to despair and defeat. His fast, fierce service, which had been the foundation of his success the previous year, began to look less effective and he moved slowly. The criticism began to grow. It was not until he played Nicola Pietrangeli on a blazing day in Milan in the Davis Cup that the Sangster of 1962 showed a gleam of the promise of 1961. He lost that match, but at least it looked as though he was enjoying playing lawn tennis again.

He says now: 'I knew that I had a lucky draw in 1961 and that I was not up to the standard of a semi-finalist. I said afterwards that I would not be surprised if I had a bad year the next year, but it might not have been so bad if I had not been ill. I knew that I had a lot of work to do on my game, but I began to think that I had got to win at all costs. The luck seemed to go against me, too. The other guy's shot would just clip the base-line, or he would get a net cord, or I'd get a bad call on a vital point. I began to think that I had had all my luck the year before. It's just a phase one goes through.'

After Milan, the progress was slow again until suddenly in Rome two months ago Sangster stepped back into the first rank of the challengers at Wimbledon. He became the first British player since the war to reach the quarter-finals of the Italian Championships and he came close to beating Emerson. In Paris, Emerson beat him again but only after Sangster had broken another British record. He became the first British singles semi-finalist since Austin in 1937. The French, taking their usual lofty view of the standard of hard-court play in Britain, had not seeded him.

If it had not been for lawn tennis he might have been a lawyer. If he had not failed a Spanish examination, he might not have played lawn tennis. 'I had the opportunity, through lawn tennis, to go to Cambridge, but I failed in Spanish. I could have gone back to school and taken it again, but that would have meant that I would have been 24 when I finished studying and all this would have gone by the side.' Instead he went to Australia, where the sight of the power and pace of his service won golden opinions from all sorts of judges. 'The best British prospect since Fred Perry' was the verdict. It was ironical that when he wanted to return to Australia last winter, the LTA who were sending a team did not pick him. They said he was 'too old'.

Service is still the most notable part of Sangster's game. It seems, he thinks, to have grown in importance with all the publicity that it has received. 'When I was younger, I used to think of myself as a touch player. I went in for a lot of half-volleys and fancy stuff. Then I went through a phase where it seemed to be fun to thump the ball at 200 mph. I think that I am learning all the time. I used to serve fast but not sensibly. Now I am more accurate.' Among other things his service has brought him a life which at the moment keeps him travelling for nine months in the year. Since last Wimbledon he has played in the USA, South America, the Caribbean and in most of the larger European countries. Like most players, he finds that every country consists mostly of tennis clubs and tennis courts.

'You travel but you are with the same people all the time and everybody speaks English. I had seven years of French at school and four years of Spanish. . . . Unless I go sightseeing the first time I go to a country, the sightseeing never gets done. One spends every day at the club.' He thinks that he can probably go on playing until he is 30 if he keeps fit. He would like to work on public relations for some big firm and, if he could find someone who would allow him to work part-time, he would like to start soon so that he could learn about the job.

The players he admires most are Rosewall, 'who got over the disadvantage of being small', Laver, 'no matter what the score is he always keeps going' and those like Seixas and Billy Knight who do everything by hard work and guts. 'I think that on the whole I admire those who have less talent and work hard more than those who have loads of talent. Which do you admire most? The millionaire who has his millions left to him or the millionaire who works for every penny?'

* * *

Margaret Smith
Takes a Rest

The Australian Margaret Smith Court carved out her career in two spells. The first was from 1961 to 1966 – half a dozen years of rich success. She then retired, temporarily, as it happened, for she returned after a year to do as much again, becoming in 1970 the second woman to achieve the traditional Grand Slam – holding all four major singles titles in the same year. This study was written in 1967.

Margaret Smith, the first Australian to win the women's singles title at Wimbledon, announced yesterday that she was retiring from competitive lawn tennis. All through the last European season – the least successful of her six years of touring – she made no secret of the fact that she was growing tired of playing and travelling. The first great Australian woman player, Miss Smith captured all the prizes she was likely to and was clearly running short of ambition. Her list of successes is wonderfully impressive. In 1960, at the age of seventeen, she won the Australian Championship (which no one has ever taken from her), beating Maria Bueno, the reigning Wimbledon champion, in the quarter-finals. 'I was so surprised', she said, 'that for three months afterwards I couldn't hit a ball in court.'

Then, two years later, she led the Australian breakthrough in the women's game. She became the first Australian to win the women's titles in Rome, Paris and at Forest Hills; her Wimbledon victories came in 1963 and 1965; and her record in mixed doubles, usually with Ken Fletcher, is one of the best the game has known. All that eluded her was the Grand Slam. She won the great titles but never, like Maureen Connolly, in the same year and as time went by she seemed to find it more and more difficult to play on hard courts.

Last season it was also plain that she was less fit than she had been on her earlier trips to Europe – and that was important, for until then absolute physical fitness had been a major reason for her swift advance to success. As Christine Truman remarked after a Wimbledon semi-final: 'I looked at her and she looked so fit that I thought "Crikey!" ' Sometimes when Margaret Smith, formidably strong and swift, a big girl who moved astonishingly quickly, occupied a court, it was difficult not to think of her as an athlete first and a lawn tennis player second.

With her physique and capacity for hard work, she could have played any game superbly. It was a lucky accident that she lived near a tennis club at Albury in New South Wales and luckier still that one of the coaches who took her in hand was Frank Sedgman. He gave her a masculine approach to the game, based on the lessons that he had learnt in serving and volleying his way to a Wimbledon title. Margaret Smith's lawn tennis was created after the image of his own. She trained with him, worked for him as a typist and, like him, she wasn't happy if her service wasn't thundering down at full-pace or if she wasn't dominating the court from the net. All this was a painstaking preparation for success and she must have felt flattered that for the first time the methods which had brought Australia success in men's lawn tennis were being applied intensively to a woman's game. Hitherto, it had always seemed to Australian women players that no one with any sort of power at home cared twopence whether they played abroad or not.

Thelma Long, Nancy Bolton and Lorraine Coghlan all achieved moderate amounts of success, but no one noticed anything until Margaret Smith, wearing a floppy white hat, beat Maria Bueno 7-5 3-6 6-4 on that hot and humid day at Brisbane seven years ago. Then suddenly everyone was cheering. As soon as it was clear that Australia had a potential women's champion at Wimbledon, the women's game there came to life.

The trouble was that the burden of combining the roles of national idol, pioneer woman, supertrained athlete and lawn tennis apprentice proved a little too much for Miss Smith. There were people who thought that sometimes she was ungracious; there were many times when the awful nervous strain of being expected to win showed itself. It was no wonder that she seldom looked happy on court and only on this last tour, when nothing mattered quite so much, has she seemed relaxed off duty. 'You have to remember', one of her friends said once, 'that she is still very much a girl from a country town to whom everything happened very quickly. Things might have been easier for her if she had come from a city like Sydney.' She was not an easy stroke-maker; she was not one of the game's great tacticians and even at her peak she relied overmuch on her strength and speed. It was no wonder that she came to grief when she met subtle strategists – like Ann Jones, who reduced her to agonies of cramp at Roland Garros in 1961, or Vera Sukova, who ended her best hope of the Grand Slam – on hard courts, who refused to let her make the most of those attributes.

It may well have been her failure to fulfil her own high hopes that was at the root of her celebrated dispute with Nell Hopman, who managed her first tour abroad in 1961, which embroiled the Lawn Tennis Association of Australia and made her even more of a national heroine. The next year she returned to Wimbledon and lost on the first day to Billie Jean Moffitt. A year later she avenged that defeat in the final. Then came a defeat by Bueno in one final and revenge the next year. For a time the Smith–Bueno duels made up the most exciting rivalry in the game, but although the Australian usually won, Bueno remained the popular favourite. Miss Smith's retirement, added to the present eclipse of Miss Bueno means that there is more room at the top for the younger generation.

*   *   *

Margaret Smith Court (II)

Margaret Smith became Mrs Barry Court in 1967 and, returning to the game, continued to further her reputation as a supreme athlete. This is David's second study, written in 1977.

Margaret Court, the most successful player in the history of women's tennis, announced her retirement yesterday at the age of 33. Her decision follows a six-month absence from competitive play during which she had spoken of seeing visions of the Virgin Mary and angels. She is now involved in religious work in her home city of Perth, Western Australia. This marks an unexpected end to a remarkable career. Margaret has always been a devout Roman Catholic but she was also the most formidable competitor in one of the least charitable of women's worlds. She was down-to-earth, and practical, tough and determined, not at all the kind of girl you would expect to hear voices or see visions. When the news of her mystical experience filtered through to the US from Australia, the other women on the Virginia Slims tour expressed total bewilderment.

She retired for the first time in 1966, saying that she was tired of 'the rat race of international tennis', and then returned a year later with a husband, Barry Court, an international yachtsman and the son of Western Australia's Prime Minister. She recovered her enthusiasm for the game, and maternity – the birth of two children, a boy now four and a girl aged two – did not stop her from playing and winning. But yesterday she said: 'I shall not play any more tournament tennis. If I had been meant to play tennis again God would have led me to it, but it is no good playing if my heart is not in it. There might be a lot of money involved but that does not matter. Retirement is my final decision. Wimbledon and Forest Hills mean nothing beside my beliefs.'

Her visions have been widely publicised. She has given long TV interviews on the subject. Last autumn she announced that she was leaving the tour because she was expecting a third baby, but she had a miscarriage. In December she said that she saw a vision of the Virgin above the door of her children's bedroom. 'I said to myself, "Margaret, you're seeing things". Then I looked again, and Our Lady was there.' She had other visions afterwards.

She continued to practise her tennis. Her coach told reporters that she was playing as well as ever and she was confident that she could regain her old place at the top of the women's game. She won the last of her 92 major international titles – a record for any woman – at Forest Hills in September when she and Virginia Wade defeated Billie Jean King, who followed Maria Bueno as her chief rival, and Rosemary Casals in the women's doubles final. She won the Wimbledon singles three times, including the longest women's final, 14-12 11-9, against Mrs King in 1969, Paris and Forest Hills five times each, and the Australian singles eleven times, starting in 1960 and including a sequence of seven successive years.

Undoubtedly she was the strongest, fittest, and most athletic woman the game has yet known. She served and volleyed relentlessly and she also had a great ability to reach out suddenly and hit winning forehands in moments of crisis. Like Maureen Connolly she achieved the Grand Slam of the four great titles, and 1970 was her peak year. She comes high in any order of lawn tennis merit, but below Connolly because of those terrible flutterings of nerves which sometimes beset her. Connolly never allowed herself to look as vulnerable. Marriage relaxed her as did success. Religion seems to have done so too. In her recent TV interviews she talked about herself with a calm fluency, which was quite new.

*　*　*

Maureen Connolly

Maureen Connolly, from San Diego, was the first woman to achieve the Grand Slam, winning all four major titles in a calendar year. She was unbeaten in singles in three visits to Wimbledon; she was twice winner of the French Championships, once of the Australian, and thrice victor in her own National Championships. And she did all this before her twentieth birthday. Then her career was cut short when she broke her leg in a riding accident. Her life was cut short also, for she was only 34 when she died of cancer on 21 June, 1969, leaving a husband and two children.

Someone once asked Maureen Connolly, the most relentlessly successful champion since Suzanne Lenglen, what was the funniest experience in her lawn tennis career. 'I never had one', she replied. 'My tennis was always a very serious business.'

On Saturday she died, aged 34, in hospital at Dallas at the end of a long fight against cancer. She had been ill for three years. Until recently she had continued to coach and to play, and she had never lost her interest in the game and the players who were her friends. When Maureen retired from active competition – after a riding accident which damaged her right leg in 1954 – she wrote, commentated, and advised on tennis. The shrewd wit and the sharp mind were revealed, which had been hidden from the public in all the years when she had seemed to be nothing but a grimfaced little girl who kept on winning matches.

In a way, the riding accident may have been the luckiest thing that happened to her. For it enabled her to escape honourably from the burden of defending all the titles that she had won so early. In 1953, at eighteen, she had become the only woman in the game to bring off the Grand Slam of winning the four great singles championships – Australia, Paris, Wimbledon, and Forest Hills – in a year, and when she retired she had been champion at Wimbledon and at Forest Hills three times. In tennis, there would have been nothing left for her to do as a player but continue to win the titles that she had already won. The only world that was left for her to conquer was ordinary life. Falling off Colonel Merryboy, her favourite horse, made that both easy and possible. A year after the accident she married Norman Brinker, who had been a US Olympic rider, and they had two daughters, now aged twelve and ten.

As a player, she was invulnerable because of the strength and accuracy of her groundstrokes. She was a model of dedication, tenacious, and a wonderful competitor. At thirteen she became the youngest player ever to win the US Junior title and from that moment every senior reputation in the American game – Louise Brough, Margaret Osborne, Doris Hart, and Shirley Fry – was imperilled by the advance of the formidable prodigy from San Diego.

In 1951, at the age of sixteen, she beat Miss Fry 6-3 1-6 6-4 to win Forest Hills. After that, for two years, there was nothing but victory all the way. She was a perfectionist and she worked doggedly for her success on the practice court. In her autobiography she told part of the background to this sudden rise to the top. Her relationship with her mother was never easy. She quarrelled bitterly with 'Teach' Tennant, her coach, as Alice Marble, another of Miss Tennant's pupils, had done. Teddy Tinling, her dress designer who was one of her closest friends, said yesterday: 'Drama was never far away from her. On the whole, she was a sad, sad, girl.'

Life as a tennis player became easier for her in the last relaxed year when she travelled with Nell Hopman, a relaxed and enthusiastic Australian. In California, she had been brought up to hate and destroy her opponents. 'Nell taught me to win and yet to love', she said. At home in Dallas players whom she liked were invited to stay with her and among those whom she coached was Ann Jones. When Ann reached the final at Forest Hills two years ago, a telephone call to Maureen in Texas was part of her training ritual.

In the general verdict, only Lenglen and Helen Wills Moody rivalled her as a player and Maureen, if she had continued, might have won more titles than either of those great players. Suzanne died on a Wimbledon semi-finals day, Maureen on the eve of a new Championship.

*   *   *

Hazel Wightman

H azel Hotchkiss Wightman looms large in the history of tennis. Born in California on 20 December, 1886, she had a notable career before the First World War. She donated the trophy for the annual match between British and American women that bears her name, and took part in the early contests.

She died, respected and loved, on 5 December 1974.

Mrs Hazel Hotchkiss Wightman, the donor of the Wightman Cup, who died at Boston, Massachusetts, on Thursday, aged 87, was one of the most formidable and respected competitors in the history of lawn tennis and a considerable influence on the game in America for more than 60 years. She was a tireless and determined match-player, who never lost her enthusiasm for watching, discussing or teaching tennis. A Californian who went to New England when she married in 1912, she won the US singles title four times, being unbeaten between 1909 and 1911 and then regaining it in 1919. She was six times US doubles champion and she won the Wimbledon title in 1924 with Helen Wills, one of the many champions whom she helped and advised.

Altogether she won 48 US national titles. The last was the US Indoor Doubles in 1943, when she was partnered by Pauline Betz. That was her tenth success in that event. She might have collected even more titles if her schedule of match practice had not been interrupted by the birth of five children. Certainly, she felt that she would have done better in her only match against Suzanne Lenglen if it had not been for maternity. 'She beat me 6-0 6-0 at Wimbledon, but I had only just returned to the game after having a baby and would have loved to have had a second go at her', she said regretfully, looking back over an interval of 50 years.

She was a fine volleyer and always thought that her great virtue on court had been speed. 'I have always been small, but I was always fast and had courage', was her own verdict. She played in the early Wightman Cup matches and then captained the American team. The first contest was staged to celebrate the opening of the new Stadium Court at Forest Hills in 1923. She had wanted the event to be a multi-national women's tournament, but instead it became an annual match between Britain and the United States. The 50th year of the competition was celebrated in Boston. The match was played at her own club, Longwood, a short distance from her home, and the mayor paid tribute to her by proclaiming it 'Hazel Hotchkiss Wightman Day'. In front of a crowd of 5,000, the British consul read a letter from the Queen announcing that she had been awarded the CBE.

Mrs Wightman looked frail then, but she watched every shot of the match and talked about it vigorously afterwards. She was still coaching children in the area then and more senior players also went to her for advice. ('The other day Arthur Ashe came to ask me to look at his service. . . .') They were given nuggets of common sense like, 'If you can't control yourself you will never control the ball' or 'You have got to be master of the ball, but remember when you play a match it is your friend. It is your only ally. The ball doesn't make mistakes, you do.'

* * *

Ode to Billie Jean

At the Championships of 1975, David had occasion to reflect on the achievements of Billie Jean King. As it happened it was not the swan song of that great player at Wimbledon: she did not play her last singles there until the semi-final round in 1983. But her last singles championship, her sixth, was won in 1975.

Court Five isn't one of Wimbledon's great spectator courts. If you want to watch there you have to get there early and you'll probably have to stand, but two hours before the start yesterday it was surrounded by women. They outnumbered the men there by about seven to one. They were waiting for Billie Jean King to make what she says will be one of her last appearances in the singles at Wimbledon. 'This is my last major title. I am not playing singles at Forest Hills and I am not playing Wimbledon next year. I will definitely not come back next time even if I win', she says.

It wasn't much of a match. She beat Julie Anthony, a fellow Californian, 6-2 6-3, but Mrs King made it into an occasion. Whenever she missed a shot there were small shrugs of the shoulder and practice backhand swings. She was always busy. Even when Miss Anthony hit a good shot Mrs King upstaged her by the extravagance of her reaction. When she herself won a spectacular shot, she basked in applause. Ted Tinling, who has done so much to help her to polish her image, called her 'Madam SuperStar'. This was a superstar's minor performance, but she still gave her supporters the full treatment.

In some ways this has been a difficult week for her. Virginia Wade beat her in the final at Eastbourne a week ago, which cannot have helped her confidence, and since Wimbledon began, her leadership of the Women's Tennis Association – the players' union which she played a major part in founding – has been under heavy fire. She is the president and, with Gladys Heldman, then the editor and publisher of *World Tennis*, the influential American magazine, she risked the wrath of the US Lawn Tennis Association and pioneered the women's tour five years ago.

That was a perfectly timed move. Even she can't have guessed how exactly the women's breakaway movement in the game would fit the mood of the US in the early 1970s. Tennis was booming, taking over from golf as the top middle-class game, and Women's Lib was in its infancy. The male chauvinists of the USLTA took the view that: (a) women's tennis wasn't worth watching; (b) women deserved only about one-tenth of the prize-money men received.

Mrs Heldman obtained the backing of the Phillip Morris organisation which was launching Virginia Slims, a new cigarette aimed at the woman smoker, and their sponsorship was enough to support the girls in their battle against the USLTA. They have proved their case that the women's tour now draws more spectators and larger TV audiences than men's tennis in the US, and last year Chris Evert, who took over from Mrs King as the ruler of the women's game there, earned $261,460 in a year. But Mrs King herself has probably earned more than any other sportswoman in history.

All that is a measure of Billie Jean's achievement. She has been the big star and the principal publicist of the women's game. Two years ago her victory over Bobby Riggs answered those who took the view that a middle-aged court hustler (and Wimbledon champion) could be superior to the best woman in the business on a tennis court. She has been a great volleyer, a shrewd tactician and a tough match-player. Wimbledon has been her showpiece. 'The Old Lady's House', Rosemary Casals, her doubles partner, called it, and the Old Lady has won plenty of medals there. She has been singles champion five times, and collected nine doubles titles and four mixed. Her total of eighteen is just behind Elizabeth Ryan's record of nineteen in the years between the wars. All she has to do now is to overtake that target.

*   *   *

Ken Rosewall

This study of Ken Rosewall was written in October 1976, following the publication of Peter Rowley's biography of Rosewall, *Twenty Years at the Top*. David had recently abandoned full-time journalism to become a creative participator in events as General Secretary of the International Tennis Federation. Rosewall, a deeply satisfying player for those who like to see the game as poetry in motion, was one of the few obviously all-time 'greats' who was never Wimbledon singles champion.

Twenty Years at the Top. It is the right title for a book about Ken Rosewall. The marvellous thing about him is that his talents have lasted so long. He played at Wimbledon first in 1952 when Frank Sedgman, Dick Savitt, Jaroslav Drobny, Eric Sturgess, and Vic Seixas were ruling the Championships. In 1974 he reached the final there for the fourth time. He had outlasted his contemporaries and the generation which followed them.

Lew Hoad was betrayed by his back; Rod Laver's left arm lost its strength; Tony Roche's series of injuries forced him into secondary stuff like Team Tennis; and Roy Emerson, lean, keen, and trained to the last ounce throughout the 1950s and 1960s, gave up serious competition to become the darling of the summer tennis camps. But Rosewall stayed on, a survivor from the age of Hopman, when all the Australian kids looked stringy and short-haired, in the world of Connors and Borg where the courts are paved with dollar bills.

Perhaps he is the last of the old-style professionals. Easy, fluent shots; grace and speed of movement; intensity of concentration. Nature gave him a great deal, even if it did not endow him with Hoad's ability to summon up thunder, lightning and absolute majesty of shot. Ken is a genius who is only 5ft 7in and weighs only 140lb. A ghost with a rapier in his backhand. His are the quiet virtues of tennis. On his good days it is a pleasure to watch him slip into his best attacking rhythm. His smashes, passes and volleys are object lessons in the art of placement, but the serve is a weakness and its vulnerability (particularly the tendency to double-fault) has always been most marked on days when he is under pressure. The child was father of the perfectionist.

The most interesting parts of Peter Rowley's new biography (Cassell, £4.50, 239pp), which is the fruit of a great many fascinating conversations with the player himself, deal with Rosewall's tennis education. Samuel Smiles would have admired it as a study in self-help. Rosewall *père* was a grocer in a modest Sydney suburb. Ken, an only child, was presented with a shortened racket when he was three. At five, Bob Rosewall stopped the little boy hitting double-handers and made him use his right hand. He bought a dozen tennis books and started to turn him into a champion. 'From books I taught Ken Fred Perry's forehand and Don Budge's backhand. The volley, overhead and lob he developed naturally. We would get up at four and five in the morning. We would spend weeks hitting only one stroke at a time. I would drop a handkerchief on the ground and he would hit to it.'

The child practised volleying against a white wall with a painted advertisement, and on another side of their house his father dug away a slope so that the earth was flat enough for him to practise his groundstrokes. His mother, who broke a hip playing tennis, made sure that his white clothes were immaculate. When he was nine he entered his first tournament and lost to the winner. At eleven he won the Metropolitan Hard Court Championship, defeating a boy two years his senior and over six feet tall in the final. 'In my heart I thought I had a champion, but I never told him that', said Bob Rosewall.

He enjoyed the distractions of rugby and cricket. Bob Rosewall told him: 'Ken, if you quit rugby and cricket and concentrate exclusively on tennis, I think you have what it takes to be a champion. Or you can be good in all sports, but champion in none of them. Think it over for a week and let me know.' Three days later Ken told him: 'Dad, I want to be a champion.' The sessions of two or three hours of practice in the early mornings continued. 'The reason I got to the top is due to many sacrifices by my parents and later by my family. When I was a youngster of eleven, twelve or fourteen I used to go to bed at 8 p.m. and get up to play tennis with my father at 5 a.m. before he went to work and I to school.'

Jack Kramer watched him beat Hoad 6-0 6-0 when they were twelve-year-olds. Ted Schroeder asked him what he thought about them. 'We had better get the hell out of the way before these kids get much older because they'll be beating our ears off', said Kramer. Seventeen years later he remembered that match: 'It was just like it generally is. Lew makes all the miraculous shots and Kenny wins all the matches.'

He suffered from eczema. Slazengers gave him a job. Carnation Milk sponsored him and Hopman chose him and Hoad for the Australian

Davis Cup tour of Europe and the United States in 1972. Bob Rosewall told him: 'If Mr Hopman tells you to change this stroke or that stroke, listen, but afterwards you only do what you feel is right.' There are touches of asperity whenever Ken mentions Hopman in the book. The pupil doesn't remember that particular teacher with absolute charity.

He fell in love. He met Wilma McIver, from Brisbane, when he was fourteen, began writing to her (one hundred letters in three months) and sending her chocolates. When he was on tour he carried eight photographs of her, and Lew and the other boys used to tease him by hiding the one that he kept on his bedside table. When he was 21 they were married.

He won the first of his two French and four Australian titles in 1953, and the following year he was runner-up to Drobny at Wimbledon. Most people remember that final because of the overwhelming support that Drobny, the sentimental favourite, received. The Centre Court reckoned that Rosewall, the elegant teenager, belonged to the future, but it was Drobny's turn because the Australian would soon be making a habit of winning the title. Ken, taking his usual commonsense view, merely thinks that his strategy was mistaken: 'I was badly advised. Harry Hopman was the team coach. I'm not saying that he advised me badly but you have read that he went out and found Lew Hoad and me and developed me. He did try to help my serve, but he had no effect on my backhand or forehand. "Dumb" is the way I'd describe my game against Drobny. I should have come to the net on my serve and return of serve. I'd serve to his backhand and instead of following it to the net he'd hit a soft, deep return and come in to the net himself, knowing I wouldn't come in.'

Rowley quotes plenty of analyses like that. Ken's views on his own and other people's tennis are those of a dedicated professional. It is always a joy to watch a match with him. His insights are always practical. He can get a ball through the eye of a needle and he tells you why other people can't.

He lost in the 1956 Wimbledon final to Hoad, but then spoilt Lew's Grand Slam by defeating him in the final at Forest Hills. When that match was over he amazed even those who knew him by going to a side court and practising serving with Don Budge. Soon afterwards he turned professional. On the pro tour he overtook Hoad, gradually overcame Gonzales ('On my first tour with Gonzales I felt as though I was being thrown to the lions'), and then began his marvellous rivalry with Rod Laver, with so many great matches hidden away in the small one-night-stand towns of the American professional circuit.

Looking back, it is impossible to see why we allowed so much brilliant lawn tennis – the sort of stuff which should have been shown to crowds in the world's great stadiums – to go to waste. If the game had been open to the professionals in 1960 (as it was so nearly) Rosewall's name wouldn't be on the list of talented players who never quite won the men's singles at

Wimbledon. As it was, we had to wait for Open tennis until 1968 and his late harvest was remarkable. Aged 33, he beat Laver at Bournemouth in the game's first Open final, and went on to win Paris in that month of June when the rioting students could almost have thrown their stones into Roland Garros. He regained the Australian in 1971 and retained it the next year. He won South Africa, ruled Forest Hills in 1970 and WCT at Dallas in 1971 and 1972. Newcombe beat him in one more Wimbledon final in 1970 and Connors, punishing that medium-paced serve, knocked him out in 1974, a year when the Centre Court was awash with emotion, and repeated his overwhelming victory in the final at Forest Hills.

The veterans are waiting for him now. He will be 42 next month and doesn't think that he can go on playing against younger players. 'You have to be realistic. My career is waning because it is physically and mentally impossible for me to play as much as I know I should.'

It has been a remarkable career. If Wimbledon, the biggest prize, eluded him, he ends as the most respected competitor in the game, a player for those who relish its beauties and its disciplines, the perfect professional. Rowley's book illustrates that well. The champion's character was moulded in those 5 a.m. practice sessions with Dad: 'Youthful tennis training has to be good and stays with you for the rest of your life – the same as if you learn good manners', Ken remarked once. Every would-be Rosewall ought to have that engraved on his tennis racket.

* * *

Elizabeth Ryan

Elizabeth Ryan was born on 5 February, 1892 at Anaheim, California, and died on 6 July, 1979. She had collapsed in the dressing room at Wimbledon the day before her record of nineteen Wimbledon titles was broken when Billie Jean King took her twentieth. Miss Ryan, who never married, became a London resident and was arguably the most assiduous competitor in the game. In nineteen seasons she competed in at least 366 tournaments, won all three events in 90 and was a triple finalist in 164.

David was secretary of the International Tennis Federation when he wrote this obituary.

It seems that Wimbledon's greatest women players are at their most vulnerable during the Championships. Lottie Dod died in the middle of Wimbledon 1960; Maureen Connolly on the eve of the 1969 tournament; Suzanne Lenglen in the second week of the 1938 Championships; and last Friday, the day on which Martina Navratilova beat Chris Lloyd to win the

1979 title, Elizabeth Ryan, the most successful woman doubles player in the history of Wimbledon, collapsed and died at the All England Club. She was 87 and had lived in London for most of her life.

Her contemporaries talked about her range of shots with awe. 'Who can doubt, when they see Miss Ryan scoring time and again with her drop shots, that this is a most useful stroke?' wrote Gordon Lowe in 1924. Her volleys and smashes were equally formidable, and so was a deadly chop, particularly effective on wet grass.

Miss Ryan learnt the game at her home in Anaheim, and came to England with her mother and her sister, Alice, in 1912. Ted Tinling, one of her closest friends, in *Love and Faults* – an autobiography somewhat surprisingly not yet published in Britain – once asked her how she had learnt to volley at a time when most of her contemporaries preferred the safety of the base-line. She told him that when she was fifteen she had played her sister in a final at Vancouver. There was a rough patch on the court, and Alice profited from it in shrewdly-placed shots. Elizabeth decided that she could only stop this by meeting the ball before it bounced.

Her first appearance at Wimbledon was in 1912. Her rivals did not regard her as a serious contender, but she held two match-points against Mrs Hillyard, one of Wimbledon's greatest early champions, before losing 3-6 8-6 6-3 [in the quarter-finals]. She never succeeded in winning the singles, although she reached the final twice, losing to Miss Lenglen [1921] and to Helen Wills Moody [1930]. But as a doubles player she dominated the post-war Championships.

She and the French champion, Miss Lenglen, held the title from 1919 to 1923, losing only one set in the five years, and then, after a year when Miss Lenglen was absent through illness, regained it in 1925. She was also champion with Mary Kay Browne (1926), Helen Wills Moody (1927 and 1930) and Simone Mathieu (1933 and 1934). Miss Ryan won the mixed doubles title seven times between 1919 and 1932. She was four times doubles champion in France, the United States doubles and mixed champion in 1926, and [mixed] champion in 1933. Her only major international singles victory was in Rome in 1933.

She was proud of her record of nineteen Wimbledon titles, and had watched Billie Jean King, another remarkable match-player from California, drawing closer to it every year. It was ironic that she died the day before Mrs King overtook her by winning the doubles with Miss Navratilova. Not long ago she told friends that she hoped she would take her record with her to the grave. That was what happened. Miss Ryan died as she had played, determined not to be beaten.

POLITICAL
ISSUES

Locking the Stable Door

Open tennis was a long way off when the British LTA held its annual meeting in 1958. David's report highlights the growing concern at the difficulties of trying to impose old standards on leading players.

The new rules which give greater control over expenses received by amateur players, both at home and on overseas tours, were approved safely at the annual meeting of the Lawn Tennis Association yesterday with the politest of criticism from the floor.

This probably was because all kinds of disarming appeals for 'a fair trial' for the new rules, which limit expense-paid play abroad to 150 days a year and lay down strict rates for subsistence payments, had come from the council platform. The president, the Duke of Devonshire, pointed out that the new proposals followed the line set recently by the International Lawn Tennis Federation. They were an attempt to find a suitable compromise between the old conception of amateurism and modern conditions, and they were the result of very careful deliberation. The LTA had given a strong lead in Brussels when they were formulated and the council asked for them to be passed because they felt that it was the duty of every association to see that international rules are observed. 'We belong to the international federation and therefore we must support them', said the Duke.

The old rules had been criticised frequently as vague, perhaps 'deliberately vague', but the new proposals were clear and precise. There was nothing new in the idea that amateur players should be controlled, and social and economic changes since the war had forced them to revise the old conceptions of amateurism. 'How many people can afford to play lawn tennis for love nowadays without a private income? And for that matter how many people have got private incomes?' asked the Duke. He continued: 'There have been many faults in the past, but we are making an honest attempt to keep a line of demarcation between amateurism and professionalism and yet, at the same time, helping both amateurs and professionals. It is obviously a compromise and obviously fault can be found with it, but we do ask everyone to give it a fair crack of the whip.'

The chief critic was D. J. Erlebach (Kent), who suggested that the new rules changed the meaning of the word 'amateur' from 'semi-professional' to 'semi-part-time-professional'. He was afraid that the more attempts were made to clamp down on the 'full-time amateur', the more likely it was that the best players in the world would be driven into the professional ranks. There was a real danger that the control of the game would pass out of the hands of the amateur associations and into those of the professional promoters, who were there to make a profit.

It was more important, said Erlebach, that amateur control of all players should be retained than they should try to make conditions of definition for the particular word 'amateur'. If all full-time players were, subject to reasonable control, allowed to earn what they could, then the drain of talent would be stopped and the standard of championships and leading tournaments maintained. Most people believed that open tournaments were bound to come sooner or later. The LTA ought to 'think again before it was too late'.

A. D. Knight, the father of the Northamptonshire player, W. A. Knight, said that he wanted to put the players' point of view. Under the new rules they would be allowed only to receive expenses for 240 days' play at home and abroad. Who would employ them for the remaining three or four months of the year? The rules were approved with about half a dozen votes against.

The honorary treasurer, H. Garton Ash, expressed some concern about the falling-off in the profits from Wimbledon. The LTA's share had fallen from £59,058 in 1955 and £57,509 in 1956 to £48,087. That, he said, showed the desirability of finding additional sources of income for the work of the association.

*   *   *

The Big Push Fails

Open tennis was expected to come about at the annual meeting of the International Federation in Paris in 1960. The move had the support of the 'big four', Great Britain, the United States, France and Australia, and the narrow defeat came as a shock to many. Revelation of the farcical background to the defeat came later. The motion for reform lost by five votes: three were lost because the delegate who was to cast them was occupied in arranging an excursion on the *bateaux mouches*, another because the delegate was asleep, and a fifth because the delegate was in the lavatory. On such absurdities Open tennis was delayed another eight years.

The International Lawn Tennis Federation lost its courage this afternoon and, surprisingly and disappointingly, refused to approve the proposal to allow experimental Open tournaments next year. The proposal failed to gain the two-thirds majority necessary to change the rule, which at present forbids amateurs and professionals to compete against each other, by five votes. It will almost certainly be raised again at next year's meeting in Stockholm.

The voting was 135 in favour and 75, mainly from the smaller countries, against. The United States and Australian representatives voted for the proposals according to mandate, but the knowledge that both these major lawn tennis powers looked upon the prospect of Open tournaments with only moderate enthusiasm may well have stiffened the opposition. Most of the Iron Curtain countries abstained, and altogether only eighteen of the 57 member countries supported the proposal.

The day's debates lasted, apart from a three and a half hour break for lunch, for six hours and, in general, the meeting was a sorry affair for those who have been calling for the expansion of the liberalisation of the game. As had been expected, no vote was taken on the proposal to establish the new category of 'authorised player', halfway between amateur and professional. This scheme, which had been in a large measure the work of J. Borotra, the new president of the Federation, was shelved for two years and the matter will be reviewed by a new committee, made up of members of the Federation's board of management.

At the press conference afterwards, Borotra said: 'I am not a depressed man, but some of you perhaps think that I should be in view of my personal feelings on this matter. I never give up, although in the past I have been beaten very often. This is coming up again. We must find a solution and I have no doubt that something will come from the discussions of the new committee. We must take steps to ban hypocrisy and defend the true amateur.'

The retiring president, J. Eaton Griffiths (Britain), who was chairman of the special sub-committee of the Federation which put forward the proposal for authorised players, was reminded that he had said recently that chaos would ensue if the proposal was not carried. He replied: 'If everyone acts according to the present laws there will not be chaos but your guess as to whether the rules will be better obeyed in 1961 than they were in 1959 is as good as mine.'

To an outside view, it seems that several large and influential nations – Britain and France are honourable exceptions – are quite happy to go on for years talking and theorising, but taking no positive action to prevent abuses and invasions of the laws governing expenses. A French journalist asked, rather wickedly, whether Borotra did not think that two years was too short a time for the management committee to study the matter and find a solution.

The Federation also rejected the Russian proposal to include lawn tennis once again in the Olympic Games. Lawn tennis events were held during the Games between 1896 and 1924, but the pressure of the world lawn tennis calendar and disputes about the demarcation of authority between the Federation and the International Olympic Committee brought them to an end. East Germany was refused membership, because the Federation regards Germany as a single entity and Ecuador was warned that she would be expelled if she did not pay her membership dues.

* * *

The British Revolution

A decisive event of the French Revolution was an oath taken in the tennis court in the Tuileries on 20 June, 1789. The point of no return in the British revolution took place on Thursday, 14 December, 1967, in the Amateur Fencing Association's headquarters in a corner of Queen's Club, London, at the annual meeting of the Lawn Tennis Association. It changed the face of the game.

History was made with only a small amount of argument at the annual meeting of the Lawn Tennis Association in London yesterday. In less than two hours the distinction between amateurs and professionals was abolished, notice to quit on 22 April was served on the International Lawn Tennis Federation and the way was cleared for an Open Wimbledon in July – all by an overwhelming majority.

The only serious debate was on the question of whether the ILTF should be given four months or a year to come to terms with Britain's

demands. On almost every other point the meeting was toughly resolved. There were menaces from Australia (a speech from Mr Ben Barnett,
former Test wicket-keeper, on behalf of the ILTF and the LTAA, was full
of threats of suspension and isolation and must have cost both bodies any
hope of winning friends and influencing people) and pleas from
Denmark for a postponement of action. But these and all other arguments
for delay were submerged in a great wave of emotional support for the
stand which the LTA Council and, behind them, the All England Club
had made. At the end there were only five votes against the proposal to
throw amateurism overboard.

The official line was changed slightly. In October the LTA set the date
for their declaration of independence as 1 January. Since then the ILTF
have offered the olive branch of a sub-committee and promises of reform.
Yesterday's meeting agreed to give the Federation until 22 April – two
days after the next meeting of the ILTF's management committee – to
produce these. Then, no matter what the ILTF say or do, Britain will go
ahead and the first Open tournament in the history of the game will be the
British Hard Court Championships, the LTA's own major tournament,
which begin on that morning. There will be one or two minor amateur
events in the spring before this but the new delay – this limited test of
good faith – will give the British circuit time to adjust itself to the change
and the All England Club a proper opportunity to organise the first Open
Wimbledon.

Mr Derek Penman, the chairman of the Rules Committee, forcefully
put the case for reform; the main object was not that they should have an
Open Wimbledon but that they should remove sham and hypocrisy from
the game. An Open Wimbledon followed inevitably from this decision,
but it was not the main reason for it. 'For too long we have been governed
by a set of amateur rules which are quite unenforceable. We know that
so-called amateur players bargain for payments grossly in excess of what
they are entitled to but without which they cannot live. We know that
tournament committees connive at this, otherwise there would be no
players at their tournaments. We feel we owe it not only to ourselves but
to our players to release them from this humiliating and hypocritical
situation and to make it possible for them to earn openly and honestly the
rewards to which their skill entitles them.'

Hypocrisy, he continued, was by no means confined to players and
tournaments. Although a considerable amount of lip service was paid to
the ideals of amateurism, there was a considerable gulf between the views
expressed by some delegates and the action taken by their national
associations. 'How, for instance, can the USLTA reconcile the payment of
£3,000 per annum to members of their Davis Cup team with their profes-
sed views on amateurism? We have tried peaceful means and failed. Now
we feel that we can no longer endure the present situation.'

No one except Mr Barnett – 'no support from the LTAA and no Australian players in British tournaments' – and a few rather confused voices questioned the validity of Mr Penman's arguments. But the timing of the unilateral declaration of independence caused more discussions. Mr Alan Heyman, Denmark's representative, put the case for waiting until 1 January, 1969. This would give time to rally support from other other nations. 'If you delay for a year, you will have done your duty with a clean conscience.' Mr P. F. Jones (Tally Ho!, Birmingham) supported this and Mr Tony Mottram (Woodborough, Putney) was afraid that British tournaments, deprived of overseas players, would become less interesting. They might find that young players lacked the incentive to improve. If we waited for international support until 1969 the revolution might be bloodless and more effective. Mark Cox, British Davis Cup player, thought that a delay of four months would be fair to current players and would enable them to arrange their tournament engagements.

Eventually, the amendment calling for 1 January, 1969, as the starting date was put by Mr John Archer (Hurlingham), who feared that if we moved without allies now we might find ourselves facing a 'lawn tennis Suez'. Mr John Eaton Griffiths, the British vice-president of the ILTF, preferred 22 April. That would give the Federation four more months to find a solution and there would be no hint of a British retreat. If we put off action for a year, the ILTF would still do nothing and 'everyone would say Britain's down the drain again'. On that note of nationalism, the vote was taken and British tennis moved to the brink of its new age.

* * *

The United States Rally to Support Great Britain

Under the heading 'Hands Across the Net from America' David reported the meeting of the US Association in Coronado City, California, in February 1968, where there was support for the British stand. Had not the United States come to Britain's support, there is little doubt that world opinion would not have come down on the side of the radical reform.

After five days of tortuous manoeuvring and lobbying, of secret discussions in hidden corners of what must be the largest hotel on the Pacific coast, and straight talk and hard negotiation over dry martinis in the sun, the United States Lawn Tennis Association finally came out with what Britain must regard as an ideal resolution on the problems of amateurism and Open lawn tennis. They have given the International Lawn Tennis Federation an ultimatum – 'change the rules at the special meeting next month or we may resign and urge other nations to do the same' – and they want national self-determination on Open tournaments and a substantial revision of the amateur rules. They are not committed to follow the British line completely because far too many administrators here want to retain the distinction between amateurs and professionals, but they do want to give a free hand to Britain and to any other country which feels the same.

A month ago the Americans were talking about 'saving Britain at Coronado City'. Now the mood has changed completely to one of active support for Britain. The conservatives here have been routed. At yesterday's meeting one delegate complained that they were 'putting a shotgun' to the ILTF's head, and in the end it turned out that the delegates were quite delighted to do this. Sixteen sections with 102,064 votes were in favour of the resolution, and only one – the Middle States (Pennsylvania, Delaware, and parts of New Jersey) with 9,978 – against. After the special meeting of the ILTF, the USLTA will meet again to hear a report from Bob Kelleher, their president, and take any further action that they may think necessary.

The whole meeting has been a triumph for Kelleher. He and his supporters, who include most of America's better present-day players, have managed their campaign brilliantly. Tentatively and after much agonised deliberation, the USLTA voted for Open tennis in Luxembourg last year. Kelleher, a Los Angeles lawyer and one of the few recent US Davis Cup captains to win not merely a match but a Challenge Round, was pro-Open, but he made no significant contribution to the debate, and one of the two delegates who went with him was notoriously anti.

No one expected the US attitude to change after that, and when the British announced that they were going to act independently, Victor Denny, the US vice-president of the ILTF, voted to suspend them at a meeting of the ILTF management committee. Kelleher made official noises about the British action being precipitate, and his conservatives grew angry with Britain for trying to force a change on the tennis world after being beaten in a democratic debate. People here and in Australia who had never talked much about the ILTF before and had certainly never seen it in action suddenly became Dr de Stefani's loyal supporters, mainly because they were afraid of change even though the need for change in tennis had been increasingly apparent in recent years.

Tennis is booming in America. Most of Kelleher's young supporters wanted Open tennis because they believed that it makes the way clear for even greater advance. With the tide running for reform, Kelleher, taking great care not to frighten the moderates, began his campaign. If some people thought him lukewarm at the start, there was no doubt about his strength at the finish. No one who is close to him ever believed that when it came to the crunch he could have done anything but support the British. Once the USLTA had been jolted into thinking about the matter, and it became clear that sides would have to be taken, Kelleher toured the sections explaining the alternatives and sounding out opinions.

The first sectional returns were good; there was plenty of support for Open tennis and for allowing American players to compete at an Open Wimbledon, but it was by no means certain that a resolution that was strong enough or constructive enough to offer a useful basis for future action would get through the meeting. Kelleher wanted something which would force the LTA to move and help Britain without splitting his own association. The resolution, as it stood at the end, gave him complete authority on the spot to say: 'We are leaving.'

Just as the USLTA was about to move into conclave, the news came through that Australia were in favour of reform but only with the consent of the ILTF. This disconcerted the 'hawks' here and Kelleher thought that the proviso about the ILTF must weaken any stand which Britain's friends took at the meeting. Soon afterwards Britain's ambassadors, Derek Hardwick and Derek Penman, arrived highly elated by the Australian decision. 'More than we expected', said Penman. And when further investigations showed that the Australian decision was much more fluid than their formal statement had suggested, the Americans took heart again.

It has been generally agreed here that the visit of Hardwick and Penman has been a key factor in the American decision. In Australia they addressed the LTAA and answered questions for half an hour, mainly from three judges who were anti-reform. 'As soon as we explained that we didn't want to interfere with anyone, that what we wanted was home rule for everyone in the game, they agreed and it was plain sailing', said Hardwick. Here they were invited to attend the meeting, but declined. 'Our work had been done', said Penman. It had consisted mainly of 'meeting the right people', explaining and setting minds at rest.

The most important discussion of all was on Wednesday with Henry J. Benisch, last year's president of the West Side Club which stages Forest Hills, who was representing the Eastern section, the largest of all. He arrived ready to cast 19,000 votes against the resolution. He ended by seconding it yesterday. 'We don't want to change Forest Hills', he was told, 'we want to give you the chance to improve it'.

Kelleher made only one tactical error and the way it was redeemed showed the competence of his staff-work. Some time before the meeting he gave an interview to *Sports Illustrated* in which he said that he had become president simply to stop the job going to 'one of the backward old goats – some New Englander dedicated to tennis but completely out of touch with the sporting picture of America'. The large headline was 'an open minded boss for a bunch of old goats'. This was published on

Wednesday just when the 'old goats'' votes were vital. When Kelleher's lieutenants heard about this they were horror-stricken. Quickly they bought up every copy on the hotel news-stand and sped round Coronado City snatching up copies of the magazine. Not one single 'old goat' mentioned it.

Arrangements are now being made for a summit conference, probably in Paris next weekend, between Britain, Australia, France, and the United States, and even more radical moves are being rumoured. Strong whispers could be heard from the top brass of the USLTA that the Americans would soon be putting forward a plan to reform the Davis Cup, and the Australians would jump to support this.

Billie Jean King was here and is said to be greatly tempted by the professional offer made to her by George McCall, who will announce his main plans in the next four days. It is now known that Frank Sedgman intends to come back and play the British circuit next season and was last seen in Kansas City with the 'Handsome Eight' and looking decidedly ruffled. They had had unhappy discussions with David Dixon, their promoter, about the way their tour is being staged. The latest innovation is that the line-judges have been given whistles and blow every time the ball goes out of play.

* * *

Open Tennis – Ten Years On

There was no more acute observer of tennis politics than David. Here he writes on the progress of the game a decade after the abandonment of the old, long outdated, amateur framework in 1968.

Some of the sports headlines of 1977 looked oddly familiar. Kerry Packer broke into the comparatively quiet world of cricket and immediately anyone who had studied the intricacies of tennis politics in the first ten years of Open competition found that it was like a journey back into the past: 'Millionaire tycoon plans independent circuit', 'Top stars sign big contracts', 'Cricket bosses ban rebels', 'Judge sums up on players' freedom plea'. If the stories in the British and Australian papers reached Dallas, Lamar Hunt, the head of World Championship Tennis and the part-organiser of a similar revolution, must have regarded Mr Packer's progress with a certain amount of wry irony.

The parallels were surprising. Secret negotiations. The establishment taken by surprise. The game's major international competitors hurrying to sign for the new promoter without giving their countries a chance to bargain for their services. Packer promising dramatic new developments in the presentation of a hitherto conservative game. Fanfares of publicity. Even a lecture to the recruits from John Newcombe, one of the oldest of the WCT old boys, on the art of projecting personality in a professional sport. And, finally, exactly as happened with WCT at the beginning, disappointing crowds and television ratings, with a depleted conventional Test series between India and the Australians who had stayed with the national cricket association attracting more public support.

It was all very reminiscent of the smoke-filled rooms in which the representatives of the International Tennis Federation and the Grand Slam tournament bargained with Mr Hunt and George MacCall, the former US Davis Cup captain, who headed a rival professional group. As in the cricket controversy, the established authorities controlled the traditional stadiums and the tournaments which tennis enthusiasts were in the habit of regarding as important and the promoters, offering rewards which the amateur officials could not match at that time, commanded the loyalty of most of the star players.

The public is a curious animal. On the whole, it doesn't like innovations. The storm of criticism aroused by Mr Packer's large cheque book and his novel ideas for the game (cricket by floodlight and the amplified grunts of fast bowlers as they delivered the ball) was comparable to a good deal of the reaction to Mr Hunt's entry into the world of tennis. To begin with, he was unknown to most of those with whom he was negotiating. He was a highly respected administrator in other sports in the United States, but tennis was a new game for him and he had to learn quickly about its international structure.

At first, it seemed that he was going to concentrate on the 'show-business' aspects of the game. The first tour of the 'Handsome Eight', as WCT dubbed the eight very presentable players whom they signed first, in 1968, with coloured clothing (what, not 'all white'!), courtside commentaries during rallies, interludes of song and dance, and solicitation of spectator participation, was a disaster. It did not attract the new audiences that WCT expected and the new method of presentation simply alienated the tennis community.

It was ahead of its time, of course. If those of us who shivered in an ice rink on the first night of WCT in Kansas City [David's account of this occasion appears on page 140], as the tournament died its theatrical death and optimistic ideas froze silently, had been able to look into the future, we should have understood that we were not so much attending the start of a men's pro tour as taking part in an experimental viewing of the kind of ideas that produced World Team Tennis six years later. But all we asked ourselves then was what colour, noise and popcorn had to do with the cathedral hush of the Centre Court at Wimbledon or the Stade Roland Garros on great afternoons of high drama. There may be an audience for Team Tennis. Its promoters have searched hard enough and moderated some of their ideas. But WCT couldn't find that pool of new spectators on that first tour and WTT have yet to show that their league can be financially successful.

WCT moved quickly towards orthodoxy because it was clear that that was what the public and their players wanted. Hunt's emergence as a promoter – and one about whose financial credentials there could be no doubt – may also have helped the die-hards of the old amateur game to accept the idea of Open tennis. The great amateur tournaments could survive when, as in the Kramer days, there were no more than half a dozen top players on the professional circuit. By the early 1960s, it was almost taken for granted that the Wimbledon champion would turn pro as soon as he had asserted his supremacy in the amateur game. If he gave up his title, the great excitement at the Championships would be to see who would be his successor in the royal line. But when WCT completed their raid on the ranks of the national associations, it meant that events like Wimbledon, Paris and Forest Hills had to open their gates to the professionals or face the possibility of seeing their men's titles go to a player ranked as low as sixteenth in the world.

Action of some kind was necessary to preserve the status of the great tournaments. That was the political case for Open tennis. The moral case was even stronger. By 1967, the old system of 'amateurism' was totally discredited. The leading amateurs were subsidised by an expenses system and other direct and indirect payments which often made it possible for them to earn far more money than the pros. Herman David, who was then chairman of the All England Club and of the Championships Committee at Wimbledon, described that kind of 'amateurism' as 'a living lie' and the British Lawn Tennis Association, whose new chairman, Derek Hardwick, believed passionately in Open tennis, declared itself ready to defy the International Federation and stage events in which the professionals and those amateurs who wanted to break down the barriers between the two sides of the game could compete together. So far Mr Packer has not managed to win that kind of support from the cricket establishment.

Those were the heady days of idealism in tennis. The story has been less shining and straightforward since then. The International Federation, faced with the defection of Wimbledon, its most important tournament, compromised, allowing a limited number of Open events as an experiment, but frowning on a British proposal that the amateur–professional distinction should be abolished and replaced by a single 'player' category. That caused confusion. There were arguments about compensation and control with WCT, which resulted in all WCT players being banned from the 1972 Wimbledon, and in 1973 – nine months after the formation of the Association of Tennis Professionals, the players' union – many of the leading players stayed away from the Championships as a protest against an ITF decision to suspend Nikki Pilic for refusing to play in a Davis Cup match for Yugoslavia.

The game's public image has suffered from those disputes, but mostly they were by-products of the explosion of interest in the game which Open tennis helped to accelerate. Golf, another game which develops great international individual stars, evolved its method of government slowly and carefully and so avoided the kind of struggles for power that have marred the first years of Open tennis. In ten years tennis has to build up a system of the kind that golf has spent more than half a century perfecting. And if the great expansion in public interest in the game taxed the resources of the administration, the ITF, ATP and all the other groups involved in the international circuit had to learn for their part how to deal with prosperity.

The first Grand Prix, a series of linked tournaments with jackpot prizes at the end, offered the players a bonus pool of $150,000 and its winner $25,000. By 1974 that had risen to $500,000 with a first prize of $100,000. Last year it was $1,450,000 and Guillermo Vilas, who finished first, took a reward of $300,000. This year the pool will be $2 million, and the leader will collect $350,000 at the end of the year. Altogether, there will be some $10 million at stake in the men's events of the Colgate Grand Prix.

The increase in the Wimbledon prize-money is equally revealing. The British tournament does not pay its men as much as the US Open, which takes particular pride in keeping the dollar on top, or the French Championships, which have to meet the challenge of Team Tennis, but the amounts offered to the players by the All England Club have risen from £26,150 in 1968 to £217,540 last year and £279,023 this year. Rod Laver, the tournament's first Open men's champion, received £2,000 and Billie Jean King, the women's winner, £750.

Last year Bjorn Borg's first prize was £15,000 and Virginia Wade won £13,500. The men's champion this year will be even more fortunate – £19,000 – the top woman will get £17,100. The players aren't the only beneficiaries. The Lawn Tennis Association, which depends heavily upon the profits from Wimbledon for its task of promoting the game in Britain, has received extra money from the 1977 tournament and if the public is being asked to pay more for admission to the matches this year £1.5 million is being spent on improving facilities at the ground.

Those statistics give an indication of the expansion of the game in Britain since Open tennis began. The American statistics, which suggest that there are more than 30 million occasional tennis players in the US, are even more impressive. But some warning notes have been sounded recently. Although there was no shortage of tournaments willing to put forward $175,000 for 'protected' status in the Grand Prix this year, there were some complaints from those who feel that prize-money is too high.

Announcing Wimbledon's increased allocation to the players, Sir Brian Burnett, the chairman, said: 'I think it is time we called a halt to this rapid escalation. If more money is available, it should go to the middle bracket of players or be ploughed back into the game. Some of the money at the top is quite fantastic. It is almost indecent. One effect of these high prizes in the singles is that some of the leading men are no longer interested in the doubles. The British public enjoy the doubles as much as the singles, but many players are now content to concentrate on the singles.'

Wimbledon had added in the extra money this time in order to keep up with its Grand Slam tournaments. 'Prize-money at Forest Hills in 1977 was 18 per cent higher than Wimbledon's and I understand that they are increasing again. The French Championships are 27 per cent higher than ours for the men, although it is much less for the women. One has to keep pace with this to hold our position in world tennis.'

Certainly, the rewards are high, but if thirteen million viewers in Britain alone watched Borg beat Connors in the men's final and more than nine million saw Virginia Wade win on an afternoon when Britain was supposed to be working, who can argue with the players' claim that very high skills deserve very high rewards? An athlete's earning life is short. Can he be blamed for asking to be paid at a rate which is in proportion to the amount of public attention that he can command?

But then Wimbledon is a special case, like the US Open, Melbourne, Rome, Paris and the other great national tournaments. Those are the events which draw big crowds because of their traditions. If the boom which Open tennis brought suddenly stopped, and sponsors began to melt away, they are the events which have the best chance of survival.

And their strength has been reinforced because they have learnt the public relations skills which organisations like WCT, Virginia Slims and Colgate brought to the game. Open tennis has helped the national associations to learn the art of promotion, to sell tickets and to modernise their attitudes to the game. That is probably the best benefit of all because it helps the club player by spreading the gospel at grass-roots level.

*   *   *

Time of Acrimony

If, in the late 1980s, the administration of the international game is reasonably harmonious (though not without many problems), the historical record would be incomplete if the danger of a serious split in the early years of Open tennis were overlooked. Any student of the history of the game will appreciate David's shrewd assessment of the events which led to John Newcombe being barred from the defence of his Wimbledon singles title in 1972.

The saddest aspect of lawn tennis in 1971 was that events followed the path predicted by those who had believed all along in the inevitability of a clash between the International Lawn Tennis Federation and Lamar Hunt's World Championship Tennis group. The year began with a patched-up peace and ended with complete polarisation. From 1 January, 1972, the ILTF banned all WCT players from their courts and tournaments, which meant that Open tennis – the cause of the game's great expansion and the enormous increase in the money available to players and tournaments – had come to an end. The halt may be only temporary and negotiations may yet bring Rod Laver, Ken Rosewall, John Newcombe and their fellow contract professionals back to Wimbledon this June, but even if there is a truce, the year's disagreements show that the old days of idealism are over.

To understand what has happened, it is necessary to dig into the history of the dispute. Britain's original concept of Open tennis in 1967 was of a circuit in which all tournaments would be open to all players, and the competitors (neither 'amateurs' nor 'professionals' but 'players') would be rewarded according to their results. There would be no guarantees, no payments under the table, but prizes for the successful and incentives to sharpen the enthusiasm of those who challenged them. It was argued that a circuit conducted under those conditions would not depend too much on its old aristocracy and would offer plenty of opportunity for young players to make reputations for themselves.

It seemed an ideal way to attract spectators and run tournaments fairly but, for several reasons, this has not happened. In tennis, at the start of Open competition in 1968, the independent players were controlled by amateur national associations whilst the professionals were in two groups, George MacCall's National Tennis League – which held the contracts of Laver, Rosewall and most of the older touring pros – and WCT, a younger organisation, originally David Dixon's 'Handsome Eight' but later a more conventional touring party. The groups were merged soon after Lamar Hunt, with his new executive director, Michael Davies, took full command of WCT.

There was a measure of goodwill at the start, but no one could forget that the old guard of the ILTF had agreed to Open tennis unwillingly. Refusing to follow the British idea to its conclusion, they had compromised by establishing the category of the 'contract' or 'touring' professional and limiting the number of tournaments open to pros. The professionals grumbled but accepted the fact that they needed the publicity, the rewards and the excitement of big Open tournaments.

Fear of WCT was for a long time a major motive behind the Federation's actions, binding together the old reactionaries and the new idealists. Both groups wanted WCT to disappear, for a variety of reasons: the falling status of the Davis Cup; jealousies between players; suspicion that Mr Hunt with his non-tennis background, plus an executive director who had not always been the British LTA's favourite son, might work against the game's best traditions, and – most of all – the question of money.

For a long time the ILTF believed that instead of asking for fees for the appearances of his players at tournaments (which cut across the no-guarantee ideal), Hunt would run his organisation by taking a percentage of their winnings. When he showed no sign of doing this and when, after two superb years of Open tournaments, his best players began to weary of the strain of playing in all the Federation's events, the ILTF introduced, with WCT's co-operation at first, the Grand Prix, a linked series of tournaments with a jackpot prize at the end.

The Grand Prix, suggested by Jack Kramer and sponsored first by Pepsi-Cola, was soon overshadowed when WCT announced a similar jackpot competition of their own. The World Championship of Tennis burst upon an astonished ILTF who felt affronted that they had not been told about it in advance of the press announcement at Forest Hills in September 1970.

Mr Hunt said that he wanted his players to concentrate on this twenty-city series and, in order to bring his strength up to the necessary 32 players, he captured, among others, Arthur Ashe and Bob Lutz from the US Davis Cup team. The ILTF, exploiting to the utmost the power and importance of Wimbledon, might have forced a breach at the end of that year, but a British initative – somewhat reluctantly supported by the ILTF's management committee – brought about an armistice. WCT agreed to play in a number of Grand Prix tournaments in 1971 and Wimbledon was still open to them.

For a time in 1971 there was real reason for optimism. The Italian Championships, a joint venture between the Italian Federation and WCT, proved a tremendous financial success for both groups. WCT sent 32 players and a number of Europe's leading independent competitors took part. There were record crowds and everyone regarded the experiment in co-operation as offering guidance for the way in which WCT and other ILTF members ought to work together.

Unhappily, the French Open, which was solely an ILTF tournament and not a part of WCT's twenty-city series, was very different. Laver, Rosewall, John Newcombe, Tom Okker and other leading WCT players did not enter, pleading fatigue, injury or simply dislike of the idea of two long weeks at the Stade Roland Garros. Lamar Hunt tried to persuade his players to carry out WCT's side of the bargain, but could not find a way to ensure that they would compete. The French claimed that this proved that no one could trust WCT and that the truce had been worthless.

The dispute flared with alarming ferocity at Wimbledon. Using Paris as a prime example of the need for a fixed agreement with WCT, the ILTF wrote to Mr Hunt, suggesting that it was important to formulate a joint schedule in which 'your tournaments could dovetail with ours in such a way that the calendar would allow you to meet your commitments'. 'We are convinced', the Federation's letter went on, 'that there is no room in the world for two conflicting lawn tennis circuits such as the ILTF Grand Prix and the WCT Championships. We feel, and we hope that you agree, that these two circuits should be merged into one world-wide competition....'

But there was to be no agreement. Discussions about sharing tournaments broke down. The ILTF said that WCT had asked for $24,000 a week to play at Wimbledon and other major championships, although later Mr Hunt stated that their price had been no more than $5,760 a week. All kinds of other emotional issues arose, such as whether or not WCT were attempting to dictate to Wimbledon on such questions as television contracts and the kind of ball used. There was a disastrous press conference, which the ILTF tried to end in a mere fifteen minutes and might have done so if Richard Evans of the *Evening News* had not spoken out strongly for a proper examination of the issues involved. The ILTF announced that they were proposing to exclude WCT from all their tournaments and courts from 1st January, 1972 and this threat was carried through at the annual meeting at Stresa a week later.

Once war had been declared both sides took up belligerent positions. In Mr Hunt's view, WCT's stubbornness was justified in the face of the actions the ILTF had taken. The ILTF made a determined attempt to increase the amount of money at stake in the Grand Prix in order to stop further defections to the professionals. When Pepsi-Cola, possibly worried by the dispute between the two sides, hesitated before renewing their sponsorship of the Grand Prix, the ILTF promptly produced the Commercial Union Assurance Company with even more money.

Ilie Nastase, who had beaten Laver in the final of the Embassy British Indoor Championships, turned down a large professional offer. Players like Stan Smith, Clark Graebner and Cliff Richey stayed in the ILTF camp. Jack Kramer, formerly the boss of the professional circuit, joined the Grand Prix committee, together with Derek Hardwick, one of the few ILTF administrators who has a real vision of the way the Federation ought to develop its strategies.

In February of this year morale in the WCT camp was high and attendances at their tournaments were large. At the moment it does matter to them if they don't go to Wimbledon because they still see it as the world championship – but that feeling may diminish in a year or two when Mr Hunt has built up his own circuit.

There is plenty of ground for compromise. Both Mr Hunt and the ILTF talk continually about acting for the good of the game. The best they could do for it would be to make peace.

* * *

The Wimbledon Boycott

The boycott of the Wimbledon Championships by members of the Association of Tennis Professionals in 1973 was the most traumatic happening in the history of that meeting. Wimbledon's own reaction, voiced by the All England Club's chairman, the late Herman David, when the decimation of the men's entry was confirmed, was: 'There will be no recrimination.'

At the end of the 1973 French Championships, after Ilie Nastase had beaten Nikki Pilic, a French official came into the press-room with a hastily printed notice. This announced the International Lawn Tennis Federation's rejection of Pilic's appeal against the nine months' suspension imposed on him by Yugoslavia for failing to play in their Davis Cup match against New Zealand at Zagreb three weeks earlier. It caused the explosion which spoilt Wimbledon, involved the ILTF and the Association of Tennis Professionals, the players' union, in a short but expensive lawsuit, soured the relationship between the players and the administrators, and seriously damaged the public image of lawn tennis.

Throughout the dispute both sides seriously underestimated each other's strength and resolution. Here was another of the game's growing pains. Because the ILTF delayed the introduction of Open competition for so long, the money and the problems of control and organisation have all come at once. These have to be solved quickly.

The Pilic affair concerned a player's right to refuse to play for his country. He had turned professional in 1967 with World Championship Tennis and now he was eligible to play in the Davis Cup again. Pilic made a series of conditions about this, but at the end it was plain that Yugoslavia expected Pilic to appear. He did not make the journey, Yugoslavia lost a match which they had seemed certain to win, and Pilic became the national scapegoat. Certainly, the Yugoslavs had a grievance against the player for, if he was going to say no, he should have said it earlier and more plainly. However, a nine months' suspension was savage, and many people, including ATP, regarded the idea that a man could be ordered to play for his country as feudal.

Yugoslavia had announced Pilic's suspension at the start of the French Championships and ATP immediately threatened to support him by boycotting the tournament. At the insistence of the French the ILTF allowed him to appeal and play, and both Pilic and the Yugoslav Federation agreed to accept any decision that they made. In the end the emergency committee reduced the suspension to one month – a period which covered the Italian and German Championships, and the first week of Wimbledon.

Pilic held a press conference and announced that whatever happened he was going to play in Rome. ATP threatened another mass walk-out and the Italian Federation, faced with the financial collapse of their tournament, accepted the ultimatum. They argued that if the ILTF had acted fairly, they would have suspended Pilic on 2nd June, when he was still a quarter-finalist in Paris, instead of putting the onus of carrying out the decision upon them. When the ILTF replied that they had taken the reasonable course of allowing Pilic to complete the tournament in which he was playing, the Italians replied that their tournament had, in fact, begun on 2nd June. Pilic lost to Patrice Dominguez, and a month later in Warsaw the Italian Federation was fined for defying the official ruling.

Up to then, ATP had received considerable public support. They were a new organisation, and, in the Pilic affair, they were showing their power for the first time.

When Pilic arrived in England two weeks before Wimbledon, it was plain that it was going to be difficult to avoid a collision between the ILTF and ATP. ATP tried to assert Pilic's liberty of action by seeking an injunction to restrain the All England Club and the ILTF from barring him from the Championships. That failed, and ATP's board of directors then said that they had no alternative but to carry out their threat of a boycott unless Wimbledon allowed Pilic to compete. Herman David, the chairman of the All England Club, had been a frequent critic of the ILTF over the years, and ATP hoped that he would act independently again. However, he took the view that, for the time being, the ILTF was the best governing body the game had. At some time in the future ATP might be ready to take over their role in the tournament game, but they still had to prove themselves as a representative group.

Wimbledon, he said, hoped that the members of ATP would support the tournament, but if they decided against that, the Championships would still go on. However, ATP, against a mounting wave of criticism, decided to continue the boycott. Compromises were suggested. If Pilic withdrew voluntarily, would the ILTF drop its rule that a player *must* represent his country if required? Eldon Griffiths, the Minister of Sport, tried to mediate. A joint disciplinary committee, on which both players and administrators would be represented, was proposed, but the ILTF refused to budge.

Many people felt that the situation could have been saved. If it was a battle for the control of the game, it was also a battle in which both the contending sides shared a great many common interests. ATP wanted the

Federation to use a more professional approach in the organisation of the tournament circuit, and the Federation felt that the players ought to be prepared to play for their countries. But no one could draw them together.

Nearly 80 players withdrew from Wimbledon, but Ilie Nastase and Roger Taylor played in defiance of the boycott. Their gesture was supported enthusiastically by the public and the bulk of the press, even though ATP ultimately fined the players £2,000 each. ATP member Ray Keldie also played, but was fined less. There were strange names in the draw for the men's singles and Jan Kodes won the title, but the crowd was the second biggest in the Championships' history, and the British triumphantly made the best of a bad job.

* * *

Davis Cup under Threat

In 1976 both the Davis Cup and the Federation Cup became embroiled in the international tensions occasioned by the problem of South Africa. It was in the summer of that year that David changed from his post on *The Guardian* to the political 'hot seat' as General Secretary of the International Tennis Federation.

In 1976 the political scene in lawn tennis – which has always seemed as contorted and complicated as that of Westminster, the Kremlin or Capitol Hill – was invaded by real live politicians from the great (unsporting) outside world. They were not particularly obtrusive, but they made decisions which helped to sour the atmosphere of the year. Mixing sport with politics became fashionable. The Olympic Games at Montreal, with the dispute over Taiwan and the African boycott, set a pattern which was followed in tennis.

Once more, South Africa's right to play in the Davis Cup was at issue. Mexico, who had beaten the United States for the second year in succession, again refused to play South Africa in a semi-final of the American zone. The United States Tennis Association reacted angrily, threatening to withdraw from the 1977 competition if the Davis Cup nations, at their annual meeting in London during Wimbledon, did not pass a resolution to suspend automatically any country which withdrew for a political reason.

This required a change of rule, and the American proposal failed narrowly to gain the necessary two-thirds majority. The USTA then announced that they would leave the competition, while Britain and France declared that they also would not play in 1977. For the best part of a week it seemed that the Davis Cup had lost the three countries most involved in its long history.

In the post mortems that followed, a number of criticisms were made of the way in which this situation had arisen. Some speakers – including Stan Malless, the President of the USTA, who made the main speech for his country – were said to have been inaudible; other delegates complained that they had not understood the significance of the resolution; and there was another section which, while agreeing with the aims of those who wanted to strengthen the rules, objected to being presented with an American ultimatum. There seemed to be three main groups at the Savoy Hotel. Those who voted uncompromisingly for 'no politics in tennis'; those who disliked the idea of governments making rules for sportsmen, but accepted ministerial interference as inevitable because so many national federations were under direct government control; and those who simply found the South African government's apartheid policy unacceptable . . . even though the South African Tennis Union claimed to have established a framework for progress towards multi-racial tennis in their country.

Thus a crisis had been reached in the affairs of the Davis Cup. The possibility that the Americans and their supporters might use this chance to launch a new streamlined competition was discussed in some newspapers. However, the threat of a serious breach was removed by an initiative on the part of Pablo Llorens, the president of the Spanish Federation. He suggested that the Davis Cup nations should regard 1977 as 'a neutral year'. The US, France and Britain should enter the competition, he argued, and in the breathing space other countries would be given a chance to consider fully the American arguments. There would be further discussion of the problem of political withdrawals at the 1977 meeting. If no satisfactory solution was found then, it might, said Llorens, be found that other major countries joined the group of protesting nations.

Llorens's compromise was discussed at an informal session of the Davis Cup nations after the annual meeting of the International Lawn Tennis Federation at Monte Carlo. Britain and France agreed; the American delegation conferred, and then finally accepted the plan.

The peace that followed was short-lived. Six weeks later Russia, Czechoslovakia and Hungary withdrew from the Federation Cup, the women's team tournament, at Philadelphia in protest against the presence of South Africa and Rhodesia. The Committee of Management of the International Lawn Tennis Federation, pointing out that all three countries had known that South Africa and Rhodesia were in the competition when they entered, suspended them from the 1977 Federation Cup and ordered them each to pay $10,000 for the damage caused to the tournament by their absence. The Philippines, who had withdrawn from a Plate match against Rhodesia, were asked to pay $2,500. They paid immediately. The negotiations with the Russians, Czechs and Hungarians over the management committee's ruling lasted longer. All three countries were warned that they would not be accepted for any team events organised by the ILTF and its member-nations until they had paid the outstanding costs. 'When a country enters a team event, it must fulfil its obligations to that event or face the consequences', said Derek Hardwick, the president of the ILTF.

That meant that the Hungarians – who were the holders – and the Czechs would miss the Saab King's Cup (an event for which the Russians had not entered) and that all three countries would be barred from such valuable junior and intermediate events as the BP, Galea and Annie Soisbault Cups. The Davis Cup, as an event governed by the Davis Cup nations, was not affected by that ruling.

The USSR paid back their air fares to Colgate Palmolive, the sponsors. The Hungarians guaranteed payment as the King's Cup drew near, and eventually the Czechs decided to pay in full, but both countries joined the USSR in calling for a special meeting of the ILTF to discuss the Committee of Management's decision.

Soon after the ILTF had dealt with that situation, the 'neutral year' compromise was disturbed by the USSR's refusal to meet Chile in a Davis Cup semi-final. Sweden's match against Chile at Bastad in 1975 had been difficult enough. Police had almost outnumbered spectators because of a threat to kill Jaime Fillol, Chile's leading player. It was expected that the Russians would have difficulty in meeting Chile, but there were hopes that the match might be played on neutral territory. Eventually, however, the Russians pulled out, cabling the following statement: 'USSR Lawn Tennis Federation declares its refusal to participate in Davis Cup tie against Chilean tennisists. The whole world knows bloody terror still going on in Chile. Human rights violated. USSR Lawn Tennis Federation expresses indignation at appalling crimes committed by Chilean junta.'

The Davis Cup nations' committee decided by a majority of six votes to two that the Russians had 'endangered the competition' and suspended them for the 1977 tournament. A two-thirds majority had been needed for that action. W. Harcourt Woods, the chairman, said that it was blatantly obvious that the USSR had withdrawn because of a naked political decision. The Russian cable had been 'much more the language of politicians than of sportsmen' and his committee had felt that the government of the USSR was trying to spoil the competition for a political purpose.

'We decided that the competition had been endangered because one government was interfering with the event because it disliked the policies of another government. When a government tries to use an international sport in this way, the committee believes that the sport has the right to protect itself by refusing it the means to make cheap propaganda and that

understanding between member-nations is best promoted by free competition', he commented.

Having used one rule to suspend the USSR for a year of play, the
Committee of Management decided to ask the nations for a new rule
which would automatically suspend for a year any country which failed
to carry out its Davis Cup programme. That, said Woods, would leave no
member-nation in any doubt about the penalty involved in conceding a
walk-over. Only natural disaster should, he thought, be accepted as an
excuse. Kenya, who withdrew from a 1977 match against Turkey because
New Zealand were playing in the Davis Cup (a decision taken in the wake
of the African boycott at Montreal), were suspended from the 1978 competition.

* * *

The US Move to Flushing Meadow

For nearly 60 years United States tennis and the West Side Club, Forest
Hills, New York, were partners. The long-standing link was broken
when in 1978 the USTA built a new facility, also in the Borough of
Queens, at Flushing Meadow. It was successful from the first.

The tennis world had one major cause for celebration in 1978 and in some
ways that may have been the most important reason for jubilation for half
a century. Making a grand gesture of confidence in the future of the
tournament game, the United States Tennis Association built and opened
their new National Tennis Centre at Flushing Meadow.

They found the money, and they beat the clock and the weather. They
risked embarrassing failure – there would have been considerable loss of
face if they had been forced to return to Forest Hills after a difficult parting
– and succeeded in their task amid the greatest chorus of enthusiasm and
approval that the USTA had known in 97 years of existence. They built a
new and modern home for the US Open, the first major stadium built for
the international game in 50 years, in spite of all the fears of the pessimists
who thought that the labour unions might be obstructive and that the
jungle of New York's city politics might stop a wonderful idea from
becoming reality.

It was a remarkable achievement. They took a decaying stadium (originally the Singer Bowl, that later became the Louis Armstrong Stadium),
and turned it into the best-equipped arena for the public viewing of tennis
in the game today. Aesthetically, it may not be as elegant as Wimbledon

and it may also be far too close to the main runways of La Guardia Airport. But even the All England Club must be looking enviously at the way in which the crowds at Flushing Meadow can move freely along spacious walkways between the courts, without the problems of congestion that Wimbledon is now trying so hard to cure.

The British are building new courts and increasing the size of the Centre Court, but even with those extensions the All England Club will be faced with the problems of over-popularity and over-population. Up to now they have always led the way in the provision of facilities for their great tennis public, building bigger and spending more than any of their rivals. At one time they considered building a new second centre court to replace the present number one court, but that plan seems to have been shelved. While the USTA stayed at Forest Hills, which had one huge stadium court and quite modest supporting facilities, Wimbledon's supremacy was undisputed. However, now that Slew Hester, the president of the USTA and the organiser of the swift and highly successful operation at Flushing Meadow, has turned his dream into steel and concrete, the All England Club will have to keep on looking warily across the Atlantic to see whether any other new developments are threatening their place at the top.

Flushing Meadow, on a sixteen-acre site leased from the city for fifteen years, has a stadium court with 19,000 seats and a secondary court with 7,000. Altogether, there are 25 outside courts and there is also a large nine-court indoor complex. According to their contract with New York, the USTA can use the stadium for 60 days a year for their own events and the rest of the time they will operate the new centre as 'a public facility with the same scope as a private club'. The whole aim is to involve the playing public as closely as possible with the stadium – so that they feel that it belongs to them as well as to the great players who appear there during the US Open. That is a very worthy piece of tennis democracy.

*   *   *

The Growth of Sponsorship

The most striking feature of tennis in the 1980s is the amount and extent of sponsorship by commercial interests. Sponsorship is not new. It existed in the most modest days of the game when local tournaments talked local tradesmen into taking a page advertisement in the programme. Now millions of dollars are involved.

As the year wore on, it became increasingly apparent that 1980 will be remembered as the year of the Japanese sponsor. The world outside the game may be troubled by the chill winds of recession and depression, but it is comforting to report that in 1980 several of the most important areas of international tennis received new protection and reinforcement on the professional scene from the arrival of a number of Japanese companies who saw tennis as an important vehicle for world-wide advertisement. It is easy to understand the reasons for their enthusiastic support of the circuit. In Japan itself, tennis was booming. The United States, producing players and highly publicised events in abundance, was the biggest commercial market of all the game's main centre of growth. In other affluent areas of the world – particularly in Western Europe – nearly all the national associations affiliated to the International Tennis Federation were reporting a healthy increase in the number of new clubs being built and steady increases in club membership and court occupancy.

This popularity was reflected in the publicity and increasing newspaper space given to the game. New tennis magazines appeared. The sport was easy to televise and attracted large audiences – a French survey taken late in 1980 suggested that it was the most popular of all the sports televised in that country – and all the profiles of the average tennis player produced by the advertising agencies suggested that he was likely to be a highly desirable customer for their products. Seen from the commercial point of view, a connection with tennis seemed like sound business for the leading companies of a country with such a strong export trade as Japan.

The most important sponsorships were undertaken by the Nippon Electric Company (NEC), a major telecommunications and electronics group. Their first venture into tennis sponsorship came at the start of the year when they replaced Colgate Palmolive as sponsors of the Federation Cup, the women's international team competition. Towards the end of the summer of 1979, Colgate, who had been the sport's principal supporter, had begun to sever their connections with tennis. They gave way to Volvo as sponsors of the men's Grand Prix and withdrew from the Federation Cup, which they had backed since 1976. Before they made that decision, Colgate had discussed with the ITF the possibility of staging the 1980 competition in Italy, but when they pulled out the Federation accepted an offer from the Rot-Weiss Club in Berlin, and NEC, who had signed a three-year contract, took over as sponsors. This change of support made little difference to the destiny of the competition. The United States, relying on Chris Evert Lloyd, Tracy Austin, Kathy Jordan and Rosemary Casals, won the trophy for the fifth successive year, and for the sixth consecutive year Australia were beaten in the final.

From the sponsorship of the main women's team event, NEC moved on to become the first overall sponsors of the Davis Cup in the tournament's 80 years of existence. Their agreement with the ITF followed a major reform of the competition. Over the years there had been a number of proposals for changes in the Davis Cup format, most of them variations on the idea of preliminary matches leading to a play-off for a handful of qualifying nations at a single venue. These suggestions had been regularly rejected by the competing nations, who made it clear to the committee of management of the ITF that they preferred the opportunity to play ties in front of their home crowds. Removal to a neutral venue would, it was argued, destroy the special atmosphere of the Davis Cup. The benefits from such a change might be enormous, but the competition itself would become merely another of the game's 'exhibition' events. The excitement of competing amid the vociferous support of a whole nation – an advantage demonstrated by the Czechs at the end of the year in Prague – or of taking away the prize on an enemy's ground would disappear if the tournament were played on neutral territory.

The debate was familiar enough to the Federation's committee of management when they considered the state of the competition in April. Their principal aim, in looking at the possibilities for change, was to make it easier for the public to understand its progress. There had been frequent complaints that the average tennis supporter was confused by the fact that each year's tournament took sixteen months to play. The preliminary rounds of the 1980 event had been played in the late summer of 1979, four months before the United States and Italy met in the 1979 final. It was essential, the committee felt, to find a formula which would enable the whole competition to take place in a single calendar year.

Eventually they settled on a proposal for a two-tier format for 1981. The top sixteen nations in 1980 would play in a non-zonal tournament for the main trophy. The four zones – American, Eastern and two European – would be retained for the other 40 teams. The winners in each zone would be promoted at the end of the year and the four worst losers from the main competition relegated. This suggestion was accepted by the annual meeting in Vienna in July and soon afterwards NEC, offering $1 million in prize-money to the competing nations, undertook the sponsorship of the event. The winning team will receive $200,000 and the runner-up $100,000. Announcing the agreement, Philippe Chatrier, the president of the ITF, said: 'All this should reinforce the event and help us to assure its future. The Davis Cup is the oldest multi-nation team event in sport. We have done well to preserve its traditions for so long in a tennis world that has changed so tremendously in the last twelve years. The new arrangement with NEC will help us to maintain its position in the forefront of the sport.'

NEC's sponsorship of the Federation Cup and Davis Cup was followed by the announcement that Toyota were taking over the women's Series from Colgate. Originally they had been negotiating for the organisation of the Series in 1982 at the end of the Colgate contract, but then Colgate made it known that they were prepared to end their sponsorship at the end of the 1980 Series. Canon, another Japanese company, also agreed to give substantial support to the World Championship Tennis circuit. All this, together with Seiko's involvement in the men's Grand Prix tournaments in Tokyo and Hong Kong, Daihatsu's support for the women's indoor tournament in Brighton, and the Bridgestone and Toray events in Japan, means that Japan has a considerable and growing investment in the game. Their influence will be increased still further this year when the Federation Cup, moving into Asia for the first time, is held in Tokyo in November.

The acceptance of sponsorship was not the only change in the Davis Cup. The adoption of the new format gave the ITF an opportunity to examine some of the problems involved in its organisation. Before the start of the main competition it was announced that neutral chair umpires should be appointed for each of the non-zonal ties unless both the countries involved in a tie agreed to accept local officials. This is an attempt to take off some of the pressure now being exerted upon line-judges and umpires by increased crowd participation. That was a problem at a number of ties last year and it came to a head in the final at Prague between Czechoslovakia and Italy, when the British referee, Derek Hardwick, complained about attempts to influence line-judges by supporters of both teams. Czechoslovakia, relying heavily upon Ivan Lendl who, only two years ago, was the world junior champion, won the trophy for the first time with a 4-1 victory over Italy, who thus failed in the final for the third time in four years.

* * *

ATP Makes Demands

The following is taken from David's review of events for 1982, when he was writing from the standpoint of his post as General Secretary of the International Federation. He covered the events leading to the retirement of Bjorn Borg.

Compared with other recent strife-torn years, 1982 can be regarded as a time of stability and even of some moderate progress in international tennis. It began with two major crises – the Association of Tennis Professionals announced that the three players' representatives would withdraw from the Men's International Professional Tennis Council at the end of the year, and the Council itself, amongst great public controversy, was seeking a fair solution to the problem of Bjorn Borg's refusal to accept the full commitment of ten tournaments required for participation in the Volvo Grand Prix.

ATP's threat to leave the Council stemmed from WCT's departure from the Grand Prix in 1981. There were those among the players who argued that they would derive greater benefit from adopting a neutral position – which would give them the best of both tennis circuits – than if they merely allied themselves with the Grand Prix. Those voices prevailed for a time, but in the end it was not an argument which appealed to the majority of ATP members. The Grand Prix, with its 90 tournaments, offered more opportunities of employment to the players than the more restricted WCT format, and co-operation with the MIPTC gave ATP a genuine share in the government of the game. After protracted discussions, ATP decided to stay on the Council and Philippe Chatrier, as president of the ITF, and Marshall Happer, the Council administrator, worked out an agreement with them which promised a steady increase in prize-money over five years, provided that the tournament game continued to grow and international financial conditions remained stable.

ATP's negotiators made a particular point about the large increase in tournament revenues that might be expected from cable television in the near future. Their original demand was for 15 per cent of TV revenues to finance the work of the ATP. The Council felt that this should be the players' own responsibility, and pointed out that the money from cable TV still had to materialise. If the optimistic forecasts proved true, said Philippe Chatrier, it would be right that a fair share of the extra money should be added to the prize-money offered. But, in setting the levels of reward, he felt that television income could not be considered in isolation. It had to be regarded as part of the general pattern of expansion and prosperity in the tournament game. 'Television revenue is only one of the sources of income needed to finance the circuit. It cannot be considered separately. If there is a sudden shower of TV gold, the benefit will be reflected in the levels of prize-money in the years to come.'

Borg's refusal to accept the Grand Prix entry requirements left him with the alternative of qualifying for the events in which he wanted to play. He made no secret of his unhappiness about this when he appeared at Monte Carlo and Las Vegas, where his performances were disappointing. The Council met at Monte Carlo during the tournament to make a few last fruitless efforts to find a solution. If Wimbledon or one of the other Grand Slam tournaments had taken an independent position on this matter, the Council would have been seriously embarrassed, but the great championships supported the rules and, after Las Vegas, Borg chose to withdraw from all Grand Prix tennis for the rest of the year. He felt that the Council had been unfair in refusing to allow him to rest for three months and then play in only seven tournaments in what remained of the year. The Council's view was that they could not make a special rule for Borg when 198 players out of 199 (Vijay Amritraj also decided not to accept the commitment of ten tournaments) had accepted the Grand Prix ruling.

They put their case plainly: 'Our aim is to ensure that the top players compete in enough tournaments to give those who invest in the promotion of Grand Prix events a fair share of available talent, without infringing too much on the players' liberty of action.' Both Borg and the Council suffered from this confrontation.

The Council, accepting that there was a case for helping a player who genuinely sought to rest from the circuit for a stipulated part of the year, modified the rules for the 1983 Grand Prix accordingly. They also gave Grand Slam tournaments the right to offer wild cards to their recent champions. Borg indicated at first that he would play a full schedule of tournaments in 1983, but, after appearing in a few exhibition matches, announced that he was again withdrawing from the circuit.

It seemed that he was unable to rediscover his zest for competition and found difficulty in maintaining the dedication that had made him the best player in the world for so long. His statement, as reported from Bangkok where he was playing in an exhibition match, left open the prospect of a return to the courts at some time in the future, but that was a very small crumb of comfort for his millions of admirers. Can he ever come back again? To all intents and purposes, the statement from Bangkok announced the retirement of a great athlete at the early age of 26.

THE OLYMPICS

Tennis and the Olympics

D avid was assiduous in his work to take tennis back into the Olympic Games. In the first of two essays he charts the course by which tennis ceased to be an Olympic sport after the Games in Paris in 1924.

We swept out of the Olympic Games in 1926 after one of those thumping great rows that occasionally shake the sporting world. Tennis, as usual, believed that it knew what was best for itself. The International Olympic Committee disagreed. There was an explosive confrontation between two Belgians, the Chevalier Paul de Borman, the International Lawn Tennis Federation's principal spokesman, and Count Henri Baillet-Latour, the president of IOC, and in a puff of chalk lawn tennis, one of the original sports at the first modern Olympic Games in Athens in 1896, returned to a circuit founded firmly on the supremacy of Wimbledon, Forest Hills, and the Davis Cup.

At the time both the ILTF and the IOC were growing increasingly conscious of their powers. The ILTF – which didn't drop the 'Lawn' from its title until half a century afterwards – was thirteen years old and determined to assert its authority and independence. The IOC was busily turning de Coubertin's philosophic notion of an international sporting movement into a strict reality. Who knew what was best for tennis? The IOC, who expected all International Federations to accept their rulings, or the ILTF, who felt (basing their view on the evidence of experience) that tennis could well be a mystery to those who understood the control of other sports.

The organisation of the last full Olympic tennis competition in Paris in 1924 pleased nobody except, perhaps, the United States, who won all the gold medals. Vincent Richards beat Henri Cochet in a five-set men's final and then partnered Frank Hunter to defeat Cochet and Toto Brugnon in the doubles. Helen Wills took the women's singles and won the doubles with Hazel Wightman. Then Mrs Wightman and Richard Norris Williams, the captain, beat Marion Jessup and Richards in the mixed. It was the first time that the US had competed in Olympic tennis since St Louis, 1904, when B. C. Wright and E. W. Leonard captured all the (men only) medals. Altogether, 27 countries were represented at the tournament in Paris. Pretty international, on the face of things, but when the organisation was put under scrutiny you understood why de Borman, abrasive and short-tempered, complained.

Ayres Lawn Tennis Almanack tells the story of the last Olympic tennis tournament in terms that range from sarcasm to invective and righteous anger. The heat was sweltering (no one could blame the IOC for that) but the choice of the venue added to the general discomfort. Instead of playing at one of the famous French clubs, the tournament was held 'on a waste stretch of ground near the athletic stadium . . . with results inimical to comfort and convenience of the players'. When the American team arrived, they found 'unfinished and unfurnished courts, dressing-room accommodation of the rudest and most inadequate description, and attributes which would not have been tolerated even at the meanest of their home tournaments'. After protests, there were improvements, but the reporter felt that the initial mistake had been that of allowing the tournament to be organised by officials without experience of international tennis tournaments.

The complaints multiplied when play began. Some courts weren't watered and the players rallied through dust clouds. Others were hosed down while matches were in progress on neighbouring courts, distracting the competitors, who also suffered from undisciplined photographers and noisy refreshment sellers. 'Vacillating' umpires allowed themselves to be influenced by partisan spectators, and spectators found 'only the crudest arrangements. This was deplorable since the quality of the play was some of the best ever seen in France, and Paris was full of people of all nationalities anxious to see it.' The British correspondent's final verdict was that, even though the organisation was 'unco-ordinated and inadequate', the tennis triumphed over the defects in the arrangements and the results generally reflected international form.

But once the gold medals had been distributed, the ILTF began its attempt to reform the system and ensure that in future governing bodies of sports should have the right to control their own events in Olympic tournaments. Tennis, de Borman argued, knew its own business better than the kind of organisers whom the IOC had appointed in Paris. There

were other arguments about the definition of amateurism and the pres-
tige and precedence of the game's traditional events, but basically de
Borman was determined to enforce the ILTF's right to control its own
Olympic events.

Tennis, supported by seventeen of the eighteen International Federations present at the Olympic Congress in Prague in 1926, asked that at
least one delegate from each sport should be included on the International Olympic Committee. (The eighteenth sport, which opposed this
suggestion, was athletics which already had a seat on the IOC.) Tennis
also asked that each International Federation should be given the right to
control the material organisation of its own sport and look after its
technical organisation. In other words, no more of those vacillating
umpires or courts watered at the wrong time. De Borman backed down
slightly over the word 'control', changing it eventually to a proposal that
International Federations should 'work in co-operation' with the organising committee, but he still lost.

The proposal was rejected by a large majority and the IOC even turned
down a suggestion that presidents of International Federations should
have seats reserved for them in the members' stand. De Borman, convinced that there was not the slightest prospect that Baillet-Latour would
surrender anything to tennis, went back to his Federation and in the end
they produced a four-part ultimatum. They would withdraw from all
future Games unless:

1. The ILTF was granted one representative at least on the IOC.

2. The ILTF was allowed to co-operate in the technical and material
organisation of tennis at the Games.

3. The definition of an amateur adopted by the ILTF should be
accepted as far as tennis is concerned.

4. The holding of an Olympic Games in any one year should not
cancel or supersede the holding during that year of any officially
recognised lawn tennis championships or competitions, and the
Olympic Games should not be regarded as 'a championship of the
world in tennis'.

No one should underestimate the importance of the fourth stipulation.
Tennis's own controversy over the ownership of the 'world championship' titles had only just been resolved, opening the way for the USLTA to
join the ILTF. Wimbledon and Forest Hills, the contenders for the title of
the supreme championship, had agreed to stop fighting over a form of
words and to work out their rivalry silently. They could continue to
improve their tournaments until everyone recognised which was the
more important of two great grass-court events. There was no need to be
explicit ... if the end-products were peace and the establishment of an
authoritative governing body. And if Britain and the US, the holders of
the Davis Cup, agreed on what was best for the game, why should they

trouble themselves about their relations with the IOC? Certainly, they were ready to accept de Borman's hard line.

The situation was complicated further by another of the Prague decisions. The IOC asked all Olympic sports not to hold their world championships in Olympic years. De Borman and his fellow delegate, Karl Robetin, commented:

'As far as we are concerned, the events which would come into question, although they are no longer known as "World's Championships", would be the Davis Cup, Wimbledon, Paris, and Forest Hills. We should therefore be faced with this extraordinary situation: while we are asked to abandon our most important events, which testify annually to the importance of our sport, in favour of the Olympic Games, we are refused as an International Federation the supreme right of controlling the material organisation which would ensure the events being properly conducted; and in giving up so much to the Olympic movement, we should even be refused a seat on the Committee which manages these Games, that is, the International Olympic Committee.

'It is obvious that there is a complete lack of understanding between us and the IOC, that we view matters from a totally different point of view, and that no effort has been made to meet our legitimate demands, which we consider cannot be abandoned without prejudicing the authority and prestige of our Association.'

The ILTF considered their report and decided that unless the IOC agreed to de Borman's recommendations tennis would be withdrawn from the 1928 Olympic Games. In the years since then, both the Olympic movement and tennis have prospered. The other international federations, which had shared de Borman's view that sports should be given the responsibility of organising their own events inside the Olympic framework, negotiated their share of power from the IOC. Tennis was accepted as 'an Olympic sport', which meant that many national associations could receive financial assistance from their governments, but did not compete again until 1968, when it was a 'demonstration sport' in Mexico.

By a coincidence, that was also the year when the ILTF finally agreed to Open tennis. If a number of countries still wanted us to press forward with our Olympic claim, most of the larger countries were more enthusiastic about the solution of the problems of professional competition and the inevitable expansion of the game. Two years ago, however, the ITF applied formally for reinstatement in the Games programme. If Los Angeles won the Games, we argued, Southern California, with its one million tennis players, would be a perfect place for tennis to return to the Olympic fold.

We felt that we had solved most of the questions which divided us from the IOC. They had approved our rules on 'amateurism'. We were, like soccer and boxing, two sports which have stayed in the Games, a sport with a small, rich and highly publicised professional élite, and millions of amateur players. Inclusion in the Olympic programme would give a new incentive to those amateurs.

Philippe Chatrier, the president of the ITF, discussed this question at a meeting of Olympic Programme Commission in Lausanne. It was argued sometimes, he said, that an Olympic tennis competition, played under the present rules governing amateurism, would lack many of the game's greatest heroes and would not therefore attract spectators in the way that our traditional tournaments attract crowds.

If, however, tennis were a part of an Olympic festival, he believed that it would give amateur tennis a dignity and prestige that it lacks at the moment: 'This is a serious problem for us. At the moment there are comparatively few incentives for the amateur player. If he possesses talent it is difficult for him to resist the temptation to turn those talents quickly to profitable ends by becoming a professional immediately. Unluckily, many of these young players are not good enough to earn a living from the game and disillusion sets in.

'The ITF does not regard that as a healthy situation. The Olympic incentive would help us to combat it by offering the young amateur a reason for not committing himself too quickly to the professional game. If we can offer an ambitious young player the possibility of representing his country in an Olympic competition, of becoming a national hero and earning a gold medal, then we can hope that he will feel that the financial sacrifices are worthwhile and that any decision to turn professional will be made with maturity of mind and a much greater knowledge of the real problems involved in a life wholly devoted to sport.'

Under our present rules, Chatrier claimed, we feel that we can offer the possibility of good competition to an Olympic programme. Already, tennis events in regional games, conducted under the auspices of the IOC, had proved popular with audiences in many parts of the world. Olympic tennis would help to unite the world game: 'In many countries, when funds are allocated the money goes primarily to Olympic sports. If tennis were added to the programme, it would be easier for our national tennis federations to obtain money for new courts and better training programmes. That is something which is more important to our poorer federations than to those which represent developed countries.'

* * *

How the Olympics and Tennis Need Each Other

In this second essay on the Olympics, David records his impressions of the Olympic Congress in Baden Baden in 1981 and his views on how tennis and the Olympic movement need each other's qualities.

There is a passage in one of those presidential election campaign tomes by Theodore White in which he describes how John F. Kennedy greeted so many prospective voters that halfway through the primaries his hands were so raw and swollen that he had to stop shaking hands.

For anyone who is seeking the admission of a sport into the programme of the Olympic Games, an Olympic meeting like the congress at Baden Baden turns into a prolonged bout of hand-shaking. You are a candidate. You smile. You seek to influence IOC members, NOC members and representatives. You listen to the gossip. Your old friends, the journalists, hearing whispers from decision-making voices, pass on to you hopeful snippets of near-truth. After a time you begin to think that everyone must be growing bored with your obsessive pursuit of a single goal.

The curious thing at Baden Baden was that from the start everyone seemed to take it for granted that tennis and table tennis would be added to the programme for the 1988 Games. Except us, of course. Juan Antonio Samaranch, the president of the IOC, had said as much in a television interview with the BBC the day before the congress started. 'My wife back in Cardiff says that people keep ringing her up and telling her what a good job I've done', said Roy Evans, the president of the International Table Tennis Federation. 'No one here has even told me which day the IOC will be even discussing it.'

They and we needed a two-thirds majority when the matter came to a vote at the meeting of the IOC which followed the congress. We counted favourable heads. Before the meeting we had asked all national tennis associations to seek the support of their Olympic representatives, and there had been a great many promises of help.

For tennis, there were big reasons for the readmission of tennis to the programme: the universality of the sport, the growth of participation and public interest, our history (Baron de Coubertin had regarded us as suitable for the first modern Olympics in 1896), and the simplicity of our requirements (make a court, put up a net, find rackets and balls and with such unsophisticated equipment you can play until you are 85).

There were also reasons against us. We had walked out after the 1924 Games, telling the IOC that it did not know how to organise a tennis event. For some countries, we were still an élite sport (East Germany, for instance, wins medals for almost everything but pays little attention to tennis). And we faced the big question of eligibility. Who would play in an Olympic tennis tournament? The world watches Borg and McEnroe in the Wimbledon final. Would the Games or tennis itself benefit from an Olympic tournament without the best players in the game?

In all the ITF's own heartsearchings over the Olympic issue, eligibility has always been the major question. For anyone who attended the Olympic movement's own debates at Baden Baden, it is clearly the IOC's biggest problem. The pressures for an Open Games are growing. The IOC invited a group of athletes to the congress.

They asked how they were expected to reach the standards, both of performance and conformity, required from a modern Olympic competitor and still keep in line with Rule 26, which establishes the present principles of eligibility. We aren't the only sport which has a strong professional section and a huge base. Boxing, cycling, soccer, basketball all have great professional stars and yet all make a considerable contribution to the Games.

We made our bid for reinstatement on the basis of our present amateur rules. 'No more than $100 in legitimate expenses plus travel.' We reckon that we could produce an attractive tournament for the Games even now without stretching those regulations. American college players – who produced a Wimbledon quarter-finalist this year [Tim Mayotte] – Eastern Europeans, who have kept their status for reasons of official philosophy, and bright youngsters who haven't yet chosen to take the plunge into professionalism.

Tennis makes a habit of producing young masters. Three years ago Ivan Lendl and Hana Mandlikova, last year's Grand Prix runner-up and the current champion of France and Australia, were the Junior World Champions. We are a demonstration sport in Los Angeles in 1984. We ought to be able to give a pretty good demonstration of our game.

But the ITF's whole strategy in this matter has been based not on 1984 – demonstrations are important but they are not like being on the programme and winning gold medals – but on 1988. We looked particularly at boxing. The pattern was for the young boxer to compete in the Olympics, represent his country, win his medal and then, if his ambition took him that way, to seek a professional title. If a sequence like that worked for Muhammad Ali, why shouldn't it do equally well for the Borgs and McEnroes of 1988?

It would stop kids turning pro too soon and would enable tennis to join with almost the whole of the sporting world in the pleasure and comradeship of the biggest of all athletic festivals. It would mean much greater national commitment to our game in many countries and considerable additional publicity. We put these arguments carefully to the representatives of the IOC and in the end we convinced them. Or perhaps it wasn't we who convinced so much as the actual strength of worldwide tennis. When we did our handshaking and lobbying, the response we received time and again was a tribute to the popularity of the game. Asians, Africans, South Americans all complimented us on the expansion of tennis.

'It is a beautiful game', said a Russian. 'I wish that I was young enough to learn it.' We began to understand the strength of our case. The politicians have been buffeting international sport. One more world game is a further reinforcement for the belief that sport does more for the brotherhood of man than all the rhetoric produced by the political machines. We had been outside the family. Now we had shown that we wanted to belong to it again.

As for eligibility, the IOC is re-examining the fundamental principles again with each international federation individually, seeking solutions that will work for each sport. In his first year of office Samaranch earned tremendous respect for the shrewd way in which he united the Olympic movement and sought tough and practical answers to the problems which the IOC had been vainly trying to solve for the last decade. At the meeting of the General Assembly of International Sports Federations in Monte Carlo, the president of an important federation said: 'You have been very clever. For years we have been asking the IOC to produce an answer to the eligibility question. Now you have turned the tables and have asked us to come to you with an answer.'

It is a decision which helps tennis and at the same time sets us a challenge. We have to look carefully at rules and to decide, after consulting all the various forces in the game, what kind of system we want to propose to the IOC. Obviously, we want our Olympic tournament in Seoul – and indeed, our demonstration in Los Angeles – to be as strong as the rules allow. 'Amateurism' is a word which has more or less disappeared from the rules of many federations. Competitors are allowed to earn large sums of money without jeopardising their Olympic status. One answer might be the evolution of an 'Olympic player' category. This works in some sports. Not the whole hog, but a fairly efficient animal. Whether some variation of this compromise would work in tennis is another matter.

Seoul is a long time away and much can happen on the way or in rule-making between now and 1988. 'You have to take your place at the head of the queue and that gives you a big opportunity', a journalist told Philippe Chatrier in Baden Baden. That sums up the situation. It offers a chance to encourage our players, entertain our public and win new converts to our game.

All that handshaking and canvassing was worthwhile.

*   *   *

INDEX